ARCHETYPES FROM UNDERGROUND

ARCHETYPES FROM UNDERGROUND
NOTES ON THE DOSTOEVSKIAN SELF

LONNY HARRISON

WILFRID LAURIER
UNIVERSITY PRESS

This book has been published with the help of a grant from the Canadian Federation for the Humanities and Social Sciences, through the Awards to Scholarly Publications Program, using funds provided by the Social Sciences and Humanities Research Council of Canada. Wilfrid Laurier University Press acknowledges the support of the Canada Council for the Arts for our publishing program. We acknowledge the financial support of the Government of Canada through the Canada Book Fund for our publishing activities. Funding provided by the Government of Ontario and the Ontario Arts Council. This work was supported by the Research Support Fund.

Library and Archives Canada Cataloguing in Publication

Title: Archetypes from underground : notes on the Dostoevskian self / Lonny Harrison.
Names: Harrison, Lonny, 1974- author.
Description: Paperback reprint. Originally published 2016. | Includes bibliographical references and index.
Identifiers: Canadiana 20240358627 | ISBN 9781771126700 (softcover)
Subjects: LCSH: Dostoyevsky, Fyodor, 1821-1881—Criticism and interpretation. | LCSH: Archetype (Psychology) in literature. | LCGFT: Literary criticism.
Classification: LCC PG3328.Z6 H37 2024 | DDC 891.73/3—dc23

Cover and text design by Sarita Mielke and Daiva Villa, Chris Rowat Design.

© 2024 Wilfrid Laurier University Press
Waterloo, Ontario, Canada
www.wlupress.wlu.ca

Every reasonable effort has been made to acquire permission for copyrighted material used in this text, and to acknowledge all such indebtedness accurately. Any errors and omissions called to the publisher's attention will be corrected in future printings.

No part of this publication may be reproduced, stored in a retrieval system, or transmitted, in any form or by any means, without the prior written consent of the publisher or a licence from the Canadian Copyright Licensing Agency (Access Copyright). For an Access Copyright licence, visit http://www.accesscopyright.ca or call toll free to 1-800-893-5777.

For Roy and Ziggy

Contents

Acknowledgements ix
Note on Transliteration xi

INTRODUCTION
Dostoevsky's Types and Archetypes 1
A Brief History of Archetypes 8
Dostoevsky as an Archetypal Writer 10
On Dostoevsky and Mysticism 14
Chapter Summary and Overview 18

CHAPTER 1
Foundations of the Dostoevskian Self 23
"They Call Me a Psychologist" 24
Modernity and the Problem of the Modern Self 29
Reading Dostoevsky "Religiously" 34

CHAPTER 2
The Divided Self 39
The Problem of Duality 40
The Romantic Divided Self 46
The Doppelgänger Motif and Antecedents to *The Double* 48
Dostoevskian Dialectics 62

CHAPTER 3

Dostoevsky's Underground   73
The Archetypal Unconscious   77
From Revision of *The Double* to *Notes from Underground*   79
Feminine Archetypes: Mother, Madonna, and Femme Fatale   84
The Law of Personality and the Law of Love   91

CHAPTER 4

Dostoevsky and the Shadow   99
"Karamazovism"   101
The Coincidence of Opposites   104
Intelligentsia: Illness and Apocalypse   111
Inertia and the Decomposition of Consciousness   114
Dostoevsky and the "Russian Idea"   118

CHAPTER 5

Myths of Transformation   125
Russian Folktales and the Question of Genre   126
Myths of Death and Renewal   131
The Hero Myth   134
Self as Vision of "Moments of Eternal Harmony"   143

CONCLUSION

Dostoevsky beyond Duality   149

Notes   155
Bibliography   185
Index   193

Acknowledgements

The list of people I truly wish to thank is a lengthy one. In the limited space allotted here, let me recognize the individuals who were directly involved in bringing the present work to fruition, and a few others near to me who made it possible.

Thank you Donna Orwin, Robin Feuer Miller, and my professors at the University of Toronto, who held me to the highest standards of academic rigour during my doctoral studies. Thanks to Bill Barnett for his careful reading of an early draft of the manuscript and helpful suggestions, without which this book may never have seen the light of day. Special thanks to Caryl Emerson for reading the copy-edit and offering her generous endorsement of the book.

My most heartfelt thanks go to my colleagues and students at the University of Texas at Arlington. To my colleagues for your spirit of warmth and collegiality, and my students for surprising me daily with your precocity, hard work, and dedication. Enormous thanks and gratitude to my chair, Christopher Conway, for his indomitable energy and unswerving support of my scholarly work and professional goals.

I am forever indebted to friends and family, without whom I could not have made the first step on this journey. Thanks and boundless love to my wife, Maggie, for helping to discover the doorways, and walking the paths with me that led to here. Love and endless thanks to my mom and dad, who instilled the belief in me that I could do anything I put my mind to.

I am most beholden to the editors and staff at Wilfrid Laurier University Press for their enthusiastic and efficient work of turning my manuscript into the present book. My sincerest thanks to Lisa Quinn, Blaire Comacchio, Robert Kohlmeier, Clare Hitchens, and Mike Bechthold.

This book has been published with the help of a grant from the Federation for the Humanities and Social Sciences, through the Awards to Scholarly Publications Program, using funds provided by the Social Sciences and Humanities Research Council of Canada. Thank you to these agencies for the generous support.

Finally, I would like to acknowledge earlier versions of some of my ideas presented in this book that have been previously published. Special thanks to the respective editors and publishers for granting permission to make use of the following works:

"The Numinous Experience of Ego Transcendence in Dostoevsky," *Slavic and East European Journal* 57, no. 3 (Fall 2013): 388–402.

"Reasonable to Ridiculous: The Inward Gaze of the Modern Self in Dostoevskii and Vladimir Odoevskii," *Canadian Slavonic Papers 55*, nos. 3–4 (September–December 2013): 343–363; copyright © Canadian Association of Slavists, reprinted by permission of Taylor & Francis Ltd, www.tandfonline.com on behalf of Canadian Association of Slavists.

Note on Transliteration

I use the Library of Congress system of transliteration from Russian to English, except in the case of common spellings of personal names, such as "Dostoevsky," "Belinsky," or "Nastasya."

For authors whose works are published in Russian, I revert to "–ii," as in "Dostoevskii," or "Belinskii," in the notes and Bibliography.

All translations are my own except where otherwise indicated.

INTRODUCTION

Dostoevsky's Types and Archetypes

All of Dostoevsky's characters, in their febrile determination to turn ideas into action, behave like people who have heard Christ's warning, who deeply believe it, and yet are deeply evading it.

—James Wood, *The Irresponsible Self*

Dostoevsky indicated time and again that he was interested in creating character *types*—human types that were unique and individualized but endowed with a capacity to express and embody the whole of humanity. He would say of his second novella, *The Double* (1846), that its ill-fated protagonist, Mr. Golyadkin, mirrored by his double, Golyadkin Jr., "was a character of tremendous social significance, which [I] was the first to discover and proclaim."[1] Golyadkin Jr. was his first and most important "underground type" [*moi glavneishii podpol'nyi tip*].[2] Later Dostoevsky would declare that, in spite of the work's failed execution, he had never brought a more important idea to literature.[3] For years he intended to revise and improve the work, but by the time he began to, in the early 1860s, a new project had begun to take shape—one that would bring the underground to the fore and draw in the elements around it with centripetal force. Ultimately Dostoevsky abandoned his revisions of *The Double* in favour of writing *Notes from Underground* (1864).

Regarding Mr. Golyadkin's more famous and notorious successor, the so-called Underground Man, Dostoevsky wrote in his preface to the novel

1

that "types such as the creator of these notes not only could, but are bound to exist in our society, taking into account the circumstances that have shaped our society."[4] In part Dostoevsky meant us to see the protagonist as a "social-cultural type" who was "the inevitable outcome of the conditions of Russian society."[5] He was following the convention of the invented but allegedly present and actual portrait of a significant social type, such as Aleksandr Pushkin had famously captured in *Eugene Onegin* (1833). The *Handbook of Russian Literature* observes that "it was Pushkin who, drawing on a plethora of European and Russian literary and social precedents, taught subsequent novelists... *what* sort of actuality to capture and *how* to encode it."[6] In similar fashion, in the preface to the second edition of his own landmark novella of 1841, Mikhail Lermontov wrote that "*A Hero of Our Time*, gentlemen, is indeed a portrait, but not of a single individual; it is a portrait composed of all the vices of our generation in the fullness of their development."[7] The Underground Man, then, was a social-cultural artifact, the inevitable outcome of social conditions that had formed his personality, "one of the representatives of a generation still surviving."[8] He is recognized as a parody of the attitudes of two distinct periods—the radical 1860s and the romantic, idealist 1840s.[9] In effect, he "dramatizes the dilemmas of a representative Russian personality attempting to live by the two European codes whose unhappy effects Dostoevsky explores."[10]

Dostoevsky's social-cultural types are related to his own country's development and adaptation to the major strains of thought and literary modes of the secular modern West. Russia was at the time in the throes of a crisis of national identity that was paramount in the minds of its writers and thinkers throughout much of the nineteenth century. It propelled virulent debates between Dostoevsky and rival factions of the left-wing intelligentsia, while all parties at the same time responded to thinkers and writers of the West, who informed parts of their world view. This problem, along with Dostoevsky's views on his nation's historical development and the character of its people, will be taken up at various points throughout this volume to provide a backdrop to the literary issues under examination. I'll argue that Dostoevsky's social-cultural types, his take on Western ideas, and his feelings toward his nation's people and their national identity are only pieces of a larger picture and the beginning of a longer story.

Bearing in mind the importance of Gogol's social types, and the impact they had on Dostoevsky's early creations, Dostoevsky's characters, too, have often been regarded, by the author's contemporaries and by later generations alike, in terms of their social import. But it is worth noting that Dostoevsky was critical of Gogol's types when he avowed that the Gogolian type "is only half the truth, and half of the truth quite often is a lie."[11] His own reputation as the embodiment of the social conscience of Russian Realism notwithstanding, Dostoevsky often reminded us that for all his concern with social types, they are only half the truth.

As a realist writer, Dostoevsky worked with social-cultural types, which have been recognized in Makar Devushkin, Mr. Golyadkin, the Underground Man, and other character creations in Dostoevsky's wide repertoire. As a "realist in a higher sense," as he once called himself (see Chapter 1 for more on this), he worked in a realm more deeply seated in the human psyche—the realm of archetypes.

Let's take an example from *The Brothers Karamazov*, his last novel. Here Dostoevsky interlaces his underground motif and symbolism with a classification of characters sometimes known as *Karamazovshchina* (roughly, "Karamazovism"). This represented both a new type and a development or unfolding of the underground type. *Karamazovshchina* is a denominal term that Dostoevsky used in the text of *The Brothers Karamazov* itself. Rakitin speaks the word during his court testimony, in Part 4, Book XII, Chapter 2, where he refers to the "muddled Karamazov way, which no one can understand or make any sense of."[12] It was Maxim Gorky who first drew attention to the term, in two 1913 articles, interpreting *Karamazovshchina* as denoting the extreme degree of irresponsibility and cynicism.[13] In Robert Belknap's classic study, *The Structure of "The Brothers Karamazov,"* Belknap speaks of inherent relationships, "clusters of attributes" within which characteristics and their opposites are inherent in one structural system. Qualities and traits form clusters, the most prominent of which is the Karamazovan nature. Both Gorky's and Belknap's treatments of the culmination of Dostoevsky's signature type expand on the idea of the atypical case that nevertheless represents the whole. While neither of them named it so, I argue that the signature type devised by Dostoevsky—from the underground to the Karamazovan nature—can be regarded as an *archetype*.

Archetypes help us grasp Dostoevsky's penchant for atypical representations of the whole. The Karamazov brothers, like Dostoevsky's other underground types, exhibit characteristics and play roles that map onto archetypal images and patterns that I investigate throughout this volume. One line of investigation in this study is the trajectory that ties Dostoevsky's so-called *underground type* to his final hero, Alyosha Karamazov. I will argue that the dynamic play of forces that catalyze transformation—the same forces that drive vitality and change in archetypes—is the structural and thematic focus of these characters and the themes of vitality and change in Dostoevsky's works.

To begin to identify archetypes and observe how they function in Dostoevsky's work, I take a preliminary look at some of the issues examined at length throughout this book: how Dostoevsky viewed art, life, the self, humanity, and the people and traditions of his native Russia. I believe that examining these trajectories and mapping their intersections allow us to see an image of (and patterns of) Dostoevskian archetypes, and lead us toward answers to the ultimate question: What is the Dostoevskian self? By that I mean the self as Dostoevsky understood it and depicted it in his writing. I argue, moreover, that the idea of self is *itself* an archetype made up of a variety of archetypal images and motifs. I approach my question from a variety of angles and make my analysis in the pages that follow. While still a young man with literary ambitions and with his great work ahead of him, Dostoevsky wrote, "Man is a mystery. [The mystery] must be solved, and even if you spend your whole life trying, do not say the time was spent in vain; I occupy myself with this mystery, because I want to be human."[14] In spite of its clichéd ring and the relative youth of the author when he wrote it, this irresistibly quotable remark is often repeated because it is easy to see it at the core of the author's singular obsession. The young Dostoevsky's pledge to discover the root of the human mystery is carried through his fiction in dramatizations of the profound truths of human existence in all their paradoxical variety. Although not a professional philosopher, Dostoevsky wrote about humanity as a philosophical problem. Man as mystery is his topic—a riddle unsolvable, yet worth devoting one's life to. In essence his was a Romantic quest, an imperative to discover something urgent and consequential, yet tragically unrealizable and remote to human understanding. The genuineness of his dedication to pursuing the unknown and undiscoverable is borne out in Dostoevsky's mature works, in which social types no longer suffice, as the author delves ever deeper into the human psyche, the unconscious, the otherworldly—the arcane realms that would become virtually synonymous with the Petersburg novelist's name.

It is instructive to consider how Dostoevsky articulated his aesthetic paradigm in later years, writing in the voice of the seasoned and now renowned veteran author of the *Diary of a Writer*. More than merely the accurate depiction of what is seen, realism is for Dostoevsky a search for the *essence* of what is seen:

> "One must portray reality as it is," they say, whereas reality such as this does not exist and never has on earth because the essence of things is inaccessible to man. He perceives nature as it is reflected in his ideas, after it has passed through his senses; therefore we have to give more credit to the idea and not be afraid of the ideal.[15]

Dostoevsky knows that our cognition of reality is contingent upon what we perceive as it passes through our minds and emotions. In fact, he used the word *realism* pejoratively when referring to those contemporaries of his who seemed to neglect this simple fact. He spoke of his own brand of realism more as a metaphysical concept than a literary technique, closer in kind to Platonic idealism than literary realism.[16]

This philosophical perspective shaped Dostoevsky's fiction. His writing by and large deals in the conflicts and tensions that are the fruits of passions and sensations. His characters are ruled by emotions and especially that combination of emotions and *ideas* that is the source of much dramatic friction in his novels. For Dostoevsky knew that to understand rationally is to see only a fraction of the picture. To *feel* is a greater form of understanding, since ideas have an emotional matrix, and humans perceive in large part with the emotional body. With vivid evocations of atmosphere and especially vacillations of mood and temper that Dostoevsky presents, the reader is engaged in a visceral way so that he or she experiences a story on a deep psycho-emotional level.

The interesting thing is how Dostoevsky conceives of an idea as having an essence all its own that can infuse the soul. This notion is described in the *Diary*:

> Ideas fly through the air, but always according to laws. Ideas live and are spread according to laws too difficult for us to grasp. Ideas are infections, and do you know that in the general mood of life any idea accessible only to a highly educated and developed mind can suddenly be transmitted to a coarse being who has never cared about anything and immediately infect his soul with its influence?[17]

By extension, our emotions and mental images are the result of "infection" with ideas that have a sort of life of their own. They operate according to fixed laws even if those laws are too complex for our comprehension. These are the deep-running waters of spirit and consciousness that Vyacheslav Ivanov wrote of in Dostoevsky—the seething torrents of thought, emotion, and experience, struggling in dynamic dialectic in perpetually recurring cycles of myth and tragedy.[18]

Human emotions, ideas, consciousness, myth and tragedy—these accounts are taken from the context of Dostoevsky's later writings, as the veteran writer inhabited his persona of the diarist in *Diary of a Writer*. But it might be seen that they shed light on his earliest work as well. One of the ironies in Dostoevsky's early publishing history is his being hailed as a brilliant new talent working in the area of social realism and soon after drawing criticism for writing that strayed from the aesthetic aims and qualities of the emergent Natural School. The problem, which I take up in detail in Chapter 2, is related to these twin notions that the essence of things eludes our understanding and that the laws governing the spread of ideas are often too difficult to grasp. Contemporary social realities as depicted by Belinsky and his Natural School were for Dostoevsky only part of the truth. With his own character types he reached for farther-ranging, more profound truths that would be sustainable over time. As Robert Louis Jackson observes, "Type for Dostoevsky is the artistic medium through which the artist reveals the dynamics of reality, the configuration not only of the past, but also of the future, as it is disclosed in the indications of the present."[19]

Again, Dostoevsky's work in this sense is rooted in the best traditions of his nation's literature. Harking back to Pushkin and Lermontov, his depiction of authentic types and their reality has much to do with the dynamics of transformation. It is significant to all of the literary portraits after Onegin, as Yuri Lotman notes, that the concretization of the "rupture" is a catalyst in the transformation of the individual in Russian society.[20] Rupture would come to define the experience of many of the leading roles in the great tradition of Russian Realism, drawing much of its inspiration through the succeeding decades of the nineteenth century from Pushkin and Lermontov. For Dostoevsky, catalysis and transformation are keys to the principle of character type.

Dostoevsky would enlarge on this principle until his last work. In the preface to *The Brothers Karamazov* (1880), the hero Alexei Fedorovich is introduced as an "indeterminate" [*neopredelennyi*] and "undefined" [*nevyiasnivshiisia*] type; he is an "odd man" [*strannyi chelovek*], even an "eccentric" [*chudak*]. While the odd man is often a particular and isolated case, he nevertheless sometimes "bears within himself the heart of the whole, while the other people of his epoch have all for some reason been torn away from it for a time by some sort of gale of wind."[21] The aspect of rupture presented here—the paradox of Dostoevsky's atypical hero who represents the whole of humanity—has been studied. Bird, for example, remarks that Dostoevsky's characters are "profoundly individual, eccentric, even improbable," and explains that, while empirical data may be synthesized into a roughly coherent unity, that unity may be mistaken or illusory, torn away from the whole. "Paradoxically, the improbable hero Alyosha might turn out to be more essential, more real, than his more typical brethren taken for empirical reality." Dostoevsky depicts emerging individuals rather than those who figure into normative Russian society.[22]

My own analysis, broader than that, places Dostoevsky on a trajectory that marks a period of great change in the Western science of the mind and the understanding of the self. Dostoevsky's creative art and its impact fall between two critical points in history for the human mind and self. They are, in the words of historian Richard Tarnas, when "the Copernican revolution impelled and symbolized the outward-moving ascent and construction of the modern self that began in the Renaissance and brought forth the Enlightenment," and "the depth psychology revolution reflected the inward-turning descent and deconstruction of the self that commenced at the end of the nineteenth century and brought forth the postmodern era."[23] In this book I discuss the history of the emergence of the modern self in some detail, as well as Dostoevsky's response to it and his role in the deconstruction of the self that led to the depth psychology revolution.[24] Additionally, I view Dostoevsky within the Russian context, taking into consideration his nation's historical development, its position vis-à-vis Europe in the nineteenth century, and its unique attitudes regarding the modern self.

It is somewhat surprising that until now no sustained critical analysis of Dostoevsky's work and its basis in archetypes has been undertaken. Except in rare examples, the term *archetype* has been used only in the conventional sense in relation to Dostoevsky's writing, as a generic model or prototype after which similar things are patterned. For example, in Laurie Bernstein's work the archetype of the saintly prostitute based on the figure of Mary Magdalene is explored as a feature of several of Dostoevsky's female characters.[25] In the entry on Goethe in *The Dostoevsky Encyclopedia*, it is suggested that "Faust, Gretchen, and Mephistopheles served as archetypes with which Dostoevsky often identified his fictional characters."[26] In other instances, the protagonist of "White Nights" might be called the archetypal dreamer (Dostoevsky called him a dreamer type: *mechtatel'*), or the Underground Man considered an archetypal outsider or alienated individual.

Beyond this conventional sort of association, Dostoevsky's archetypes draw on symbolism and allegory, as when he includes in his stories religious and folk archetypes of the Devil, or that uniquely Russian concept the Holy Fool [*iurodivyi*]. To understand Dostoevsky's use of archetypes we must therefore turn to a wider concept that posits an archetypal model based on the structural patterns of myth, as in Alexandra Rudicina's "Crime and Myth: The Archetypal Pattern of Rebirth in Three Novels of Dostoevsky."[27] Rudicina interprets the organizing pattern of violence and murder in a selection of Dostoevsky's novels in terms of the dynamic of rebirth through transgression, followed by suffering and expiation, which is central to the founding myth of Christianity.

We can see that there are several conceptual frameworks within which to interpret archetypes. As I develop this theory of archetypes in Dostoevsky, my approach most closely resembles the latter example, as I draw on the concept of archetypes used in depth psychology and comparative mythology, informed by the work of Carl Jung, Joseph Campbell, and, more recently, Richard Tarnas.

Let me preface my analysis, however, by saying that my intention is not to apply a Jungian or Campbellian analysis to Dostoevsky. Jung developed a theory of archetypes based predominantly on the psychoanalytic interpretation of dreams, and Campbell studied world myths and archetypes related to the hero's journey or the so-called *monomyth*. Both have been criticized for essentialist claims, unsubstantiated generalizations, and oversimplifications purporting to be universals that yield cross-cultural insights into the human condition. Neither theory suffices in itself as an approach to Dostoevsky, and it behooves me to use them with caution. Nevertheless, they provide helpful signposts, and I'll temper this caveat by acknowledging that the work of archetypal researchers such as Jung and the historian and archetypist Tarnas, whose synopsis of the history of archetypes I cite below, are indispensable for interpreting modern myths. For I view Dostoevsky's work, in a way, as just that: a collection of modern myths. Moreover, Jung in particular is useful in a historiographical sense, as he and Dostoevsky shared some of the same sources, particularly German Romantic Idealism. I'll examine these correlations as I discuss archetypes and their implications in greater detail throughout this book. In the end, archetypes can help us redefine our understanding of the prominent place Dostoevsky maintains within Russian Realism, as well as his relationship to Russian national identity and its faith. Archetypes help to explain why these elements of the Russian character were so important to Dostoevsky.

A Brief History of Archetypes
In the Freudian model, civilization is imperilled by wild, atavistic instincts, which we need to suppress. By contrast, in the work of Freud's disciple C.G. Jung, the work of individuation involves the coming to awareness of a so-called *shadow self*, a necessary part of a whole and integrated personality. Just as Dostoevsky designated Alexei Karamazov an "odd man out," so for Jung is the uniqueness of the individual paramount: "The individual psyche, just because of its individuality, is an exception to the statistical rule and is therefore robbed of one of its main characteristics when subjected to the leveling influence of statistical evaluation."[28] Furthermore, Jung's study of religion, mythology, and the symbolism of ancient and modern civilizations led him to the discovery that the unconscious spontaneously personifies in primordial images and symbols, which he called archetypes.[29] For Jung, archetypal patterning makes up a blueprint-like structure of human thought and behaviour, one that has informed human response to life over

the generations. The unrealized self is contained in archetypal forms, until individuation (the work of self-integration or "becoming who you are") achieves a new unity, when the self "expresses the unity of the personality as a whole."[30]

The earliest form of archetypes was that of the gods and goddesses of the "ancient mythic imagination." As Tarnas writes, "In this once universal mode of consciousness, memorably embodied at the dawn of Western culture in the Homeric epics and later in classical Greek drama, reality is understood to be pervaded and structured by powerful numinous forces and presences that are rendered to the human imagination as the divinized figures and narratives of ancient myth, often closely associated with the celestial bodies."[31] In Plato, the term *archetype* occurs in the Philo Judaeus in reference to the *Imago Dei* (the God-image in man). It is also in Irenaeus. Then in the *Corpus Hermeticum* God is called the "archetypal light" and is similarly referenced in Dionysius the Areopagite.[32]

Tarnas traces the development of the "idea of archetypal or universal forms" through the Middle Ages and the Renaissance, arguing that it was focal to what the Scholastics called "the problem of universals," a vexing issue most memorably addressed by the ancient Greeks but that "both reflected and mediated the evolution of Western thought as the locus of intelligible reality gradually shifted from the transcendent to the immanent, from the universal to the particular, and ultimately from the divinely given archetypal Form (*eidos*) to the humanly constructed general name (*nomina*)."[33] Tarnas argues that following the Renaissance the archetypes "gradually retreated" from philosophical and scholarly discourse and then "virtually disappeared with the modern rise of nominalist philosophy and empiricist science."[34] What Tarnas calls the "archetypal perspective" retained its central role in the arts as well as the classics and the study of mythology, but for our purposes it was the focus on archetypes in Romanticism that placed it squarely within "the subjective realm of interior meaning" as the only remaining refuge permitted by the Enlightenment, in which form it entered "the modern sensibility." Thus, "The radiant ascent and dominance of modern reason coincided precisely with the eclipse of the archetypal vision." We can perhaps see how the notion of archetypes would have figured into the philosophical world in which Dostoevsky found himself by considering, as Tarnas notes, that "Kant's Copernican revolution in philosophy...focused on discovering those subjective interpretive structures of the mind that order and condition all human knowledge and experience." Such are "the a priori categories and forms" that shifted philosophical interest "from the object of knowledge to the knowing subject," thus influencing "virtually every field of modern thought."[35]

Drawing on both Kant and Freud, Jung used archetypes in a far more explicit manner than did Dostoevsky. Jung's theory of archetypes grew primarily out of his work with Freud and his own clinical research in analytical psychology. Jung described archetypes, in Tarnas's words, "as autonomous primordial forms in the psyche that structure and impel all human experience and behavior."[36] Eventually he came to regard archetypes as "expressions not only of a collective unconscious shared by all human beings but also of a larger matrix of being and meaning that informs and encompasses both the physical world and the human psyche."[37] In another of the many definitions he gave, Jung puts it this way:

> Human knowledge consists essentially in the constant adaptation of the primordial patterns of ideas that were given us *a priori*. These need certain modifications, because, in their original form, they are suited to an archaic mode of life but not to the demands of a specifically differentiated environment. If the flow of instinctive dynamism into our life is to be maintained, as is absolutely necessary for our existence, then it is imperative that we should remould these archetypal forms into ideas which are adequate to the challenge of the present.[38]

We see then that Dostoevsky inherited a centuries-old archetypal tradition that was undergoing the same radical transformation in modernity as virtually all other signposts of Western thought, and was therefore carried by the same intellectual currents that Dostoevsky struggled to navigate within the framework of Russian literary and intellectual movements. We turn now to consider more precisely the purpose served by the archetypal character in Dostoevsky's writing, from its earliest forms to its eventual maturation in the Underground Man.

Dostoevsky as an Archetypal Writer

Archetypes speak the language of stories and myth—the images that make up the great narratives of our time even as they stand in relation to more remote cultures and civilizations. That is why archetypes are studied in fields as diverse as psychology, literature, philosophy, comparative religion, and anthropology: stories are how we organize reality and give meaning to our lives. As humans we have a highly developed propensity to see common patterns. We respond to patterns that we are congenitally adapted to perceiving, and we invest them with meaning in stories, myths, and symbols. We project our own cognitive and emotional forms by imposing the energy of the psyche—imagination, ideas, belief systems, goals, desires, or fantasy. Myths and folk tales are descriptions of unconscious processes, which can be conduits to coping with change, uncertainty, traumatic experience, or growth. They draw audiences out of their own circumstances to enter a completely different world and have novel experiences.

In literary studies, the best-known theorist of archetypes is Northrop Frye, for whom an archetype is "a symbol, usually an image, which recurs often enough in literature to be recognizable as an element of one's literary experience as a whole."[39] Frye investigated archetypal symbols or conventional elements of literature and narrative patterns related to myths. Such largely symbolic elements are not precisely what I mean when I identify archetypes in Dostoevsky. Dostoevsky's archetypes are not purely narratological in the Fryean sense; they are not (or I should say not *merely*) structural principles that recur in works of literature as images, metaphors, myths, symbols, and plot, which relate to one another as a set of conventions. In Dostoevsky, I argue, archetypes are aspects of *personality* that carry meaning by virtue of being invested with ideas of self, nation, God, tradition, and primordial truth.

Jung, Campbell, Frye, Tarnas and other archetypists provide models for examining archetypes, and contribute in many ways to a useful archetypal heuristic. However, here I treat their work as hypotheses rather than prescriptions as I define my own theory of archetypes in Dostoevsky. I use the archetypal approach only as a probe that is gradually deconstructed in the process; while Dostoevsky trades in archetypal images and narratives, they do not serve clinical, therapeutic, or anthropological purposes. We must bear firmly in mind that Dostoevsky was a fiction writer and topical journalist. There is a difference between literature and life or praxis, a line that I intend to demarcate clearly. In Chapter 1 I address the tradition of interpreting Dostoevsky's life and writing from a psychological perspective and discuss potential problems involved in adopting such an approach.

As I begin to explore the range of archetypal themes in Dostoevsky, in spite of the caveats above, I must first anticipate objections from those who would contest the validity of Jung's research, given that his reputation has to an extent been tainted by his association with the New Age movement, which some argue was rooted in this thought and with which his work is now linked. His life and works are often regarded with suspicion or even derision by positivist-minded scholars. In the main, I must justify my use of Jung's work on archetypes as a methodological framework against such critics as Richard Noll, who alleged in *The Jung Cult: Origins of a Charismatic Movement* that Jung is the centre of a quasi-mystical personality cult, the purveyor of a kind of "spiritual elitism."

Jung spent his life studying Gnosticism, comparative religion, mythologies, and alchemy. Throughout his life he recorded the images and symbols arising from the unconscious. One of his theses holds that through rigorous self-examination and inward-turning concentration, one discovers the universal self lurking in the dark recesses of the soul. Jung integrated his study of alchemy and other esoteric traditions into his modern psychological structures to achieve the realization that tension between opposites is the generative force of personal transformation. He found that the mind-body complex manifested itself in archetypal patterning in the personal psyche and found expression in innate patterns of behaviour, which personified themes in the collective realm of art, religion, and mythology. These principles are tied to the Western notion of the development of self; hence, by analogy, alchemical transmutation is equivalent to the transformation and awakening of the authentic self through the meeting of the conscious and unconscious mind.

The alleged concern is that some of the admiration for Jung's life and work is cult-like and shrouded in secrecy. Noll's own research shows, however, just how much of that spirit is derived from the *fin-de-siècle* age in which Jung developed his research and practice. Noll traces Jung's ideas back through German Romanticism and *Naturphilosophie*. Folk [*Völkisch*] mysticism is Jung's "training ground," the fount from which he drew inspiration for his theory of archetypes. For example, Goethe's Urbild ("primordial image") and Urtype are eternal and transcendent archetypes shaping man and the natural world in mysterious but observable ways.[40] Noll's warning about Jung is that the charismatic psychologist's voice could be counted among those calling for emerging spiritual and political elites to lead the Germanic peoples of Central Europe to a new "awakening" through reliance on more highly refined "intuitive" faculties.[41]

We find, however, that the same brand of speculative, metaphysical philosophy for which Noll faults Jung—the idea of an eternal manifestation of the divine essence through nature, tied to folk nationalism and folk mythologies—forms the backdrop to Dostoevsky's thinking as well. The fruits of the *Naturphilosophen* Goethe (1749–1832), Schelling (1775–1854), and Carus (1789–1869) are Dostoevsky's patrimony too—especially Schelling and Carus, whose considerable impact on Dostoevsky I examine in a later chapter. Dostoevsky would draw inspiration from the folk themselves, in their patterns of belief and in his own mystical sense of Russian national identity through its folk and their destiny, an important issue that I will take up at various later points as well. Dostoevsky might easily be criticized for metaphysical speculation and national chauvinism as much or more than Jung. I don't consider Noll's criticisms of Jung to be applicable to Dostoevsky, however, because Dostoevsky is a fiction writer, and, as I stated above, mythological tropes are time-honoured elements of story writing. Furthermore, as regards archetypes, it helps to consider that they are rudiments in the process of individuation, or the formation of a whole, integrated personality. As I discuss in various stages throughout this book, I see Dostoevsky's work in a similar light: his characters almost unanimously experience a sense of inner division, enact rolls (archetypal forms) that catalyze change and transformation, and ultimately move toward discovery of authentic self (though that process is rarely completed).

In Jung, an archetype is an explanatory paraphrase of Platonic *eidos*—archaic, primordial types, universal images from remotest times, an essentially unconscious content that is altered by becoming conscious and by being perceived.[42] Jung adds that "there are present in every psyche forms which are unconscious but nonetheless active—living dispositions, ideas in the Platonic sense that preform and continually influence our thoughts and feelings and actions."[43] Thus archetypes are dynamic factors, active, immanent forms that manifest themselves in fantasy, dreams, and impulsive behaviours and reveal their presence by symbolic images. Much like Dostoevsky on the origination of ideas, in *Diary of Writer*, mentioned earlier, Jung writes, "They have a definite cause, but that cause is remote to human understanding."[44] In another place, Jung defines archetypes as "symbolic expressions of the inner unconscious drama of the psyche which becomes accessible to man's consciousness by way of projecting."[45] These expressions are manifestations of unknown origin, mirrored in the psyche and in nature, which evince a universal quality and, according to evidence Jung found, are reproduced across time and cultures, in any time or any place in the world.[46]

Jung saw archetypes as conscious representations arising from the unconscious portion of the mind. Although they are sometimes misunderstood as definite mythological images or motifs, Jung explains that an archetype is "a tendency to form such representations of a motif—representations that can vary a great deal in detail without losing their basic pattern."[47] Thus archetypes are better understood as propensities than as static patterns: "The archetype is essentially an unconscious content that is altered by becoming conscious and by being perceived, and it takes its color from the individual consciousness in which it happens to appear." Moreover, they proceed by dialectic: "As the archetypes, like all numinous contents, are relatively autonomous, they cannot be integrated simply by rational means, but require a dialectical procedure."[48] We begin to see dynamics similar to those at work in a Dostoevsky text. This is especially true of the idea that all archetypes have a positive and favourable side that points upward as well as a partly negative and unfavourable, partly *chthonic* side that points downward.[49] Dostoevsky's *underground* is the territory of this downward-pointing dimension, the subterranean, the unconscious. Its opposite is the upward-pointing process of transformation, numinous experience, and discovery of authentic self—also Dostoevsky's terrain.

On Dostoevsky and Mysticism
One of the ruling themes of Dostoevsky's mature works is the chief problem upon which Jung's theories are based: that the loss of a spiritual sense of modern life is a problem not only of individuals but of societies, representing a self-destructive danger to modern civilization. Challenging the scientific rationalism and mechanistic views of Freud, Jung theorized that religion is a paramount psychological need, and moreover that spiritual tendencies are ingrained in mankind's mental structure, a part of the psychic reality he called the *collective unconscious*. The collective unconscious, which can be understood as an inherited repository of human experience, contributes many of the drives and impulses that inform modern identities and the individual ego. Whether or not Dostoevsky can be said to have espoused a belief in something as particular as the collective unconscious is open to debate. Certainly Dostoevsky saw a binding factor in the hearts and mental attitudes of the Russian people. Moreover, Dostoevsky provides evidence that he believed that visionary experience, and confrontations with the unconscious mind, held the potential to obtain to higher truths than the reasoning, rational mind is capable of doing. This belief is one example of the type of essentialism that can be attributed to Dostoevsky, which opens his work to investigation in the light of other essentialist theories.

Both Dostoevsky's and Jung's notions of ideas or essential forms that reveal themselves in complex and myriad ways are types of idealism. The underlying premise of idealism is the mystical doctrine that mind is more intrinsic to reality than matter. Humans are uniquely capable of grasping the structure of life itself intuitively—Dostoevsky's "mystery of man"—in its elemental forms. Beyond reason and rationality, the intuitive sense is a higher faculty of judgment, apprehending a divine intelligence, a supernatural moral order underlying the universe in which humans play a central role. The work of individuation, to use the Jungian terminology, or movement toward becoming one's true self, is a coming to understanding of those intuitions revealed via symbols arising from the unconscious, through which the archetypes express themselves. In Chapter 2, during a discussion of the foundations of the Dostoevskian self, I take up the topic of idealism as an underlying principle of archetypes.

Many have called Dostoevsky a mystic. The Russian philosopher Nikolai Berdiaev, who read Dostoevsky more assiduously than had Dostoevsky's own contemporaries, was the first to call him a "mystical realist." He writes of the immanence of divine mystery in Dostoevsky, of natural miracles, and the manifestation of intangibles. Moreover, Berdiaev explains that Dostoevsky is neither an Orthodox Christian nor a humanist. Dostoevsky's artistic vision, in Berdiaev's estimation, is a *gnosis*, or a system of knowing accessible only to the spirit and not to the rational, empirical mind.[50] To be sure, there are doctrinal features of Gnosticism that Dostoevsky did not accept and that are too consequential for him to properly be counted as an adherent. To be fair, though, Berdiaev seems to have used the term broadly, in a generic sense, referring to intuitive knowledge of the life of the soul. Thus does Berdiaev distinguish in Dostoevsky a literary method wherein the principal object of investigation comprises the unconscious motivations behind the conscious lives of human beings, in which a deeper, more authentic reality whirls in a mass of conflicting drives. Daily existence and social interaction are seen as clashes of egos and their struggle to come to harmony within the parameters of larger universal moral conflicts. The idea of transformation, in particular the alchemical *transmutation*, representing passage from one level to another, or the metamorphosis of elements into other forms, commingles active knowledge (gnosis) with imagination (presented in art and literature). Dostoevsky's conception of transformation is manifest in his application of concepts such as spontaneity, direct experience, and higher realism. These are some of the fundamentals of archetypes, which I discuss in later chapters.

As a matter of fact, Dostoevsky did not view himself as a mystic. He criticized the "spiritualism craze" entering the drawing rooms of Russian society in the 1870s because of its "mystical" character.[51] As Scanlan observes, the Grand Inquisitor berates Christ precisely for His refusal to use the power of "miracle, mystery, and authority" to hold men in thrall,[52] and in general Dostoevsky saw little room for mystical vision except in the case of revelation of the higher synthesis of being.[53] Scanlan explains that religious experience in Dostoevsky—which is not "faith" but a rationally defensible form of *direct experience*—confirms the conclusions of Dostoevsky's "philosophical" conception of God as at once a supreme being whose existence can be comprehended on reasonable grounds (as distinct from faith) and the "full synthesis of being."[54]

There are scenes in Dostoevsky's work in which characters discuss the visitation of ghosts, as in *Crime and Punishment* when Svidrigailov tells Raskolnikov about a visit from his dead wife and a serf. Their communications are brief and pointless trifles, and may indicate Dostoevsky's impression of the popular practice in the nineteenth century of attempting to communicate with the dead at séances.[55] Furthermore, in *The Devils* Dostoevsky refers to the book *From New York to San Francisco and Back to Russia* (1872), by P.I. Ogorodnikov, which gives a disparaging view of modern spiritualism in America.[56]

On the other hand, it is known that Dostoevsky was an admirer of the "occultist" scientist Nikolai Fedorov (1828–1903), although the alchemist's *Great Work* in this case was industrial transformation.[57] Books in Dostoevsky's private library give further evidence of the author's interest in the occult, or another form of it known as spiritualism.[58] Still, Dostoevsky explicitly derided spiritualism. He often discussed it with friends, and in 1876 he published his thoughts about spirits in *Diary of a Writer*:

> I think that a person who wants to believe in spiritualism cannot be hindered by anything, neither by lectures nor by entire commissions: and the disbeliever, if he really does not wish to believe, cannot be persuaded by anything. That is exactly the sort of persuasion I overcame at the February séance at A.N. Aksakov's, at least during the first strong impression. Since then, I have simply denied spiritualism, that is, in essence I have been indignant over the mystical aspect of its doctrine. (After reading the report of the academic commission's study of spiritualism, I could never be in a position to deny the spiritual phenomena which I have been acquainted with even before the séance with the medium and now, especially now.) But after that remarkable séance I suddenly guessed, or more so, suddenly realized, that it's not enough that I don't believe in spiritualism, but besides that, I don't want to believe—so no sort of proof will ever shake my position.[59]

Although modern spiritualism is overtly denigrated, and Dostoevsky does not explicitly refer to earlier forms of Western esotericism, his dialogic works map onto streams of interpretive systems known to ancient traditions and modern thinkers like Jung, who referred to "the reality of the psyche." Indeed the evidence that Dostoevsky had at least some interest in the esoteric arts should come as no surprise. Dostoevsky shared an affinity with nineteenth-century occultists, who objected to scientific materialism and impersonal mechanical rationalism, and concerned themselves with phenomena that transcend rational explanation, scientific or otherwise. Besides that, as Berry observes, "Dostoevsky was aware of the literary tastes of the period and his own writing reflected his effort to appeal to the public's taste for the esoteric."[60]

Although Dostoevsky assuredly was not an occultist, he would have encountered concepts from alchemy, Hermeticism, and Neoplatonism via German Romantic Idealism, which dominated Russian culture in the 1830s. Through Herzen, Belinsky, Vladimir Odoevsky, and others, Dostoevsky was exposed to German Idealism and the idea of the Absolute from the writings of Hegel, Fichte, and Schelling. The impact of Idealism on the young writer is difficult to overestimate, especially as he absorbed the works of his favourite poet, Friedrich Schiller. As Frank is careful to note, however, metaphysical Romanticism alone cannot be called the "source" of Dostoevsky's famous works; nevertheless, "it opened his sensibility to the early nineteenth-century forms in which man struggled to express his age-old religious questionings."[61] Still, as I have argued, Dostoevsky did not view himself as a mystic and was adamant that Russian Christianity was not mystical: "I have not presented you with a single mystical idea," he wrote, and "I define Orthodoxy not by mystical beliefs but by love of humanity, and I rejoice in this."[62] Also, "In Russian, genuine Christianity, there is no mysticism at all; in it there is only love for humanity, only the image of Christ—at least that is the main thing."[63]

Jung, too, denied that his work involved any mysticism or occultism. In a series of lectures in 1935 he said, "There is nothing mystical about the collective unconscious,"[64] that "mystics are people who have a particularly vivid experience of the processes of the collective unconscious," and that "mystical experience is experience of the archetypes."[65] Some might say that there is mysticism in the very idea of a collective unconscious. Jung believed, however, in the reality of an objective psyche (another term he used for "collective unconscious"). Furthermore, something he called the "transcendent function" is activated by a balance of the conscious and unconscious minds, which produces a shift in consciousness brought about through their union. The perfect balance between them elicits unexpected insights and a sense of self-renewal. Jung biographer Gary Lachman explains, "In the process it produces a third state more vivid and 'real' than either; in it we recognize what consciousness *should* be like and see our 'normal' state as at best a muddling through.... In the simplest sense, the transcendent function is our built-in means of growth, psychological and spiritual—it's 'transcendent' only in the sense that it 'transcends' the frequent deadlock between the conscious and unconscious minds."[66]

We may dispense, however, with the labels that Noll, condescendingly, and following "Jungians," applies to Jung, such as a "a divinely inspired human vessel for dispensing the eternal truths of the spirit."[67] Nor does my research have anything in common with what Noll calls *Jungism*, "a movement that romanticizes and spiritualizes Jung's theories but has demonstrated little interest in documenting the historical facts of his life outside of the information provided in [*Memories, Dreams, Reflections* by C.G. Jung]."[68] That work is a posthumous autobiography that Noll calls "a product of discipleship," as he believes that the "sacralization" of Jung's personality and ideas follow a style and pattern derived from the pagan biographical tradition of the "divine man." It is biography as "cult legend" that depicts Jung's life as an exemplum of his theories of archetypes and the collective unconscious.[69]

Lachman addresses these criticisms of Jung as well as other reasons for the frequent rejection of Jung by the scientific community and mainstream intellectuals. Much of the argument that Jung somehow had a messiah complex and attempted to establish a cult has been discredited.[70] After all, the same charges could be levied against Dostoevsky. If Jungians preserve an image of Jung as "a divinely inspired human vessel for dispensing the eternal truths of the spirit," so, undoubtedly, do the more extreme admirers of Dostoevsky regarding their favourite novelist.

Needless to say, I aim to steer clear of such biases. My purpose is not to make essentialist claims of my own. Whether Dostoevsky espouses an essentialist doctrine (I think he does) is another matter, which I have touched on above and take up again in later chapters. I argue, in brief, that Dostoevsky wrestles with the cognitive dissonance between modern positivism and premodern essentialism. One could say, on the other hand, that just as Jung did, Dostoevsky came to his knowledge through the experience of what Jung called *individuation*, "that difficult and sometimes dangerous process of unifying the conscious and unconscious minds."[71] We know so because the confrontation of the conscious and unconscious minds, as many instances I share below will bear out, is a chief concern of his works. Yet this is more than a personal journey. It is the story of modernity. If the principal aim of Jung's work was to overcome the malaise and spiritual alienation Jung felt had overtaken modern society, one finds a similar impetus behind Dostoevsky's works. Thus, in view of Dostoevsky's engagement with the conflicts of modernity, including questions of religious and philosophical import (from the dualistic ontology of Christianity and eternal life of the soul, through the age of Enlightenment and advent of rational materialism, to German idealism and the nature of consciousness itself), I find it imperative to trace the cultural background that informed the social and historical context in which Dostoevsky matured as a thinker and wrote his major works. To anchor my approach to the archetypes of self in Dostoevsky, I argue that the evolution of the concept of the modern self formed an essential part of Dostoevsky's response to the cultural landscape of modern Europe and European Russia.

Chapter Summary and Overview
Again, my purpose is not to find Jung's or anyone's archetypes in Dostoevsky, but to define and analyze Dostoevsky's archetypes as he presents

them in the Russian national context. Nevertheless Jung's and others' work provide useful points of comparison when we encounter ideas in Dostoevsky that emerge from archetypal research. One such idea is contradiction, duality, or the tension and reconciliation of opposites; another is the plane of action on which the opposition plays out—the unconscious, or more precisely the dynamic confrontation of the conscious and unconscious minds; the final is the outcome of that interaction—transformation. In Jung, the unconscious is an archetypal dimension, while the conjunction of opposites is the unifying principle of an integrated self. In Dostoevsky the liminal space just beyond the barrier of consciousness—the underground—is the subterranean catalyst for the psychological dramas that fester, boil, and suddenly erupt.

Jung's archetypes are active, dynamic, immanent forms. In Dostoevsky, archetypes operate as both character types and generative narrative patterns. Thus I analyze the concept of archetypes and Jung's archetypal categories of individuation—*self, shadow,* and *persona*—to inform my reading of Dostoevsky and interpret insights into the human psyche offered by his major works. The major Dostoevskian archetypes I discuss are the double, the underground type, and the Karamazovan nature discussed above, as well as female archetypes of the Russian Madonna and femme fatale. When I use the Jungian concept of archetype, however, I am not always speaking of something so concrete as character *types.* My major concern is with the ways in which Dostoevsky's fiction signifies the archetypal source of the self residing in the unconscious, with its potential to inhibit self-awareness and cause personal destruction and to enhance self-knowledge and bring about self-integration. This study maintains in particular that the underground is a literary topos in Dostoevsky's narratives that represents the unconscious mind, and that the meeting of conscious and unconscious minds catalyzes personal transformation.

Chapter 1 places Dostoevsky's works in the historical context of the evolution of concepts of the self and fundamental changes wrought by the advent of modernity. It examines issues surrounding the study of Dostoevsky from both a psychological and religious point of view. Chapter 2 addresses the problem of duality and explores the Romantic poetics that informed Dostoevsky's early writing, with a particular focus on the doppelgänger motif. This leads to a discussion of the antecedents in Russian literature that informed Dostoevsky's style and poetics, and, finally, to an examination of the dialectics found in Dostoevsky, with comparisons to socialism and Christianity, and of thinkers of the Russian religious renaissance who referenced Dostoevsky's ideas in their articulation of *dvuedinstvo,* or unity-in-duality.

Chapter 3 returns to the prominent motif and symbolism of the underground in Dostoevsky's work and makes a case study of his (unrealized) effort to revise *The Double* in the early 1860s. Against the backdrop of major national and cultural uncertainty—the "accursed questions" of the 1850s and 60s—his notebooks and drafts show that planned revisions to *The Double* morphed into new formulations of his ideas, which would form the basis of *Notes from Underground*. This chapter also examines the feminine archetypes in Dostoevsky, those that carry the symbolism of Earth Mother or the national motif of Mother Russia, as well as those that represent the shadow side of the archetype in all its destructive force. The chapter concludes with an analysis of terms Dostoevsky used in notebooks and diaries with reference to the self, such as the Law of Personality and the Law of Love, along with a discussion of other terms I find useful for making reference to the varieties of self one encounters in Dostoevsky.

Chapter 4 explores the concept of the shadow in greater depth. Connecting it to my discussion of archetypes is the esoteric concept of *Mysterium Coniunctionis*, otherwise known as *coincidentia oppositorum* or the Coincidence of Opposites—the alchemical principle of psychic opposites on which Jung wrote extensively, and which was first recognized in Dostoevsky's writing by Berdiaev. Further, the so-called "Russian idea" informs a discussion here of Dostoevsky's understanding of the self from both the individual and national perspectives.

Finally, in Chapter 5 I investigate the idea of transformation and the personal experience of ego transcendence that holds a prominent place in Dostoevsky's later novels and stories. Several of Dostoevsky's characters (namely Kirillov, Prince Myshkin, Alyosha Karamazov, and the Ridiculous Man) report experiences of a numinous quality, which promotes a feeling of unity, harmony, and oneness, concurrent with integral thinking and syncretic philosophies such as German Idealism and Neoplatonism. Further, the chapter connects variations on the themes of death and resurrection to the idea of the God-man publicized by Dostoevsky, Solovyov, Berdiaev, and others. Although some of Dostoevsky's characters report the above-mentioned numinous experiences, few reach anything that could be called higher unity. For Dostoevsky, higher unity is a transcendent ideal, one not achieved in this life, even while immortality of the soul is a necessary condition in his world view and philosophy.

The dramatic force of Dostoevsky's writing takes place in a world in which the underground is dominant. In advanced scenarios, the underground catalyzes transformation, as in such cases as Elder Zosima and his Mysterious Visitor. Expressions of the deep-rooted complexes of the psyche in Dostoevsky, however, are polar, just as archetypes are frequently dualistic. They are complex aggregates of multivalent qualities that interact and catalyze change. Dostoevsky's major characters, beginning with Golyadkin, are ideas cast as lived experience, living embodiments of a core idea dramatized amid the conflicts of modernity. They are not reducible to psychological phenomena, but as complex wholes they create multivalent patterns that map onto prominent archetypes. To investigate these archetypes cannot fail to deepen our understanding of Russia's great psychological realist of the nineteenth century.

CHAPTER 1

Foundations of the Dostoevskian Self

I tell you, I am a child of my century, a child of unbelief and doubt up to this very moment, and I am certain that I will remain so to the grave.

—Dostoevsky, letter of January–February 1854, Omsk

Soon we shall contrive to be born somehow from an idea.

—*Notes from Underground*

The iconic image of Dostoevsky is many-sided. In his own biography and as author, Dostoevsky inhabits the roles of oracular bard, revolutionary conspirator, Siberian-exile-turned-monarchist, philosopher of suffering and redemption, Russian mystic, and novelist-seer who predicted that Western socialism would be the cause of unlimited despotism in Russia and "the lopping off of a hundred million heads" (per Shigalev in *The Devils*). We are fascinated by the man and his extraordinary life, by the author and his sensational works, and by the engrossing times in which he wrote them. We are captivated most of all by the exhilarating works themselves.

But why do those works hold us so much in thrall? I venture that the reason we read Dostoevsky again and again is to plumb the souls of his enigmatic characters. As types they occupy the most variegated spectrum:

the downtrodden and abused; the dreamers, criminals, murderers and thieves; amoral nihilists and visionary prophets; holy fools and sage elders; the petty and avaricious; the wretched and despairing; the perfectly beautiful amid the morally bankrupt and outright evil. The almost mythical parade of agitated, fever-addled heroes and anti-heroes entangled in Dostoevsky's nightmarish urban dramas has become emblematic of his work. His great and remarkable talent is his facility to dramatize the emotional and psychological lives of such a diverse cast along with their weighty psychic loads. We are tantalized by the same questions that seem to tantalize and haunt them: What drives them? What do they believe? Who are they? And where is their soul?

In this chapter I ask: What is the Dostoevskian self? I'll ask what Dostoevsky meant when he referred to the self, and I begin to search for the origins of the notions that emerge from my analysis. I examine developments that separate the modern self from its ancient precursors and describe how Dostoevsky responds to the advent of the modern self in the themes that he dramatizes in his uniquely complex and multivalent manner. It is critical to understand the considerable extent to which Dostoevsky conceived of a special, uniquely Russian self as well as, in particular, the mystical folk ethos and other national and religious overtones that he attributed to it.

Put another way: What, judging by Dostoevsky's accounts, is the self made of? What do Dostoevsky's characters mean when they say "I," and what does Dostoevsky the writer mean when he uses the first-person pronoun "я" [*ya*]? I mean this in the everyday, purely indexical sense as well as in the conscious or one might say *self-conscious* sense of "I" that Dostoevsky uses when he talks about the nature of the conscious mind, the human psyche, and its place in the cosmos. This is a broad topic and a large question that brings up several others that need to be addressed in turn, and these considerations lay the groundwork for my study of archetypes in Dostoevsky. I proceed with the understanding that "self" is also an archetype, and the historical development of the Western notion of self and its Russian counterpart can be seen as an unfolding of personality along archetypal lines.

'They Call Me a Psychologist'

In a letter of February 1878 Dostoevsky wrote explicitly on the type of question I am asking. It is late in his life, and he is writing to an admirer of his work, Nikolai Ozmidov, after speculating on the question of sensory experience and consciousness:

> If it has been conscious of all this... then, therefore, *my self* is higher than all this... [it] stands to the side, as it were, above all this, judges

and is conscious of it. But, in that case, this *self* not only is not subject to the earthly axiom, to earthly law, but goes beyond them and has a law higher than them. Where is that law? Not on earth, where all come to an end and all die without a trace and without resurrection. Isn't this a hint at the immortality of the soul? If not, would you, Nikolay Lukich, take to worrying about it, writing letters, looking for it? This means that you can't cope with your *self*: it doesn't fit into the earthly order but seeks something else, besides the earth, to which it also belongs.[1]

Here Dostoevsky describes a category of self that must be seen as transcendent and noumenal. It is the self that is "higher than all this," the self that "goes beyond," that stands to the side, that has a higher law than the earthly.

Reading Dostoevsky's polyphonic novels, one is involved in a chorus of Bakhtinian double-edged discourse, engaged in the process of finding *who* the self is. Who is this dialogic "I" that defines itself pre-emptively with every utterance? Who introduces himself with "I am a sick man...I am a spiteful man. I am an unpleasant man"? Who reasons himself into becoming an axe murderer? Who imagines a Grand Inquisitor who "corrects" Christ's teachings by replacing absolute freedom with absolute tyranny? These questions ask whether there is an integral being whom we associate with the Underground Man, with Raskolnikov, or Ivan Karamazov. In each of these, and among the array of Dostoevsky's characters, how do questions of faith, reason, freedom, society, free will, historicity, consciousness, and moral responsibility contribute to the formation of personality and identity? What do personality and identity mean to Dostoevsky? Within the polyphonic range of types and antitypes that inhabit Dostoevsky's works—his narratives of the grotesque distortions of personality wrought by moral depravity and suffering—does the storyteller reveal the inviolable core of the self or is he a poet of naught but chaos and disorder?

To get at these questions we encounter inherent difficulties in reading Dostoevsky from a religious, psychological, historical, or nationalist point of view, but these perspectives often converge on common insights. Here I consider each viewpoint in turn. First, the psychological.

While some have succeeded in reading Dostoevsky from a psychological perspective, doing so is fraught with pitfalls. Traditional approaches to Dostoevsky-as-psychologist run the risk of diminishing and compartmentalizing the author's works. Yet a tradition of psychoanalytic studies has grown up around them and proven to be a fruitful branch of Dostoevsky scholarship. Ivan Ermakov, a founder of the Russian psychoanalytic school, wrote books on Pushkin (1923) and Gogol (1924) as well as an unpublished monograph on Dostoevsky.[2] The pioneering Vienna Psychoanalytic Society, which took a great interest in Dostoevsky, between 1906 and 1920 would produce Otto Rank's famous paper on the doppelgänger motif in *The Double* as well as Freud's classic study of parricide in *The Brothers Karamazov*.[3] Freud and his colleagues took a biographical approach, endeavouring to link the writer's themes and obsessions, among other complexes, to his epileptic condition, "the baneful influence of his father," and the trauma of the father's murder by his own serfs.[4]

Dostoevsky-as-psychoanalyst has occupied a host of studies, the most recent being Bernard Paris's *Dostoevsky's Greatest Characters*.[5] Paris uses a theoretical framework adapted from the psychoanalyst Karen Horney to produce remarkable insight into the complexity of Dostoevsky's multifaceted characters. Finding, for example, the Underground Man's theories inadequate as an expression of his personality, Paris regards the views of the protagonist of *Notes from Underground* to be the expression of his personality, and his personality a result of his early life. Like some other purely psychological studies, however, its drawback is its excessively clinical approach, casting Dostoevsky's characters as patients in rehabilitative therapy. Clinical psychoanalysis, while compelling, is too hermetic to serve as an interpretive framework for Dostoevsky's works. A notable exception is René Girard's *Deceit, Desire, and the Novel: Self and Other in Literary Structure* (1965), which gives a prominent place to Dostoevsky's work in an incisive examination of literary texts that exemplify the psychological need for transcendence or "metaphysical desire." Girard's analysis of *The Double* is discussed in my case study of that book in the following chapter.

Paris sees that "the complexity of the underground man's motivations cannot be adequately accounted for in thematic terms," and that "in his effort to understand his lack of a stable identity, the underground man attributes his condition to the 'fundamental laws of over-acute consciousness,' but this explanation...seems inadequate to the complexity of his behavior." More insights of a similar variety are offered:

> Like the Russian romantics he describes, he is a "broad" nature, a "many-sided" man who is full of contradictory elements. His problem is that because he contains everything, he feels that he is nothing; none of his attributes really define him.... He cannot become anything because every one of his acts, impulses and values is subject to almost immediate repudiation by the conflicting components of his personality. It is no wonder that he feels "selfless" without substantial reality. He is in fact a puppet pulled about by his contradictory compulsions who ironically takes his slavery as an evidence of his freedom.[6]

Further, in describing his fantasies, the Underground Man confesses his "shameful deeds," after which everyone kisses him and he goes "barefoot and hungry preaching new ideas." He becomes Napoleon and then the Pope, and he is celebrated on the shores of Lake Como, which is transported to Rome so that as Pontiff he can throw a ball there for all of Italy. There is self-mockery and literariness in this account of his dreams, in which he has much invested, since he has "[the] desire to vindicate himself by carrying out his dreams in reality. In his fantasies he is an exalted being, a saint, a conqueror, a lover of humankind; but in reality he knows that he is only a dreamer and despises himself for it."[7]

While these observations are astute, in my view Paris overemphasizes the role of mental health in Dostoevsky's psychological portraiture. I find his psychoanalytical approach, like the others cited above, to be too particular and clinical, as if the characters under examination were real human patients in therapy. I am interested in archetypes in their narratological rather than clinical applications. I agree with Paris that the Underground Man is a slave to his own impulses, a dreamer who despises himself as a result of the inertia caused by his "heightened" consciousness, while his inscrutable mystery, by inference, is the complexity of his own motivations and behaviour. I am most interested in how Dostoevsky's *atypical* Underground Man (an odd man out) becomes a dynamic type that represents a larger whole.

The riddle of his motivations and the complexity of his behaviours are indeed the issue. I cannot agree, however, that the Underground Man's oscillations can be traced to the effects of his early life.[8] Those oscillations are, in my view, traceable not to early life (we are privy to only a few moments from that) but to the contradictory impulses that teem in his psyche, which might be called archetypal manifestations. When his underlying complexes are exposed to the light, he and we as readers undergo transformation as the result of recognition. The complexity of the character, as of other characters and themes in Dostoevsky, is available to the reader because we experience the same dilemmas in our own inner worlds. But we wouldn't benefit as much from a psychoanalytic examination of the Underground Man if, say, we had not all experienced something similar in childhood.

If psychoanalysis alone is too narrow a field to encapsulate Dostoevsky's genius, it holds true nevertheless that, of the great Russian realists of the nineteenth century, Dostoevsky is frequently seen as the era's foremost adept in the art of psychological realism. He comfortably bears the legacy of expertise in behavioural psychology *avant la lettre*, perhaps even specializing in perversity. Surprising, then, for all the attention paid to Dostoevsky the psychologist, that the writer himself seemed to duck the label: "They call me a psychologist: it is not true, I am only a realist in a higher sense, that is, I portray all the depths of the human soul."[9] The conundrum is addressed by the twentieth century's most perceptive reader of Dostoevsky, Mikhail Bakhtin, explained here by Gary Saul Morson:

> If Dostoevsky is not a psychologist, we may ask, then who is? As Bakhtin understands this gnomic statement, Dostoevsky meant to reject the *wrong sort* of psychology, which treats people as the "ready-made" product of pre-given psychic drives. For all their similarity in some respects, Freud and Dostoevsky part company on this fundamental issue. For Dostoevsky, to understand people is to comprehend not their predetermination but their freedom. As Bakhtin describes him, Dostoevsky has never been equaled in his ability to represent a character's ongoing process of choosing, the throb of the "real present moment," when the next moment is uncertain *even for the author.* Such authorial uncertainty, which is sensed as one reads, is what endows Dostoevsky's novels with their special immediacy, that palpable "momentousness" so thrilling to his readers. It is also what defines Bakhtin's concept of polyphony and establishes it as the best way ever devised to convey the feel of human freedom.... Polyphony allowed Dostoevsky to convey his sense that the "living core" of human personality is essentially and irreducibly surprising, something that no imaginable laws or knowledge could entirely explain away. By contrast, "psychologists" give us a world without "surprisingness." In place of this living core, bursting with new life, they substitute a sort of *ready-made definitiveness,* "naturally" and "normally" *predetermined* in all its words and acts by "psychological laws."[10]

Bakhtin's delineation of the differences between predetermined psychological behaviours and the immediacy and uncertainty of spontaneous impulses marks a distinction that is critical to understanding the "living core" of Dostoevsky's art, which shares so much with archetypal psychology.

Dostoevsky was correct, of course, to remind his readers that he was not a professional clinician. By the same token, readers need to remember that he was not a trained philosopher, in spite of his propensity for addressing philosophical problems. Like Bakhtin, however, we are willing to grant that Dostoevsky understood the term *psychology* differently, when applied to his books, than later generations might. Any discussion of psychology and religion in Dostoevsky can profit from bearing in mind his peculiar definition of himself as a "realist in a higher sense," and, in a letter to Apollon Maikov in December 1868, his assertion that his conception of reality and realism were completely different from those of contemporary realists and critics. "My idealism," he wrote, "is more real than their [realism]."[11]

The importance of these statements in assessing Dostoevsky's art and his achievement as a writer of nineteenth-century realism is his discovery of the literary expression of inner mental and spiritual processes—in particular the means whereby mental complexes stored in the unconscious meet the conscious mind and become externalized behaviours, as in the study of depth psychology. I have been arguing that archetypes offer, rather than psychoanalysis per se, an effective and valuable tool for examining Dostoevsky's major works. In particular they illumine an attribute that I argue is their major concern—the problem of the modern self. Reading Dostoevsky from an archetypal perspective opens his works to a better understanding of the dynamic qualities of his characters and situations, which respond to the crisis of modernity and the problem of the modern self.

Modernity and the Problem of the Modern Self

The language of self in Dostoevsky's usage in his fictions and private and public letters is a complex business. When he refers to "I" or "my self" in the passages above, is his meaning the same as in other statements Dostoevsky made about himself or in presentations of the characters of his fiction?

All such statements are contingent upon the modern conception of belief in Dostoevsky's world. That conception lies in part in the recognition that there is on earth no perfect faith or its opposite, absolute evil. Cassedy considers this principle to be epitomized by Prince Myshkin, the good and saintly invalid of *The Idiot* (1869), and his dialectical double Stavrogin of *The Devils* (1872), neither of whom can reach the antipodes at either end of the spectrum of good and evil.[12] I'll argue that the primary duality inherent in Dostoevsky's work, this duality that constitutes the Dostoevskian self, finds its source in the conflict between the expressive unity of man versus atomistic, utilitarian thinking, which is part and parcel of the crisis of modernity and the problem of the modern self.[13] Comprehending this idea requires a closer examination of the circumstances and forces that put these paradigms into conflict.

The underlying premise of idealism, I have noted, is that mind is more intrinsic to reality than matter, that the human mind can intuit divine intelligence, and that an essentially supernatural moral order underlies the universe in which humans play a central role. The modern stance that accepts the hegemony of instrumental reason, on the other hand, created a self of disengaged reason, a product of the rational mind's self-scrutinizing behaviour. That is, trust in the rational faculties alone to arrive at certain or indubitable truth created an *apparent* self that is disengaged from autonomous personhood (that trusts in its own absolute freedom and unity with divine essence) and is disinclined to intuit divinity. Understanding itself as unfree, the prisoner of nature, bound by biological and physical laws and logical imperatives, the apparent self has no recourse but to immerse itself in the intensity of the experience of modernity.[14] In Dostoevsky, Stavrogin exemplifies the disengaged stance of the apparent self with his empiricist claim that notions of good and evil are mere "prejudice" [*predrassudok*].[15]

Broadly speaking, Dostoevsky's work is a counterweight to the modern paradigmatic character of mind following the triumph of Western secularism and scientific rationalism. Through the prism of modern challenges, including his own nation's cultural fragmentation, Dostoevsky dramatizes the search for unity even while questioning its basis. This is a characteristically Romantic quest: a sense of internal division is fundamental to Romantic malaise as much as secure unity in the great chain of being and meaning was characteristic of the eighteenth century.[16] The divided self, which gives expression to so much of the dramatic intensity of Dostoevsky's art and accounts for its frequent disconcerting contradictions, is the primary duality expressing the Romantic vision of lost unity. The chief project of Romanticism was the reconciliation of subject and object, human and nature, heart and mind, spirit and matter; for Romantics strive to discover what is unknown, or imperceptible, to the rational mind. Dostoevsky's vision in his formative years as a thinker was especially informed by Schellingian idealism. Schelling and Russian Schellingians such as Vladimir Odoevsky, who influenced Dostoevsky in his formative years as a writer, opposed the rationalist distinction between the cognizing subject and its perceived object.[17] This was a reaction to the modern stand that accepts the hegemony of instrumental reason, a product of the rational mind's self-scrutinizing behaviour.

The Romantics established a new world view out of their critique of disengaged reason: the rational mind has to open to reveal our own deepest feelings and instincts, allowing the recovery of authentic self through transcendent arts, liberty of spirit, spiritual epiphany, and utopian vision—all of which evolve in an eternally unfolding expression of the Absolute. Humans need to heal the division within themselves that disengaged reason created when it set thinking in opposition to feeling or instinct and intuition. But Dostoevsky's characters are beyond Romantic solace in feeling and recovered unity—witness the Underground Man's critique of Rousseau: "l'homme de la nature et de la vérité."[18] Philosophy is no consolation. The cultural dominant of disengaged reason in the modern age was the catalyst for a now inexorable and overdetermined secular rationalism devoid of absolute values. Europe's Scientific Revolution had ushered in the triumph of the modern mind in Newtonian–Cartesian cosmology, revealing the "true nature"of reality. Man's role in the universe could be judged by the fact that "by virtue of his own intelligence, he had penetrated the universe's essential order and could now use that knowledge for his own benefit and empowerment."[19] Following Hume and Kant, metaphysics is demonstrated to go beyond the powers of human reason. Thus, religious faith lost support from both the empirical world and pure reason, and it lacked plausibility and appropriateness for secular modern man's psychological character.[20]

In light of these developments of modernity, Dostoevsky's work reckons, above all, not with the schism between faith and reason (as it is often seen as doing) but with the problem of modern identity. The modern mind is interested in knowing not only the "true nature" of reality but the true nature of the self as well. If the record of history is any indication, self is a conundrum whose resolution has been a gradual unfolding. Art and literature have frequently provided a venue for the manifestation of archetypal patterns, which the self inhabits as part of its process of assigning meaning to its many and varied forms. As I turn to specific examples in Dostoevsky, the work of Canadian philosopher Charles Taylor and historian Richard Tarnas (whom I have already mentioned) are useful for understanding this process and the making of the modern identity.

Taylor shows that the modern problem of identity is that modernity's notion of identity differs from that of the Ancients in its radical reflexivity whereby, in place of discovering one universal human nature, human agency is defined as the self in search of itself.[21] The "virtually unanimous direction of ancient thought," Taylor explains, is that "beneath the changing and shifting desires in the unwise soul, and over against the fluctuating fortunes of the external world, our true nature, reason, provides a foundation, unwavering and constant." Thus our task as humans, our only search, is to discover the one universal human nature.[22]

The crucial capacity for the great ancient moralists was that of seeing order—in the cosmos (for Plato) or in the priority of human goals (for the Stoics). Introspection had no significance for the former and wasn't thought to be crucial for the latter. The Stoics give us an argument about reason, nature, and self-sufficiency to convince us that we shouldn't set store by ordinary satisfactions; they don't ask us to examine ourselves. For Stoics, all share in the divine Logos as a kind of brotherhood of humankind.[23] Man becomes in actuality what he is potentially by liberation from materiality. Man's rational soul can reflect the transcendent Forms and, through insight into the ultimate order, move toward spiritual emancipation.[24] The universal Logos of Greek philosophy transcended all apparent oppositions, for Divine Reason was immanent in human reason.[25]

Early Christianity has a Neoplatonic philosophical structure, since the Platonic tradition articulated metaphysical insights of the Christian mysteries. Neoplatonic divine Nous (universal Reason) is the manifested ineffable, transcendent Godhead, the One. In the Christian version, the transcendent Father brought forth his manifest image (the Son or Logos) in human form to bring creation, by means of Spirit, back to its divine essence. God's hidden mysteries are ultimately manifested in Christ.[26]

The true departure from the ancient perspective is best exemplified by the inward turn of St. Augustine. For Augustine, the Platonic Forms exist in the mind of God, the ground of reality beyond the world of senses, available only through a radical inward turning. Moreover, Platonic Ideas provide the basis for Christian thought in universal symbols, and all Platonic archetypes are contained in Christ. The soul's teacher is inner illumination; and all of us, not just a select few, are initiates.[27]

Further on, Western humanism can be seen as the decline of the ageless wisdom of God-consciousness, or Divine Intellect. The emergence of the modern mind and modern self included Aquinas's mystical principle of participation, which allowed for human striving for freedom, autonomy, intellectual development, self-realization, and finite humanity participating in infinite divine being.[28] The secure world order of the Middle Ages gradually gave way to growing individuation but at the same time, with the loss of primary ties, to a feeling of powerlessness and isolation. In psychoanalyst Erich Fromm's account, the Renaissance and later the Protestant Reformation prepared Europeans for a personality shift that contributed to the development of authoritarian social structures. The Reformation brought with it the sense that one cannot control what happens, that God is unjust; at the same time it stressed the wickedness of human nature, the insignificance of the individual, and the necessity of its submission to an arbitrary judge.[29]

Further changes in the personality take place at the beginning of the modern era. Writes Taylor, "The Cartesian calls for a radical disengagement from ordinary experience; Montaigne requires a deeper engagement in our particularity. These two facets of modern individuality have been at odds up to this day."[30] Thus most of all it is the reflexive stance of disengaged reason that is the turn in Western thought that constitutes the crisis of modern self-identity.

Taylor juxtaposes these conflicts in terms of premodern enchantment and modern disenchantment. Augustinian "inwardness" shifts the locus of orientation to inner nature, fixing a clear boundary between the psychic and the physical, or the mental and the physical. Thought and feeling—the psychological dyad—are now confined to minds.[31] The hegemony of instrumental reason in the Age of Enlightenment ushers a new moral-spiritual stance into the world. The waning of popular belief in magic reflects this turn to disengagement and disenchantment. Magic "relies on a notion that certain powers have their seat in certain substances or in certain speech acts, in the premodern sense of this relation. There is no room for this in a 'disenchanted' world, as Weber's term ('*entzaubert*') implies."[32]

Taylor goes on to argue:

> The modern ideal of disengagement requires a reflexive stance. We have to turn inward and become aware of our own activity and of the processes which form us. We have to take charge of constructing our own representation of the world, which otherwise goes on without order and consequently without science; we have to take charge of the processes by which associations form and shape our character and outlook. Disengagement demands that we stop simply living in the body or within our traditions or habits and, by making them objects for us, subject them to radical scrutiny and remaking.[33]

This revolutionary paradigm shift that takes place with the advent of modernity ushers in a problematic world view wherein the combination of introspection and disengaged reasoning upsets the perceived integrity of the self-constituting subject. The modern self is its own unique, independent entity and expression. It is the sum of one's knowledge, experience, and conditioned reason, which has no existence outside of the form that contains it. "So we come to think that we 'have' selves as we have heads," Taylor writes. "But the very idea that we have or are 'a self,' that human agency is essentially defined as 'the self,' is a linguistic reflection of our modern understanding and the radical reflexivity it involves."[34] Moreover, "We seek self-knowledge, but this can no longer mean just impersonal lore about human nature, as it could for Plato. Each of us has to discover his or her own form. We are not looking for the universal nature; we each look for our own being."[35] In other words, the Augustinian view of an innate self that is revealed in contact with the divine, which one works to bring to explicit and conscious formulation, moving from ignorance to true self-knowledge,[36] is contrasted with the disengaged subject, with its reflexive stance, exercising procedural reason and instrumental control.[37]

In sum, the world picture that emerged with the Scientific Revolution and became established in the Enlightenment

> freed the modern self from long-established structures of cosmic meanings and purposes that, while perhaps sustaining and numinous, were often problematically interpreted, shaped, and enforced

by cultural authorities—whether political or religious—whose vision was not always profound, their motives not always beyond question. We have come to realize, however, not only the great liberation but the great loss that the triumph of the mechanistic world picture brought in its wake. The liberation and the loss at the heart of modernity have been inextricably connected.[38]

The world thus imagined situates the problem of the modern self as I view it in works by Dostoevsky.

Reading Dostoevsky 'Religiously'

Dostoevsky's statement that his idealism was more real than his critics' realism was made in the context of planning the uncompleted novel *Atheism*, in which he discussed his nation's national development, the Russian land, and the Russian Christ (his plans for *Atheism* would transform into *Diary of a Writer* and his final novels, in which these topics occupied him keenly). He ties his conception of realism to this problem of the Russian self and the spiritual development of the nation:

> (The unveiling is psychological. Deep feeling. Man and Russian man.) Ah my friend! I have such a completely different concept about reality and realism than our realists and critics. My idealism is more authentic than theirs. Lord! To say all that we, Russians, have experienced in the last 10 years in our spiritual development—don't the realists nevertheless cry that it's fantasy? And yet it is primordial, true realism! That's what realism is, only deeper, and theirs only floats on the surface.... Realism is deep—no question. But their realism is only one hundredth of the real, it can't explain the true happening facts. And we with our idealism have even predicted facts. It has happened.[39]

In these statements, we find Dostoevsky combining his "more authentic idealism" and "deeper realism" with topics like national identity and the spiritual development of Russia. They indicate the extent to which the problems of modernity, nationalism, and religion are inextricably linked in his work. We therefore turn now to consider the question of religion and its implications for self-presentations in the Dostoevskian text.

Dostoevsky's impassioned engagement with religious problems perennially inspires illuminating scholarship in Russia and in the West. Yet the complexity of that engagement continues to confound, causing recent debate to centre on the persistent challenges of "reading Dostoevsky religiously."[40] The polyphonic range and dialectical uncertainty that have come to be seen as hallmarks of the Dostoevskian text ensure that attempts to cloak the author in one consistent and finalized system of belief are presumptuous at best. If in that text the issues involving religion and modernity resist consensus, then "reading Dostoevsky religiously" requires most of all, says Malcolm Jones, dynamic engagement between religious vision and the ideological challenges of the modern age.[41]

The problem is not that religious issues are indeterminate in Dostoevsky's writing, but that they are puzzlingly broad and often ambiguous. In Jones's and other recent studies, complex religious themes in Dostoevsky's fiction are approached from religious and psychological perspectives reflecting both the modern and pre-modern world, of Russia and elsewhere—but traditions or ideas indigenous to the writer's native Russia, surprisingly, are not always the dominant.

True, in later works Dostoevsky promoted the view indigenous to Slavophilism that Russia and the Orthodox Church were models for pan-human Christian brotherhood.[42] Dostoevsky's critique of Western rationalism naturally lends itself to comparisons with Slavophilism, especially given Dostoevsky's later associations with romantic Russian nationalism. Slavophilism followed the Neoplatonic line of identification with the inalienable self, which is divine, rather than the ego self. We should proceed with caution here, however, since Dostoevsky's attitudes toward the Slavophile school of thought were complex and often ambiguous. While he shared some of their values, Dostoevsky also questioned and debated the Slavophiles as much as he did the Westernizers, particularly in his journalistic writings of the 1860s.[43] On some points Dostoevsky harmonized with Slavophile thought, but on others he diverged.[44] For instance, he criticized the Slavophiles' idealization of pre-Petrine Russia but found common ground in their critique of Catholicism and the West. Slavophiles, in particular Ivan Kireevsky, thought the Catholic Church had developed in the spirit of rationalism it inherited from Rome, while Russian Orthodoxy stayed true to the spiritual traditions of the early Church fathers.

While motifs of Eastern Orthodoxy are often present in Dostoevsky's mature novels, argues Jones, its doctrinal elements, rites, and rituals are occasional and peripheral, "not thrust upon the reader's attention, thereby permitting, even encouraging readings that do not require them."[45] However, while Dostoevsky depicts "minimal religion," there is no doubt about the writer's belief in the supreme value of religious experiences in human affairs.[46] The deficiency in doctrinal and iconographic elements in the novels is made up for by the "direct impact of lived, personal testimony" of their characters' lives, even though the stories may "lack the power and authority of interpretive tradition."[47] In a related view, Cassedy shows that if we look for confirmation of Russia's native faith in Elder Zosima, the revered *starets* of *The Brothers Karamazov* (1880), we find that his creed is remote from Russian Orthodoxy, representing not only a type of nature mysticism but even possibly a heretical, ethnocentric belief.[48] In the example of Zosima, Dostoevsky proceeds from Christian doctrinal reasoning, yet the "grand synthesis with the all" that he promotes bears no connection to Dostoevsky's native religious traditions.[49] Van den Bercken's recent study also concludes that the religious elements in Dostoevsky's novels are Christian, but depart significantly from Eastern Orthodoxy.[50]

While it is true that Dostoevsky's religious ideas are often tied to Russian nationalism, insofar as the research noted above shows that Dostoevsky's religion can be placed outside of Russian Orthodoxy, several studies have compared his major themes to religious ideas across a surprisingly broad field. They verify that while Christianity is integral to some of the author's most powerful imagery and ideas, it is not a necessary condition for his descriptions of metaphysics or cosmology. For instance, Irina Kirk observed that similarities exist between Dostoevsky's hero of *The Idiot* (1869) and Siddhartha Gautama the Buddha.[51] Michael Futrell (1981) investigated Buddhistic elements in *The Brothers Karamazov*, as well as (1979) references to Muhammad and Islam in several of Dostoevsky's novels from *Notes from the House of the Dead* (1862) to *The Devils* (1872).[52] Sarah Young (2006) discovered further commonalities between Prince Myshkin's experiences and Buddhist concepts of impermanence, ego dissolution, and presentness.[53] Myshkin's qualities have even been likened to shamanism and Sufi mysticism, indicating their common source with intuitive apophatic theology.[54]

These compelling intercultural studies appreciate the breadth of religious and spiritual meaning in Dostoevsky's texts. Can there be any rationale for giving religion in Dostoevsky so many disparate accounts? Perhaps there is if it's true, as Rowan Williams argues, that religious meaning in Dostoevsky is something more malleable than doctrinaire: "What [Dostoevsky] does in *Karamazov* is not to demonstrate that it is possible to imagine a life so integrated and transparent that the credibility of faith becomes unassailable; it is simply to show that faith moves and adapts, matures and reshapes itself, not by adjusting its doctrinal content... but by the relentless stripping away from faith of egotistical or triumphalistic expectations. The credibility of faith is in its freedom to let itself be judged and to grow."[55]

Despite the undecidability of those texts and the author's oscillating positions on important questions of faith vis-à-vis reason, reading Dostoevsky through the lens of non-Orthodox traditions sheds light on points in his fiction and non-fiction that are often taken to be contradictory and irreconcilable. To my mind the problem of the modern self is the dominant theme here, in response to which Dostoevsky's recurring and unambiguous critique of modern secular reason and so-called *rational egoism* catalyzes the psychological imperative of self-transformation. Because the secular modes of thought he contests deny the importance of religious experience in the self-reflective consciousness, the numinous experience of ego transcendence is an essential transformative experience for many of Dostoevsky's important characters. Such experience is part and parcel of the journey of the archetypal hero, who is initiated into a higher realm of self-knowledge. In later chapters I discuss how and to what effect such works as *The Idiot* and *The Brothers Karamazov* dramatize this initiatory experience of inward illumination.

First, I need to investigate the sources and conditions that impacted Dostoevsky's earlier writing. His early works do not reach this level of concern with religious issues. Christian idealism comes increasingly to the fore after *Notes from Underground*, when, as secular idealism is rejected, the Christ image is embraced as a necessary ideal. However, the author's early experiments with form, particularly Romantic poetics and the problems of duality, must be seen as the basis for an aesthetics that privileges higher vision and thus a realm of experience related to the author's later religious concerns. Like the Underground Man, who had endeavoured to foster the "beautiful and sublime" [*prekrasnoe i vysokoe*], the Romantic subject wishes to perceive himself as a unified being who exists in the exalted space of ideal self. In the next chapter I turn to the poetics of Romanticism to show evidence of its profound impact on Dostoevsky and his abiding concern with idealism and the transcendent realm of the sacred.

CHAPTER TWO

The Divided Self

The nineteenth-century dislike of Realism is the rage of Caliban seeing his own face in a glass. The nineteenth-century dislike of Romanticism is the rage of Caliban not seeing his own face in a glass.
—Oscar Wilde, Preface to The Picture of Dorian Gray

We are all divorced from life, we are all cripples, every one of us, more or less.
—Notes from Underground

Throughout his public life, rumours abounded of Dostoevsky's own "personality split" as the perception of him as a sick or mad/insane novelist grew, owing to his well-known medical condition of epilepsy and supported by his provocative journalism and political thought.[1] Such, for example, are the attacks by contemporary critic Aleksandr Skabichevsky in two articles of February 1875 and January 1876. He claimed that Dostoevsky's duality had a pathological root: that "Dostoevsky lived two 'doubles,' a bright one and a dark one, whose vacillations were responsible for the alternation between lyric and frenzied passages in his fiction and journalism." Skabichevsky's theory parodied the romantic theme of the double, which in Dostoevsky's fiction is not necessarily a symptom of disease, but rather reflects the struggle between good and evil in the human heart.[2] This distinction helps to explain the difference between the literary problem I examine and psychological or pathological problems. It is not my intention to analyze the author in psychological terms, but to uncover the origins and trace the dynamics of his literary creations.

In the following pages I investigate the problem of duality as a cultural phenomenon and literary trope, while I analyze Dostoevsky's use of the double, or doppelgänger, as a principal structural and thematic motif. Finally, I look more specifically at some theoretical models I call *Dostoevsky's dialectics*. These preliminary inquiries serve as a basis for my close reading of Dostoevsky's works in the following chapters, in which I argue that the strong emphasis the writer puts on the divided self is a foundational aspect of his archetypal poetics.

The Problem of Duality

Duality as a property of human consciousness and its moral systems is fundamental to Western discourse traditions—from Heraclitus's pairs of opposites and Plato's Allegory of the Cave to Cartesian substance dualism; from Christian and Gnostic accounts of the material and spirit worlds to Kant's antinomies; from Hegel's coinage of "the Other" to the depth psychology of Carl Jung and Jacques Lacan. "Je est un autre" is the famous dualist assertion by Arthur Rimbaud,[3] and Friedrich Nietzsche in *The Gay Science* declared, "du bist immer ein Anderer."[4] Since the twentieth-century advent of postcolonialism, postmodernism, and gender studies, the discourse of duality, or *alterity*, has come to interpenetrate and at the same time integrate an ever-widening field of scholarly disciplines among the social sciences. Finally, modern science bumps up against a pervasive subject–object problem in which perception and evaluation cannot be separated from their object of analysis. Some see the duality at the core of our conscious thought structures as the chief problem of human life. "Reflection starts by dividing man within himself," says Charles Taylor, writing at the close of the twentieth century of the synthesizing power of reflective consciousness, our task as binary creatures being to overcome the oppositions that prevent the spiritual goals of life from uniting with subjective freedom.[5] The scope of the present study does not allow for a comprehensive history of the phenomenon of duality in all its myriad forms, nor could I presume, through any amount of analysis, to resolve the profusion of issues involved in this most fundamental aspect of the human condition. My task is to view the workings of subjective duality as a literary problem given archetypal dimensions by Dostoevsky. To this end I first use examples from Dostoevsky's early correspondence before considering certain cultural and historical contexts.

Evidence of Dostoevsky's attraction, in his formative years, to the paired ideas of madness and doubles is this pronouncement in the postscript of a letter to his brother Mikhail of 9 August 1838: "I have a plan: to become a madman. Let people get furious and try to cure me, let them make me reasonable."[6] His peculiar enthusiasm for "becom[ing] a madman" comes from reading Hoffmann's *Der Magnetiseur*, whose protagonist Alban scorns the moral precepts he considers to be outdated and oppressive. "It is terrifying to see a man," writes Dostoevsky, "who has the inconceivable in his power, who does not know what to do, who plays with a toy that is— God!"[7] Dostoevsky's enthusiasm for the mad Alban and, at the same time, his horror at the implications of the latter's rebellion are the kernels of ideas that come to fruition in Dostoevsky's mature writing. The issues expressed here are dilemmas that will resonate throughout his oeuvre: What are the implications of the extraordinary power humans wield by the strength of an ideologically tuned mind and reckless passion (e.g., Nikolai Stavrogin)? Can one discover the foundation of moral action by means of the reasoning faculties alone (e.g., the Underground Man, Ivan Karamazov)? Does an individual have the right to transgress the ethical strictures of society to serve his own ends, on his own terms (e.g., Raskolnikov)? At the core of these dilemmas is a question of the balance between human intellect and the passions.

In a letter written shortly after the previous one, Dostoevsky responds to his brother's alleged notion that in order to *know* more, you have to *feel* less. He calls such a notion a rash formula and emotional raving: "What do you mean by the word *know*? An understanding of nature, the human soul, God, love—that comes from the heart, not from the mind."[8] He elaborates:

> It is *reason* that conducts thought through the frail membrane into the soul. Reason is a material faculty—the soul or spirit lives by the idea that is whispered to it by the heart—An idea is born in the soul. Reason is the instrument, the machine that is set in motion by the fire of the soul—And so (this is the second point) human reason when it strays into the domain of knowledge operates independently of *feeling*, that is, of the *heart*. But if the goal is to understand love and nature, then a clear field is open to the *heart*.[9]

The primacy of thought over feeling in his brother's schemata demonstrates a rationalist and empiricist point of view that had characterized Enlightenment thought and found its fullest expression in Kant. Some of Dostoevsky's characters rail against the view—there is perhaps no greater apotheosis of the resistance to rational empiricism than the Underground Man's hostile objection: "two times two makes four is no longer life, gentlemen, but the beginning of death."[10] The Underground Man is aware that he is probably perceived as a madman for his irrational attitudes. Similarly, Dostoevsky's distinction between heart and mind, which privileges feeling over the material faculty of reason, accords with his aforementioned pronouncement that he identifies with the mad Alban. It is not that he considers insanity a virtue, but he recognizes that a society that functions on rational systems to the exclusion of feeling ignores a fundamental constituent of humanity—its complex inner emotional life. In a mechanistic universe, feeling is superfluous, and overly sentient beings must be mad.

The idea that nature, the soul, God, and love are understood not by the mind but by the heart belongs to the Romantic disposition, under whose influence madmen abound. Romantic discourse that evoked notions of the sublime, the irrational, the otherworldly, and the supernatural carried a special appeal for Dostoevsky as a young man. Frank notes the aspiring writer's tendency, whenever he is called to represent his inner life, to employ the categories of Romantic metaphysics and to cast personal problems into cosmic and world-embracing terms.[11] In the same letter as the last quoted above, one notices the marked Romantic flavour of the sixteen-year-old Dostoevsky's imagery and analogies:

> I am drifting around in some cold, polar atmosphere where no ray of sunshine has crept.... It is long since I have experienced any burst of inspiration... on the other hand, I often find myself in the same state as the prisoner of Chillon, remember, after the death of his brothers in the dungeon.... No heavenly bird of poetry will ever fly in to visit me and warm my soul that has grown cold.[12]

In the same exalted discourse, Dostoevsky muses in this letter over the dichotomy between the realm of spirit and the physical plane: "If we were spirits we would live and soar in the sphere of that thought over which our soul hovers when it wishes to fathom it. But since we are dust, men, we have to comprehend it, but we cannot embrace it all at once."[13]

Dostoevsky's language shows that his understanding of human self-awareness involves a leap into the transcendental realm. Man's understanding of the phenomena of the universe and the full awareness of his own nature are curtailed by the material conditions of his material manifestation. Therefore, human aspirations naturally aim for that higher awareness that reason—a material faculty—is incapable of grasping. The satisfaction of gaining the self-knowledge for which we yearn, sadly, is just out of reach. This tragic situation is the foundation of Romantic poetics.

In sum, the divided self is the primary duality that expresses the Romantic vision of lost unity and its recovery in utopian vision. For Dostoevsky, like the German Romantics who influenced his generation, poetry and the arts are keys to the world of experience beyond the scope of science and instrumental reason. Romanticism is also the response to perceptions of cultural malaise and a present degraded by the Enlightenment hegemony of instrumental reason and the pecuniary ethic of modern industrial society. The Romantic penchant for escape is a drive to recreate the world of harmony, to enshrine the innocence of childhood or recapture the values of a historical golden age. Moreover the Romantic aesthetic thus always operates according to a system of binary oppositions, of past to present, nature to culture, individual to society, or reality to timelessness.[14]

With these considerations in mind, it is easy to see why Dostoevsky was interested, as a writer, in the dynamics of change and transformation. For this, he had much to observe and work from: the turbulent socio-political life of modern Europe, the dense interior life of the exalted but doomed Romantic anti-hero. As an artist, his finest work is the seething cauldron, the rage of Caliban. He employs the teeming and changing flow of conscious life and subterranean, unconscious impulses as a dramatic principle—the very principle that shapes the Dostoevskian archetypes. The multi-dimensional depths of personality with dark, gothic undercurrents inform the invented lives of composite creatures, emblematic figures of Dostoevsky's angst-ridden urban folklore. Their lives and adventures unfold against a haunted urban cityscape of contrasts: its white nights and dark intentions, idyllic dreams and sordid fantasies. Their dramas catalyze in the in-between spaces of stairwells, back entrances, windows, carriages, and compartments. Their crises and epiphanies unfurl along grey and damp Petersburg avenues, its sordid tenements and crowded corner dwellings, dimly lit and stifling. The typical Dostoevskian atmospherics prompted one of the novelist's most perceptive early-twentieth-century commentators, Vikenty Veresaev, to write, "And so it goes everywhere in Dostoevsky. With their living weight the reader is oppressed by the fog, darkness and drizzling rains; an isolating melancholy fills the soul. And together with Dostoevsky you begin to love this melancholy with some peculiar, painful love."[15]

As a child Dostoevsky experienced literature with profound, direct, and intense pathos. Later in life he would reminisce, "I used to spend the long winter evenings before going to bed listening (for I could not yet read), agape with ecstasy and terror, as my parents read aloud to me from the novels of Ann Radcliffe. Then I would rave deliriously about them in my sleep."[16] In Leonid Grossman's apt summation, adventure tales and Gothic horror novels (Scott, Radcliffe, Louissa, Maturin, De Quincey, Hoffmann) showed the young Dostoevsky that in the age of reason of Voltaire and Derzhavin, some dared to break through the conventions of rationality to reveal the wonderful and terrible otherworld of irrationality.[17]

The Gothic horror novel is a genre that deserves special mention as a pre-eminent example of how Romantic poetics engaged the task of probing a human nature that is divided by good and evil. In the complex psychological drama of Gothic fiction, the discord between human passion and civil ethics is foregrounded in sensational dramas of sometimes heroic proportions. In particular, the post-revolutionary obsession with freedom that was depicted in British Gothic fiction might suggest that "even before Napoleon, the Gothic hero wished to be Napoleon."[18] Generally, Gothic novels measure the nature of human social organization and its value systems against the dimensions of the problem of evil. According to the ethical formula usually applied in the Gothic mode, evil does not exist in human nature, but is often a perceptual consequence of fabricated morality and ethics. "Whenever natural impulses act against social law," Simpson observes, "or when human nature is conditioned or repressed, the possibility of perceiving 'evil' is created."[19] Thus, the concept of sin and the question of evil that occupy the centre of Gothic themes and plot structure are treated in terms of the discord between human passions and the social laws that are meant to govern them. Humankind's innocence in the face of nature is for the most part upheld, and is coupled with a reliance on fate and religion.[20]

One of Dostoevsky's earliest experiences with the exhilaration of storytelling came courtesy of his Bible tutor. Andrei Dostoevsky recalled that the first book he and his brothers were given for reading lessons was a collection of tales from the Old and New Testaments, and that the deacon who came to tutor them was an animated storyteller with whom the boys were duly fascinated. He read and sermonized to the Dostoevsky boys with such religious fervour and dramatic zest that he couldn't help leaving a deep impression on the highly susceptible future author Fyodor Mikhailovich. The writer later informed his younger brother with great nostalgic enthusiasm that he had found a copy of the same edition of the childhood reader the deacon had used in his lessons with the boys.[21] These illustrations from Dostoevsky's childhood suggest that Dostoevsky experienced the written word, which had such profound meaning for the boy and would continue to bewitch the artist, in a twofold manner: as viscerally engaging dramatic flights of imagination, and as revelation of the divine word of Truth.

In adolescence, Dostoevsky absorbed and internalized the literatures of a broader category of European Romanticism. Parisian boulevard literature, known also as French *roman feuilleton* (by popular writers such as Frederick Sulié, Eugène Sue, and Paul de Kock) gave him colourful scenes of contemporary urban life in all the trappings of somewhat "sensationalist" prose.[22] The future author would spice his stories with grand doses of intrigue, scandal, catastrophes, and cliff-hangers. In his own country, historical novels of the 1830s adapted the trends of European Romanticism to the Russian context. Dostoevsky read such Russian imitators of Walter Scott as M.N. Zagoskin, I.I. Lazhechnikov, and K.P. Masalsky, showing his interest in this brand of contemporary Romantic nationalism.[23] Honoré de Balzac, Victor Hugo, and George Sand can be singled out as writers who dramatized for Dostoevsky the moral conflicts of an age increasingly subject to material interests, and who offered socialist and Christian moral alternatives in their stead. Owing in large part to these writers, and to visions of social harmony promoted by French Utopian Socialism and Saint-Simonian New Christianity—movements current among leftist thinkers in Europe in the 1840s and absorbed eagerly in Russia—Dostoevsky's Christianity was, by the time he was writing his earliest manuscripts, strongly social-humanitarian in orientation.[24] Furthermore, German Romantic Idealism in philosophy, art, and aesthetics was another strain of influence that proliferated among Russian intellectuals in the 1830s and 40s and made strong impressions on the budding writer. Its traces in Dostoevsky's thought and writing have been studied in some depth. Frank identifies an indoctrinating experience of Idealist philosophy as the greatest formative influence on Dostoevsky's first experiments in writing. Growing up in the first half of the nineteenth century, Dostoevsky (b. 1821) inherited both the Enlightenment love for science and reason and the Romantic quest for man's relation to the world of the supernatural or transcendent—the Absolute Idea. The precise intellectual climate created in Russia by the stirring momentum of literary and socio-philosophical trends siphoning in from Western Europe through its poets and philosophers is both the starting point and a point of departure for Dostoevsky's own debut writing in the 1840s. It should be noted, however, that Dostoevsky's "indoctrination" with metaphysical romanticism and Idealist philosophy cannot be attributed to his close study of particular texts. Rather, Dostoevsky's environment was saturated with these "ideas in the air."[25]

Dostoevsky was well versed in the foregoing literary trends and was conversant with each of their discourses. They gave him an abundance of heroes, episodes, conflicts, and intrigues to process and adapt, handling each of the elements with his characteristic exuberance and perfervid vitality. Grossman explains how Dostoevsky was trained in classical perfection of form when first hearkening to his muse; but learning from his predecessors and from the free, unfettered form of Romantic novels—owing, moreover, to the exigencies of the publishing trade and the necessity of catering to public taste—his writing style came to centre on *zanimatel'nost'* (approx. "captivation," or "captivating-ness") as an artistic principle.[26] Driven by his own zest for *zanimatel'nost'*, Dostoevsky wrung the salient tensions out of each of the genres he mastered and learned to modulate the emotional intensity in his characters and stories.

To summarize, the problem of duality is a cultural phenomenon embedded in the very fabric of Western civilization and given prominence in poetics of the Romantic Age. Dostoevsky's penchant for sensationalist prose has a lot to do with his interpretation of the trials and aspirations of the Romantic divided self, which I explore in the next section.

The Romantic Divided Self

Although many themes of the Romantic Age had reached their saturation point by the time Dostoevsky began writing in the mid-1840s, his early works show him testing contradictions that were as yet unresolved. Chief among them is the disparity between personal aims of transcendence and real-world contingencies that pull Romantic heroes into isolation, disillusionment, and despair. In response to perceptions of cultural collapse and spiritual decline, notions of the self took on unprecedented dimensions of meaning in the art and literature of the Romantic Age. The rapidly escalating pace of socio-cultural change brought pressures from industrialization and urbanization, the expansion of the bureaucratic state apparatus, and the burgeoning mercantile economy. The increasing secularization of art and culture together with the passing of traditional mores and values from social practices—not to mention the stark realities of daily life in the modernizing world—led writers and artists to depict the debasement of human dignity, with the individual as a focal point. The composite individual personality became a primary preoccupation, the object of scrutiny and analysis in science and philosophy and the subject of a broad sweep of artistic and literary expression. The aspirations of the individual in search of higher forms of self-knowledge and spiritual development on one hand came up against the concomitant drive in mass society, on the other, to perfect functional models of social organization through utilitarian ethics and mercantile interests.

As the child and product of the age, the morally itinerant Romantic protagonist experiences an irreconcilable opposition between the inner self and the outside world, from which he feels alienated and disinherited. Where Romanticism reflected cultural collapse characterized by a fundamental insecurity, the self alone seemed to offer a measure of security—but the deeper it was probed, the more it succumbed to doubt. Feeling alone in a hostile world rather than part of an integrated and organic whole, the individual relied increasingly on self-examination but found that introspection led further into isolation, disillusionment, and despair.

Accordingly, dualism and internal division are fundamental to Romantic malaise,[27] and the discordant interplay of egoism and moral sense is elemental in the cultural ethos of Romanticism.

A hostile, alien reality devoid of values and resistant to efforts at achieving personal fulfillment and happiness precipitated a flight into fantasy to escape the external world and recreate the world of harmony within one's own imaginings.[28] The acknowledgement that "the structures made by man for man" were "not really adequate to man" constituted the essential motivation of later Romanticism and gave the impetus to its literature of lost illusions. The implications for creative literature are expressed by Alex de Jonge in *Dostoevsky and the Age of Intensity*: "The malaise creates a mode of consciousness rather than a state of mind, colouring an outlook in such a way that it becomes impossible placidly to accept the here and now. This fundamental sense of ontological unease lies at the heart of the more desperate aspects of the literature of the age."[29] The new individualism of Romanticism created a sense of the self as existing or acting in opposition to the rest of the world, from which it felt traumatically cut off. Yet, as de Jonge recognizes, Romantic Age despair, while causing alienation and estrangement and prompting mental escape, also brought about a mode of consciousness marked by transcendental strivings. Internal division is fundamental to Romantic malaise, but even as it gives expression to uncertainty and disenchantment, it operates as a catalyst in the quest to reconcile the goals of the individual with the imperatives of society, and to discover fundamental ontological truths:

> The sense of being disunited is a key characteristic of the age. It is usually associated with self-disgust and disgust with the world at large. This disgusted sense of schizoid division is perhaps the most important of all Romanticism's reflections of its sense of the inadequacies of its reality. It provides the motivation for the most serious and ambitious of all the aspirations of Romanticism: the restoration of unity, harmony and synthesis.[30]

Flights of fancy born of Romantic despair with its accompanying sense of inner division combined in Dostoevsky's work to form a metaphysical striving that represented humanity's relation to a world of supernatural or transcendent forces.

At the time, in nineteenth-century Europe and Dostoevsky's Russia, modern science and philosophy were describing a mechanistic world that was increasingly hostile to mythic sensibilities of the sacred world. Positivist theorists argued that society should be transformed so as to free humankind from the shackles of superstition and dogmatism. In the world view that emerges from Dostoevsky's fiction, on the other hand, the empirical mind exists in tension and conflict with first principles and universal values that operate according to spiritual realities that he saw as anathematic to the doctrine of science. The problem of duality thus is an enduring concern in Dostoevsky's work, giving it increasingly closer ties to archetypal patterns of myth and sacred symbology in spite of criticisms from the author's pragmatic-minded contemporaries. As I draw together the strands of Dostoevsky's literary, cultural, and philosophical influences, I shift in the next section to consider a range of sources from Romantic literature that informed his use of doubling to probe the interiority of the self in its struggle with the pressures of modernity to shed the trappings of Romantic Idealism. It is striking the extent to which the origins of Dostoevsky's literary art can be traced to his youthful introduction to fiction from both Russia and beyond in Western Europe. I show that he would have had ample opportunity to contemplate the potential of the doppelgänger motif as a device with which to dramatize the inner conflict that emblematized the Romantic sensibility. This analysis will lay a foundation for my discussion in Chapter 4 of an archetypal aspect of self represented by the doppelgänger known as the *shadow*.

The Doppelgänger Motif and Antecedents to *The Double*
"Doubling" as a literary trope is related to the Romantic outlook, which I have been describing, and which Dostoevsky adapted and parodied in much of his early work and continued to exploit in his mature fiction. Among the dichotomies expressed by this duality in the mid-nineteenth century are passion and intellect, heart and mind, rational and irrational, matter and spirit, the natural and supernatural, and the fantastic and the real. The self, or rather perceptions of self, are divided in perpetual and often devastating struggles between the poles represented in these categories. Broadly conceived, Romantics want to believe they are perfectly *one*; however, failing to recognize their own doublings, they give credence to only one of the two halves—generally the ideal and sublime half, while ignoring mundane and sordid realities.[31] Below, I investigate these antinomies as they find their expression in Dostoevsky's 1846 novella *The Double* and several of its literary antecedents.

While there are no overtly philosophical or religious arguments in the book, *The Double* problematizes themes of moral idealism in the context of secular bureaucratic society in which egoism and moral relativism predominate. One aspect of self—the autonomously acting double, Golyadkin Jr.—finds success and validation in the bureaucratic culture, but he is a "wretch," a "scoundrel," a "villain"; he steals Golyadkin Sr.'s work and passes it off as his own; he lies, cheats, and whispers flattery in the ears of his colleagues and superiors. Golyadkin Sr. employs the psychic mechanism of projection onto an externally perceived adversary to distance himself from these behaviours, so as to label them with moral valuations. Others among Golyadkin's office colleagues are painted with the same brush, such as Vladimir Semenovich, his rival for the affections of Klara Olsuf'evna, who allegedly has ulterior motives, while only he, Golyadkin, is "acting openly and above board."[32] His double's and his colleagues' pursuit of ambition at the expense of others is not only disreputable, but in Golyadkin's eyes *dishonourable* and morally suspect. The ostensibly "real" Golyadkin does not successfully integrate in the bureaucratic milieu, but feels himself to be morally superior. Yet his sanctimonious pronouncements reveal an underlying hypocrisy that show him attempting to come to terms with his feelings of envy and resentment. He repeatedly claims moral superiority while denouncing the reprehensible behaviours that he apparently enacts through the rejected shadow personality. These contradictions that occasion the hero's psychic division—the cleft of his full mental and physical self into two distinct personalities—stem from the interplay of the protagonist's contradictory practices of self-imaging.

The hero's repeated confrontations with his double place the conflict of inner division at the centre of both the novel's action and its thematic concerns. To this end, in *The Double* Dostoevsky exploits the doppelgänger motif, a familiar literary device in Romantic literature. The motif highlights the anxiety that betokens a contradiction between one's inner sense of freedom and the external circumstance of subjection to necessity. Both the egoistic passion that rules *The Double*'s Golyadkin and the morally suspect mores of society he constantly condemns are indicative of this ideological framing indigenous to the Gothic mode. "Doubling," however, is a much older literary practice than this particular application would suggest. Laurence Porter argues that doubling is the generative principle of narrative: when a protagonist experiences desire toward an external object that he believes will complete him, the division between subject and object gives rise to a quest for union with the object. This is the basis of narrative action, in which the protagonist plays the dual role of performer and observer. By the time Romantics exploit the trope, doubling comes to exemplify the cultural flux that occasioned deep probing for personal identity. Radical changes in social, political, and religious institutions subverted the stable foundation upon which the personality had previously been formed. Moreover, the non-rational was perceived as a force that contributed to the shaping of current events as well as personal experience.

Consequently, "This phenomenon encouraged and sanctioned the literary exploration of non-rational modes of perception, with the viewpoint we now call depth psychology.... To the doubling of narrative subject and object, and to the reduplication of narrative line, nineteenth-century literature characteristically added the doubling of individual characters in order to portray inner conflicts, to depict a *décalage* between a character's conscious and unconscious mind."[33]

Examples of the "double technique" that would have been familiar to Dostoevsky and his readers are found in such German Romantics as Adelbert von Chamisso and E.T.A. Hoffmann, and in their Russian counterparts Aleksandr Veltman, Ivan Lazhechnikov, and Nikolai Gogol, all of whom Andrei Dostoevsky reports having numbered among his older brother's favourite authors as a youth.[34] Dostoevsky was particularly impressed with the tales of E.T.A. Hoffmann, perhaps the best-known author to exploit the doppelgänger idea. Ample research on the topic confirms the profound impact the German writer made upon Dostoevsky, exercising a deep and pervading force not only in his earliest works, where intertextual references are most abundant, but over the course of his entire literary output.[35] Surprisingly for someone as literate as Dostoevsky, the obsession with Hoffmann came as somewhat of an anachronism, since the "Hoffmann craze" reached its peak in Russia in the late 1830s. The first translations of Hoffmann began appearing in Russia in 1822, the year of the writer's death, and in 1825 the first Russian imitation of Hoffmann's manner appeared in the story "The Poppy-Seed-Cake Woman of the Lafertov Quarter" ("Lafertovskaia makovnitsa"), by the nobleman Alexei Perovsky, who wrote under the pen name Antony Pogorelsky. With his 1828 collection of stories called *The Double, or My Evenings in Little Russia* (*Dvoinik, ili moi vechera v Malorossii*), discussed below, he is credited with coining the term that refers to a *double* in the Russian language [*dvoinik*] to render the German "*Doppelgänger*" or "*Doppeltgänger*."[36]

Hoffmannism was soon to become the rage in Russian Romanticism, taking hold primarily in the early 1830s. But already with Gogol's 1836 story "The Nose," an ironic parody of the doppelgänger motif, the trend was on its way out, attested to by a rapid decline in translations of Hoffmann in popular Russian journals after 1841. Prince V.F. Odoevsky's *Russian Nights* of 1844 included stories that had already appeared in individual printings and signals the end of Hoffmannism as a mainstay of popular Russian Romanticism.[37] Dostoevsky's resuscitation of its conventions in his own *The Double* in 1846 earned him the censure of Vissarion Belinsky, the same Natural School critic who had praised the excellence of Pushkin's Hoffmannesque "The Queen of Spades" (1834). Literary modes had changed considerably, and Natural School realism was now the favoured style. Yet it is impossible to see Dostoevsky as a writer who was simply behind the times once one considers that *The Double* incorporates much more into its narrative fabric than Hoffmannian supernaturalism. The clever miscellany of interwoven narrative modes combines the heroic romance and adventure novel, Romantic sentimentalism, urban Gothic horror, and French *boulevard* literature—influences noted above. But Dostoevsky's use of the doppelgänger as a centrepiece of his work gives us pause, since, as stated above, the motif had been outmoded for a decade or more. Insight to this question should be found as I compare *The Double* to several works that appeared between the late 1820s through 1840. On the cusp of Russian Romanticism and the advent of Russian realism, each of these works involves a situation of psychic division or double figures, each according to its own formula. They are Pogorelsky's *The Double*, Veltman's *Heart and Mind: An Adventure* (1838), and Prince Vladimir Odoevsky's Gothic tale "The Cosmorama" (1840). Coupled with issues of social and moral concern, common to all of them is the struggle between heart and mind—that is, the dualistic pairing of the realm of feeling and passion vis-à-vis the reasoning, rational mind. Among the dichotomies expressed by this duality in the mid-nineteenth century, besides heart and mind, are passion and intellect, rational and irrational, matter and spirit, the natural and supernatural, and the fantastic and the real. In the remainder of this section, I investigate these antinomies as they find their expression in the antecedents to Dostoevsky's *The Double* named above, particularly insofar as they exploit the tension between heart and mind, a productive catalyst that I argue plays a critical role in the formation of Dostoevsky's conception of the divided self.

Pogorelsky debuted with the Hoffmanesque "The Poppyseed-Cake-Woman of the Lafertov Quarter," which was incorporated into the cycle of his *The Double*, in 1828.[38] The several stories making up this collection are told alternately by the narrator Antony and his alter ego, who is called simply The Double. Antony and his double trade tales that centre on themes relating to the foibles of human passion, and then, in conversation, evaluate each other's narratives in dialogues about the discord between passion and intellect. This metanarrative framework allows Pogorelsky to expose the ironies implicit in the analysis of heart and mind. For one, The Double is presented as a staunch rationalist, a mentor who lectures Antony with quasi-scientific analysis of human nature. The Double cautions against excessive belief in the supernatural (in spite of his own ostensibly fantastic nature) so that his skepticism serves as a foil to Antony's credulity.[39] One finds parallels in the meeting of Golyadkin and his double—and even Ivan with his own doppelgänger, who appears to him as the devil in *The Brothers Karamazov*—except that Golyadkin's double turns out to be a false friend and imposter, and the double in Dostoevsky's last novel is blackened by many degrees as the devil himself and the embodiment of rational egoism. In Pogorelsky, The Double is a harmless and convivial companion, albeit one who acts as a catalyst leading the protagonist toward rational self-examination.

The conflict of passion and intellect is best represented in Pogorelsky's story "The Pernicious Effects of an Unbridled Imagination" and the dialogue that follows it. Narrated by The Double, this tale sees a Russian count fall passionately in love with a sinister Spanish professor's daughter, who turns out to be a papier-mâché windup doll. In the melodramatic denouement, the count, after being deceived into marrying the automaton, goes raving mad as the professor smashes her to pieces before his eyes, shouting, "Here is your wife!"[40] To Antony's incredulous queries as to whether a man can really fall in love with a doll, The Double references Pygmalion and numerous legendary creators of lifelike automatons. "Look at the world," he remarks, "how many dolls of both sexes are you bound to meet, who do nothing and can do nothing but walk in the streets, dance at balls, curtsey and smile? In spite of all this, people very often fall in love with them and sometimes even give them preference over others who are much more deserving!"[41] The Russian count, and by this general analogy anyone sharing the same weakness, is faulted for falling prey to an "unbridled imagination" and unchecked passion.

The ensuing discussion between the two narrative voices focuses on the constant struggle for supremacy between intellect and passion. The Double teaches Antony the anatomy of intellect, along with its spiritual properties and their inversions created by vice and weakness. He defines intellect as an amalgam of several categories: common sense, perspicacity, quick understanding, profundity of thought, foresight, clarity, tact, wit, cunning, and social sense (*esprit de société*). These are compared with the vices, which are depicted in diagrams to show how they offset the qualities of intellect. The virtues (magnanimity, firmness, decisiveness, good nature, compassion, etc.) do not overpower the intellect, while the vices (malice, envy, pride, vengefulness, self-content, arrogance, etc.) can and do lead it in the wrong directions. The Double's main thrust is that one can be considered a clever person yet commit unforgivable follies. Meanwhile, envy, self-love, arrogance, and stubbornness can easily pass for intelligence, because learning, cunning, and sharpness fool inattentive and lazy people—who make up most of the population.[42]

The other stories and dialogic episodes in Pogorelsky's collection contribute similar arguments for the cultivation of virtue and reason as a bulwark against human folly. Although the literary merit of Pogorelsky's work is mediocre at best, his narratives demonstrate the clash between Romantic poetics and the spirit of rational empiricism that had come to dominate intellectual inquiry in the early mid-century. The Double's postulates notwithstanding, the problem of human consciousness and moral awareness remained shrouded in mystery. The human mind and spiritual abilities are enigmas, he explains, because the Almighty deigned to delimit human understanding of abstract matters by a sharp boundary. When Dostoevsky takes on these problems in his own work titled *The Double*, he exploits the doppelgänger motif in such a way as to accentuate the subjective experience of bumping up against that margin. Golyadkin's double wreaks his havoc just beyond the threshold of the hero's conscious awareness. Unwilling to see his double as an emanation of self, Golyadkin is unable to hold a rational debate with his twin as Pogorelsky's Antony does.

In the one instance in which he communes with his phantom clone, in Chapter VII, Golyadkin Sr. is moved by Junior's (the double's) tearful story of slander at the hands of enemies, of losing his civil post and having to walk to Petersburg and live on the streets. Won over by his guest's ingratiating manner, Golyadkin Sr. experiences compassion and a whole array of noble sentiments. Now "acting as someone's protector," and "at last doing good," he is lighthearted and joyful. Partial to his interlocutor's sentimental discourse, he dreams of exalted Schillerian brotherhood and offers reconciliation with his prodigal other self: "It's no good worrying or grumbling about this strange thing between us. It's a sin to grumble, my friend. It's Nature! And Mother Nature is generous, Yasha! I'm saying this because of my affection, my brotherly affection for you."[43] Punch-drunk and overcome with emotion, the two Golyadkins' bonding reaches maudlin heights when the double pens the epigram,

If me thou ever shouldst forget,
  I'll remember thee;
Much in life may happen yet,
  But remember me![44]

The episode betrays Golyadkin's partiality for exalted feeling, his fantasy of embodying all that is exalted and beautiful (*prekrasnoe i vysokoe*). His elevated disposition even carries over to his relations with his servant Petrushka, with whom he is usually condescending and derisive: "I want you to be happy and easy in your mind. We're all happy now, and you should be happy and contented too. And now I wish you good night. Get some sleep, Petrusha, get some sleep."[45] Golyadkin is predisposed to this harmonious convergence with his shadow self when the bond matches his fantasy of elevated moral sentiment—which for Golyadkin has the character of a lofty passion, an intoxication. In later incidents, however, when his double plays the opportunistic scamp and demon saboteur, there is no question of brotherly communion. Golyadkin wishes to make his way in society and to be recognized for gallantry, not roguery. His passion for the former makes him blind to the truth of his complicity with the shadow self who uses subterfuge and flattery while touting the ideals of chivalry. Rather than allow virtue and reason to bring his flaws to light, as Antony's double coaches, Golyadkin perpetuates a pattern of folly and anguish in the internal division of his personality by repeatedly intoning the self-shielding mantra "It has nothing to do with me."

If the double in Pogorelsky's book is a sensible, rational sort, the rogue double who hounds Golyadkin Sr. finds a truer antecedent in another work—one that had made a significant impact on the young Dostoevsky. While writing *Poor Folk*, Dostoevsky wrote to his brother Mikhail, "Have you read Veltman's *Emelya* in the last *Library for Reading*?—what a fascinating thing!"[46] The story he refers to is a tale by A.F. Veltman, who enjoyed wide popularity in Russia in the 1830s and 40s with his novels and short stories in the historical, adventure, fantastic, and utopian genres. He also wrote scholarly works on Russian and Scandinavian histories and the mythologies of Slavic tribes. Although many are written in a florid Romantic style, Veltman's works were not coloured by the Byronesque tendencies of contemporaries like Bestuzhev-Marlinsky. Many of his works are in fact Romantic parodies. He was not interested in either German Idealist philosophy or the social concerns of the Natural School; rather, his world view comes across as simple and clear, like that of a folk tale, where good and evil are clearly delineated.[47] Doubles found in Veltman's stories and novels often serve as integral components of their structural and thematic organization. In *The Lunatic: An Incident* (1834), the split-personality protagonist commits crimes while in a somnambulistic state. A double of a more folkloric cast features in Veltman's *Heart and Mind*, which Andrei Dostoevsky numbered among his brother Fyodor's best-loved books.[48] This novel exhibits a vanity fair of provincial society, which is held in the sway of the town's resident devil, or "unclean spirit" (*nechistyi dukh*), whose craft is to stir up intrigues and exacerbate the townspeople's vices. Generally *Neliogki*, as the devil is called (meaning *tough* or *difficult*, in the sense of hard-earned fate), specializes in stirring people's passions and upsetting their peace of mind: "In anyone in whom blind faith appeared, he sowed doubt; if anyone united with another in common feeling, he aroused suspicion; where quiet came to someone's heart and soul, he immediately overshadowed it with cloudlets that grow in adversity; and any place where sparks showed under the ashes, he fanned the flames—he whispered gossip and spread rumors everywhere, he confused and upset everything."[49]

Neliogki, moreover, is a plot device, an antagonist who motivates behaviours and then recedes into the background. His favourite game is ensnaring people in tangled affairs of the heart. Under his influence, all the town officials, numbering six, fall in love with and seek the hand in marriage of the heroine, Zoya Romanovna. In contrast to this banal world of petty bureaucrats who are slaves to their passions but embarrassingly inept in the art of love, the transcendence of art is upheld by the seventh suitor, the poet Porfiry, who is exempt from Neliogki's sinister art because "the Poet, who lived always in the airy plane, he didn't consider to be under his control."[50]

Veltman's text moves fluidly through the "real" world and the imaginary in a Romantic style rejected in the 1840s as outdated and sneered upon by Belinsky as stilted and far-fetched distortions of real-world concerns.[51] Dostoevsky's fascination with Veltman anticipates his own appropriation of Romantic motifs that would earn him the censure of Belinsky and other contemporaries. As one might expect, it isn't difficult to identify parallels in the two authors' adaptation of the mode. Veltman parodies the conventions of Romanticism for use in his satire of society's mores. But his satire is playful, humorous, and void of acrimony. Neliogki is personified pride, passion, and ambition that nearly everyone in Veltman's world shares. However, the unclean spirit, together with a witch who acts as his helpmate in Part Three, is more a comic jester than a hostile minion of the Enemy. Together, they toy with human passions and fate like classical gods or mischievous sprites. Like the archetypal witches and devils of Russian folklore, or personifications of *sud'ba*, the uniquely Russian concept of destiny,[52] they are not an integral part of the conscious makeup of their unwary victims, but rather external forces that tamper with the balance of heart and mind. In Dostoevsky, Golyadkin's double, like Neliogki, cajoles and minces like a playful spirit who personifies the protagonist's vices; however, the essential difference in this comparison is that Golyadkin's double most certainly is an emanation of his psyche—not an external force, but a rejected component of ego, which he has not consciously integrated. There is humour in the machinations of Golyadkin's double, but it is less innocuous than Veltman's, closer in kind to the "laughter through tears" of Gogol.

The final author I offer for comparison is Dostoevsky's somewhat older contemporary Vladimir Odoevsky. The epigraph to *Poor Folk* is taken from "The Living Corpse," a story from Odoevsky's collection *Russian Nights* (1844). Artist, intellectual, and philanthropist, Odoevsky authored literary, musical, journalistic, and educational writings. He also co-edited several journals, including Pushkin's *Contemporary* and Andrei Kraevsky's

Notes of the Fatherland. Dostoevsky makes scant reference to Odoevsky in his letters, but his familiarity with the tales of the co-editor of *Notes of the Fatherland*, in which *The Double* was first published, is certain.[53] The philosophical-romantic tales of Odoevsky are, in the words of Joseph Frank, "the literary quintessence of the Romantic Schellingian spirit of the Russian 1830s."[54] "The Cosmorama," in particular, showcases the writer's penchant for supernatural and mystical content while featuring the motifs of madness and doubles.

"The Cosmorama" is an extraordinary tale of demonic doubles and grotesque phantasmagoria that evince an alternative reality of a different sort, one where the antagonist is personified evil. The hero and narrator of "The Cosmorama," Vladimir Petrovich, is a reluctant witness to the struggle between good and evil owing to special powers of clairvoyance he gains through the use of a toy gifted to him as a boy, called a *cosmorama*. The slide-viewer box, also known as a stereoscope, used a dual-magnification mechanism to give the pictures inside a three-dimensional appearance. The mystical powers of his cosmorama allow Vladimir to see people's doubles, who communicate to him the authentic realities that lie below the surface of their conscious awareness. For example, when his family physician and confidant Doctor Bin, the giver of the toy, shows alarm at Vladimir Petrovich's insinuations about the extraordinary things he sees, the doctor's double in the cosmorama warns him:

> Don't believe him,—said the latter,—or, to put it better, don't believe me in your world. There I don't know myself what I do, but here I understand my actions which, in your world, are presented in the form of *unconscious motivation*. There I gave you a toy, without myself knowing why, but here I had the intention of forewarning your uncle—and my benefactor—of the unhappiness which was threatening all your family.[55]

The privileged gnosis provided to Vladimir Petrovich by the cosmorama reveals to him the dual aspect of truth that is hidden from the uninitiated:

> Oh, you ill-starred fortunate! You—you can see everything—everything, without the covering, without the astral shroud which *there* is impenetrable, even for me. I have to pass my own thoughts to myself by means of a series of routine trivia, by means of symbols, of secret incentives, of dark hints which I frequently take the wrong way, or which I don't take at all.[56]

Vladimir's occult knowledge, however, puts him in a dangerous position. The plot of "The Cosmorama" centres on his affair with the wife of a count whose double, whom Vladimir also sees, inhabits the count like a demon that accompanies him through life as an evil guardian monster:

> I saw Count B. at different ages of his life.... I saw how, above his mother's bed-head, at the moment of his birth, hideous monsters were writhing about, greeting the newly-born with wild joy. Here was his upbringing: a vile monster came between him and his tutor—whispering to the one and to the other confiding thoughts of egoism, nonbelief, callousness and pride. Now the appearance of the young man in society: the same vile monstrosity directs his behaviour, instils in him a subtle sharpness, caution and treachery, arranging certain success for him.[57]

The count's double aids him in slandering honest men and taking over their possessions, seducing women, ruining his opponents at cards, murdering in duels, and covering the traces of his crimes, all the while enjoying the reputation of an honest and upright citizen.

The moral insight of "The Cosmorama" is plain to see. Like a photographic negative of "The Sylph" (1837), a story by Odoevsky wherein the protagonist had witnessed the "higher self"—the plane of the exalted and beautiful—the arcane other world is in this instance the realm of veiled motivations that betray the base and evil side of human nature.[58] While in "The Sylph" a magical being admits the protagonist to the higher realm, Vladimir in "Cosmorama" accesses its mysteries through an apparatus, a window on the dualistic world. In both stories, then, an intermediary repairs the rupture between the conscious and unconscious mind, showing the potential for heightened awareness of self in this and other realities.

Odoevsky's stories are experiments in *dvoemirie* (dual worlds or "two-worldedness"), the Russian rendering of Romantic Gothic, which establishes an occult or religious system of dualism and contact or correspondence between two worlds.[59] Odoevsky's biographer discerns, however, that the writer was more concerned with the psychological potential of modes of thought and their artistic application than with the intrinsic worth of what he recognized as eccentric beliefs. This is confirmed by a note Odoevsky wrote in the 1840s: "Böhme, Swedenborg, Saint-Martin were, in relation to their time, what Alexander Dumas, Eugene Sue and others are now: talent, imagination, some sort of an unconscious striving, hints seductive to man, inexplicit concepts, beyond which is revealed an apparently deep and [illegible] love for people—beyond that—phantasmagoria."[60]

The Double exhibits remarkable parallels with Odoevsky's stories of madness, doubles, and alternative realities. In its combination of the elements of Romantic poetics with a protagonist of common bureaucratic stock, *The Double* depicts the ego struggle that underlies the surface reality of social behavioural norms. Dostoevsky's hero may not be as black and ignominious as Count B.; Golyadkin is, however, a subject whose conscious awareness is traumatized by the experience of perceiving the dualistic makeup of self, the *dvoemirie* that separates the socially constructed ego from the higher self.

Beyond *The Double* from Dostoevsky, I have discussed these examples of doubling in Romanticism and antecedents to early Russian Realism to show that the double motif is itself an expression of an archetype, serving as such in Dostoevsky's tale. A double, like any mask or persona, is a suppressed aspect of personality, which emerges to manifest the hidden aspect. The historical use of doubles as a literary device confirms my analysis. Legend and early genres of lore had treated the devil as the instrument of divine justice or as the "braggart folktale trickster"—a typical archetypal figure. The devil is a particularly strong archetype in Russian folklore, host to a whole sophisticated catalogue of demonology, which inhabits Russia's national literature as well.[61] In the nineteenth century, doubles came to be used widely in literature across Europe, in a range of roles and for a variety of purposes, making it difficult to impose a uniform interpretation on all their uses as literary devices.[62] A commonality that most share in these contexts, however, is that the double represents a suppressed aspect of personality, which is revealed to the protagonist by degrees as a result of conflict and confrontation with some form of doppelgänger. In Porter's thesis, the particular kind of doubling in which the devil is *raisonneur* and confidant to a human being, which he finds in Goethe's *Faust*, Flaubert's *La Tentation de saint Antoine* and Dostoevsky's *The Brothers Karamazov*, shows that "their devils represent an impetus, ultimately constructive, to self-awareness."[63]

The doppelgänger motif in *The Double* presents a similar challenge. The antagonist is an ego projection who mirrors the protagonist's flaws. Interaction with the double offers Golyadkin a chance to achieve greater self-awareness, particularly with respect to conscience and moral action. Moral self-awareness is an issue for Golyadkin because unconscious drives determine many of his behaviours—particularly ones that he would regard as indications of falsity, pretense, and moral transgression in others. The morning after the first meeting with his double, Golyadkin signals a marginal awareness of his unconscious projection, even if the insight is cloaked in paranoia. He admits that he always knew something like this was being prepared: "Mr. Golyadkin had long been aware that they were cooking something up, and that there was someone else in with them."[64] The revelatory moment shows a degree of understanding of the process of ego-splitting that had culminated in the fantastic events of the night before; however, the process is externalized, attributed to the machinations of deadly enemies. This hint of awareness can be compared to the catastrophic finale when the sum of Golyadkin's fears reaches a climax—as he is carted off to a madhouse, his last recorded thought is "Alas! He had felt this coming for a long time!"[65] That he externalizes the problem—suspecting all along that his enemies were conspiring to defeat him—signifies that Golyadkin is not prepared to recognize that the challenge to his moral conscience and personal integrity is an internal struggle. In the rational practice of self-justification, Golyadkin chooses not to recognize the irrational confrontation of self with self.

Nevertheless Golyadkin's traumatic confrontation introduces the aesthetics of higher vision (which I explore in Chapter 5) as foundational to Dostoevsky's poetics. Furthermore it opens the work to the rich tradition of duality myths that Dostoevsky will exploit throughout his entire oeuvre. Roger Anderson describes the function of duality myths in Dostoevsky as a preoccupation with leaps into a higher, ideal realm rather than a problem of the particular social or historical context of the characters' lives:

> Contemplating the restrictions of time, space, and their own mortality, the memorable characters try to leap beyond to a higher condition. Each would join the self with a vision of eternal constancy. What joins these characters is, first, their dissatisfaction with the empirical world and, second, a common insistence that life open onto a unitary whole that includes them personally. As a result, they are all subject to a deeply ingrained duality that they seek to resolve at any cost. They push against the knowledge of factual containment and attempt to join a cosmology of final permanence. The duality they share thus suggests a question beyond the specific programs that give it a narrative shape from novel to novel. In Dostoevsky's art duality is a structural matter, an ontological speculation in its own right.[66]

The conditions of a higher reality in myth are typically dualistic, and lead to a central paradox that the protagonist must confront and resolve. The archetypal hero of myth explores values that exist in inseparable oppositions, both sides of which compel him to action.[67] This pursuit of personal authenticity, as Anderson describes it, is synonymous with a sacred quest. In relation to his own endorsement of particular values, Golyadkin is caught between traditional and modern forms of myth-making. His allusions to the code of chivalry demonstrate a traditional frame of myth, one that functions to canonize a value system. His practice of panning the social conventions of polite society, on the other hand, is modern mythmaking—a breaking down of the canon of contemporary morals and pointing to a future in which the traditional values are re-established. Both attitudes are made explicit in Golyadkin's moralizing pronouncements, while with his escapes into fantasy, Golyadkin's invented persona and clandestine escapades quickly devolve into morbid paranoia and hallucinatory *cauchemar*. The threat of exposure is a devastating assault on his core personality, because it undermines his manufactured self. Caught thus in his cognitive dissonance, Golyadkin and his predicament serve as a foundation for Dostoevsky's archetypal poetics, as *The Double* works out his methodology for framing the interaction of the conscious and unconscious minds and narrating the personalities that come to life as their consequence.

Dostoevsky believed he had discovered a new type with his hero Mr. Golyadkin, but he was unsatisfied with his attempt to realize it.[68] However, if *The Double* was unsuccessful with critical readers, who saw it as idiosyncratic, cryptic, and aberrant in the context of the Natural School, it is nevertheless clear that its fantastic elements served Dostoevsky in ways that went unnoticed in the critical furor.[69] Belinsky may have been a shrewd judge of literary merit, the pre-eminent critic of his day, and Dostoevsky's erstwhile mentor, but one suspects in hindsight that he failed to recognize the inception of a winning formula. More recent critical judgment has acknowledged the connection between Dostoevsky's use of the fantastic and the ontological problems posed by his works. Malcolm Jones recognizes that fantastic realism "is about the intersubjective experience of reality and the elusiveness of a much sought-after, universal Truth."[70] Frank sees in Dostoevsky's method, as it develops in later works, a synthesis of the rationalism and enlightenment of the Western intelligentsia with the unconscious moral forces of the *narod* [Russian folk]. The synthesis is a foundation for the social-moral philosophy he would later develop as *pochvennichestvo*, often translated as "Native soil conservatism."[71]

In the 1840s, the shifting alliances of critical readership had come to reject abstract idealism in favour of naturalistic depiction. By combining the bureaucratic setting of Natural School realism with the Romantic fantastic, Dostoevsky undertook to counterpoise the popular sentimental and philanthropic take on the life of a civil bureaucrat with elements of the Romantic fantastic. The combination shows the tension between Dostoevsky's predilection for Romantic metaphysical idealism and his concern for the real-world social issues favoured by his readers and critics representing the Natural School. Specifically, in the famous "Vision of the Neva" episode, Dostoevsky dramatizes the vital moment when he discovered the hybrid approach he would employ to merge Romantic metaphysics with sentimental naturalism. The significance of the vision as a personal epiphany for the author is corroborated by his recounting it in three places—the 1848 short story "A Weak Heart," the 1861 feuilleton "Petersburg Visions in Verse and Prose," and the novel *A Raw Youth* (1875).[72] In the second of these, after an outpouring of details describing steam rising over the frozen river and smoke issuing from rooftop chimneys, which evoke a phantasmagorical image of an ethereal Petersburg, the author describes how his Romantic proclivities made way for a particular conflation of sensibilities:

> Some strange thought suddenly stirred in me. I shuddered, and my heart was as if flooded with a hot rush of blood that boiled up suddenly from the surge of a powerful but hitherto unknown sensation. I seemed to have understood something in that minute which had till then only been stirring in me, but was still uninterpreted; it was as if my eyes had been opened to something new, to a completely new world, unfamiliar to me and known only by certain obscure rumors, by certain mysterious signs.[73]

The transcendent moment is identified as one of artistic transformation that leads to the merging of Romantic sensibilities with the sentimental naturalism of Belinsky and the Natural School:

> They were strange, wonderful figures, entirely prosaic, not at all Don Carloses or Posas, just titular councilors, and yet, at the same time, fantastic titular councilors... some titular heart, honorable and pure, moral and devoted to the authorities, and together with him some young girl, humiliated and sorrowing, and all their story tore deeply at my heart.[74]

In this formula, Dostoevsky relates the discovery of his methodology for *Poor Folk* and its mock-sentimental hero Makar Devushkin. The "obscure rumors" and "mysterious signs" of the vision are the hieroglyphics of a new brand of realism that incorporated the heroic and fantastic modes in representations of entirely prosaic figures of the Russian bureaucracy. His "fantastic titular councilor" finds a truer form in Golyadkin, whose mock-heroic adventures challenge, more overtly than those of Makar Devushkin, contemporary representations of *chinovniki* and the evolving conventions of realism.

The conflicts of the emergent modern self are problems Dostoevsky would continue to grapple with in his fiction after *The Double*. Even if he made a profound revaluation of the radical idealist ethos of the 1840s in his novel *The Insulted and Injured* (1861),[75] he would remain at odds with the prevailing ontology of Russian intellectual society of the 1860s and 70s, with its dominant spirit of scientific materialism. Dostoevsky's fantastic realism in early writing sets the ground for the vision narrative he would employ in later works to juxtapose a vision of truth and wholeness with the modern tendency toward fragmentation. This is why some measure of self-interpretation and psychological projection are involved in the experience and articulation of visions of the good for Dostoevsky's characters. I examine the moment of transcendence as a more personal, transformative experience for Dostoevsky's characters in my final chapter and conclusion, while I continue to argue throughout this volume that Dostoevsky conceived moral ideals in terms that are inseparable from concepts of the self, as apprehensions of the external world are interlaced with perceptions of the inward gaze. What is more, the means by which his characters come to self-awareness is always a living dialectic, the equation of counteracting forces whose mutual pressure forms the cores of the archetypes. Therefore I close the present chapter with the following discussion of Dostoevsky's dialectical thought, a subject to which numerous researchers have contributed to our understanding.

Dostoevskian Dialectics
Without taking it as far as Skabichevsky's comment at the outset of this chapter, it is safe to say that Dostoevsky viewed his own life and mind as an inner dialectic. His 1854 statement quoted in my epigraph to Chapter 1 reveals as much: "I am a child of my century, a child of unbelief and doubt."[76] His art and aesthetics were, even more so than his life, based on a complex system (or systems) of dialectics. Copleston observes that "the struggle between good and evil, between, as Mitya Karamazov puts it, the ideal of Our Lady and the ideal of Sodom, the struggle between faith and its opposite, the clash between the ideal of the God–man and that of the Man–god, all these struggles and conflicts—this dialectic—proceed not in some abstract sphere of categories and concepts but in the minds, hearts and wills of human beings, manifesting the polarities of human nature."[77] The novelist does not provide any formal syntheses, or proofs, but dramatizes theses by contrasting them, leaving the reader to decide. Rather than trying to prove or disprove the existence of God, for example, he shows what it means to live with belief or unbelief. Therefore his approach to metaphysical problems, says Copleston, is psychological rather than ontological.[78]

Let me put Dostoevsky's dialectics further into context. Berdiaev, who called Dostoevsky "Russia's great metaphysician" as well as "a dialectician of genius," referred to him as a metaphysician not, of course, by virtue of any formal philosophical discourse, but because of Dostoevsky's narrative of vision and intuitive perception of truth. Berdiaev saw the dialectic of ideas as an expression of human nature, or "anthropology in motion," and Dostoevsky's ideas as possessing a significance that transcended the limits of personality. Dostoevsky's dialectic does not follow a static logic but instead navigates a shifting system of ideas as forms or expressions of life in its variety and movement. Moreover these ideas are embodied in and inseparable from the attitudes, emotions, and reactions of his characters. The ideas are expressions of the personalities of the characters and their experiences.[79] To examine the problem more closely, let us consider the varieties of dialectics that we find in Dostoevsky.

Western Duality
Cassedy shows that in Dostoevsky's system belief is ideal, it is expressed in antinomies (dual pairs) and, at the same time, is contextual. For Dostoevsky, there is on earth neither perfect faith nor its opposite, absolute evil, neither of whose exemplars, Myshkin and Stavrogin, could reach his end of the spectrum, even if he could envision it.[80] Shatov, with his Slavophilism, and Kirillov, his atheistic humanism, both preach impure, corrupted systems of belief. In place of conviction, each is lukewarm in his belief, because neither can begin to envision an absolute (as Stavrogin and Myshkin can).[81]

On the question of belief, Cassedy argues that the only thing one can say with certainty about Dostoevsky's approach to religious issues is that he *sometimes* embraced a particular set of beliefs. His narrative universe shows that a reflecting subject is contingent, owing to the instability of the believing or nonbelieving subject as well as the absolutes he or she may or may not believe. "The reciprocally heterogeneous natures of earthly beings and absolutes of any sort render unrealizable any ambition to believe perfectly or disbelieve perfectly. What's more, the unstable nature of the individual renders suspect the status of the thing that's doing the believing or disbelieving."[82]

Cassedy concludes: "Dostoevsky's mode of thought is idealist through and through, but in his own peculiar sense. Strictly speaking, there is an ideal realm, but it is "unattainable because it lies on the other side of an impenetrable wall." On the other hand, "I am obliged to stand on a path that leads to it." The earthly path is separated from the ideal realm, however, by a gap. "The gap," Cassedy writes, "is what distinguishes Dostoevsky's view from Hegel's. In Hegel's system, at whatever stage of spiritual development I find myself, I can take comfort in the fact that I am joined with the absolute by the continuum on which I stand. Dostoevsky's continuum never reaches the absolute, yet it is still a continuum that takes me ever and ever closer to the absolutes lying at either end." Thus, I exist and act at a point that is very close to the absolute, but I am never closer than very close, whether to absolute good or absolute evil. The I stands forever hesitating "between an unattainable wholeness and an equally unattainable dissolution."[83]

Gier presents Dostoevsky as an example of a *both–and* dialectic, a formula that has similarities with Hegel's synthetic dialectic and other examples of dialectical religions such as Chinese Daoism and Hindu Vedanta (Buddhism, however, more commonly follows a *neither–nor* dialectic).[84] He cites Father Tikhon's statement in "Stavrogin's Confession" (the episode excised by censors from *The Devils*) to the effect that the absolute atheist stands on the last rung but one before absolute faith. "It is especially in [Dostoevsky] where we find characters trapped between opposite tensions vying for synthesis. Dostoevsky shares Luther's preoccupation with Satan and the demonic, and he is obsessed with the dramatic coincidence of the saint and the sinner."[85]

To this point in my account of Dostoevsky's thematic approach, I have set his thinking in the context of Western duality and the collapse of the modern self versus indeterminacy and immanence. In the words of David L. Hall and Roger T. Ames, whose examples of dialectics I bring to bear on this question, "The modern self collapsed as soon as it was formed, its very apotheosis signaling its demise."[86] In comparing Western with Asian cultures, Hall and Ames argue that the concept of the self has Western European origins that give it a "culture-bound character." Because the concept was given "contrasting understandings" through "several distinct historical narratives," it has been "destabilised" by the way in which these narratives shape "actions and appreciations in disparate, richly vague manners." They cite Aristotle to argue that the Western notion of the self has not produced a "coherently defined ego or personality construct characterizing a core self."[87]

Hall and Ames argue that the "embarrassment of modernity lies in the obvious failure of the creators and purveyors of intellectual culture to demonstrate the efficacy of reason in establishing a consensual basis for our scientific, social, and political institutions." This, they note, has vitiated rational self-consciousness, which was thought to be the basis of the modern self. Rather than cohering around a reasoning core, the "elements" of the modern self "are held together by claims of aesthetic enjoyment. The...modern self returns to its origins in aesthetic plurality, but it arrives with the gift of reflexive consciousness."[88] Echoing Taylor, Hall and Ames observe that, in "the beginning, human beings were selves but they didn't have selves."[89] Alternative sets of beliefs abiding in a single person make a new accounting for irrational behaviour. When more than one set of beliefs and desires serve as the reference for explaining a set of behaviours, "the unconscious 'can [then] be viewed as an alternative set, inconsistent with the familiar set that we identify with consciousness, yet sufficiently coherent internally to count as a person.'"[90] In this way the plurality of the self plays into Dostoevsky's dialectics, but to understand his dialectical project fully we must return to the theme of Christianity. This means understanding his dialectical approach to the Christian faith, which I consider next.

'Socialism and Christianity'
Without a doubt, Dostoevsky's cosmology is Christian in orientation. Copleston confirms, as have many others, that "Dostoevsky's vision of what human life might be and should be and of human history is markedly Christocentric."[91] However, as I have already established, one finds elements of Dostoevsky's vision that cannot be found in traditional Christian metaphysics. While Dostoevsky's metaphysics has something in common with German Idealism and his dialectics bears comparison to Hegel's, it takes on dialectical complexities of its own, as we should expect.

Cassedy discusses Dostoevsky's Christianity in terms of the dialectics to which he appeals in his account of his vigil over his wife Maria Dmitrievna in the famous "Masha entry" of his personal diary, contrasting it with Hegelian dialectics, which represent a form of philosophical idealism. Dostoevsky's "two worlds" model posits a rupture that differs from Hegel's developmental dialectics, which seeks "self-knowing in God." For Dostoevsky, the earthly world is one of striving and development, while the eternal world is "timeless," "static," and "synthetic." We see Myshkin experience the unification of this rupture in his pre-seizure state, in which he calls it "the very highest synthesis of life."[92] Dostoevsky's metaphysics reveals a vision of the ideal, exposited in his own vision narratives, such as those of Myshkin, the Ridiculous Man, and others I discuss in Chapter 5.

In Cassedy's interpretation, Dostoevsky sees a paradox between development and the ideal. The ideal is the concretization of the idea, but the ideal is unattainable in this life. For Dostoevsky, humanity therefore strives to become transformed into the "I" of Christ as into his (humanity's) own ideal.[93]

The paradox can also be seen as the fusion of the individual with the *all* (or the annihilation of the "I"): "Christ's heaven" is "the fusion of the individual *I* with the collective *all* and thus represents a wedding of the contingent and concrete with the eternal and absolute."[94] In the Masha entry and Myshkin's pre-seizure state, the goal may be reached only at the cost of the self or, in other words, the "I" of consciousness.[95] The Law of Personality (see Chapter 3) stands in the way, but for Dostoevsky it boils down to the dialectic of freedom and personal choice. There is total freedom of the personality, but there is freedom also to transcend the ego, or the apparent self, to reach the higher ideal of the authentic self. The unattainability of the ideal requires one to strive for it, but one can choose not to.

These suggestions make it possible to cast Dostoevsky's dialectics in a new light. In the Masha entry we find a paradox involving ego integrity or the dissolution of the "I." Unity comes only through annihilating it, or "[giving] it over completely to each and all, undividedly and selflessly."[96] The path towards wholeness, he reasons, ends in dissolution. "Man strives on earth for an ideal, one that is *opposite* to his own nature." Ultimate dissolution is his goal. But the "I" stands in the way of dissolution. "The law on earth that there must be such a thing as an individual person is binding. The 'I' is an obstacle." In *The Brothers Karamazov*, the mysterious visitor explains that, although individuals are isolated, the end of isolation will come, when all will live in brotherhood anchored in Christian love. Indeed some of Dostoevsky's characters do begin to find a resolution of the crisis of doubt. Cassedy cites Raskolnikov and Alyosha as examples.[97]

I close the present discussion with arguments Dostoevsky posed in the uncompleted article "Socialism and Christianity," which he never published but outlined in some detail in his notebooks of 1864–1865. The projected article bears witness to Dostoevsky's feelings about the problems with socialism and the troubled history of religion vis-à-vis secular society in general.[98] First it should be noted that, from its origins in such thinkers as Henri de Saint-Simon and Charles Fourier, and in the literary works of Victor Hugo, George Sand, and others, Western socialism, which appealed to Dostoevsky as a young man and to many of his generation, had been formulated as a modern adaptation of Christianity, or its evolution.[99] But in Russia of the 1860s, with the new generation of so-called "civic critics," the radical left-wing disciples of the eminent Belinsky, socialism took a turn toward atheism. For Dostoevsky, socialism became associated with positivism, hard materialism, even nihilism, and the worst potential for tyranny and human bondage. By piecing together an approximation of the case against atheistic socialism in "Socialism and Christianity," we can draw out some clues as to how the article might have sounded.

Dostoevsky traces three stages in the evolution of human society, from primitive patriarchal tribal communities to civilization (which he distinctly labels a *transitional phase*) to consciousness of the individual self through a progressive realization of the Christ ideal—fully attainable, however, only in the afterlife. The concerns presented are problems inherent in the structural organization of modern society and in their basis in the patriarchal tradition, although they nevertheless play a critical part in the teleological process of evolving self-knowledge and moral self-awareness implied in the Christ ideal.

The socialists, according to Dostoevsky, "want to have man reborn, to *free* him, to imagine him without God and family. They conclude that, having forcibly changed his daily economic life, they will attain their goal." But if people are to be changed, Dostoevsky counters, "it will not be for *external* reasons and not otherwise than by a *moral* transformation." Addressing socialists, he adds, "You will not abandon God until you are convinced by mathematics, and the family until mothers do not wish to be mothers and man wishes to turn love into raw sex. Can you achieve this with weapons? And can one dare to say beforehand, before the experience, that here lies salvation? And with this, risk all of humanity? Western rubbish."[100]

In her excellent study of the problem, Liza Knapp explains that the Underground Man's position, much like that of Dostoevsky in his own words above, constitutes an objection to the view that all man has to do to thrive is discover the laws of nature—because *inertia* is one of the most commanding among them, and it leads only to death.[101] In other words, the laws governing matter are tyrannical and exacting, so that when, through sinning, man loses his divine attributes and becomes earthbound, subject to his own impulses and desires, he forsakes his divine heritage and becomes nothing more than matter. This is a philosophy developed in greater depth in Dostoevsky's later books, but in *Notes from Underground* its first elements are already present. Both the Underground Man and the "man of action" he criticizes submit to paralyzing mechanistic determinism. Both are materialists who bow to scientific law, ruled by inertia, which sooner or later depletes the vital force. Both have lost the capacity for free-willed, self-generated, and self-directed action, since, if human nature is determined by physical laws, then free will is superfluous.

The problem, for Dostoevsky, comes down to a question of inner freedom versus external necessity. Man's divine origins guarantee him freedom of will, but he must participate in his own salvation by struggling against natural law. That is, the law of spirit delivers man from material necessity, and faith in the resurrected Christ liberates man from his subjugation to nature (as decreed by Paul in *Romans*).[102] Man's task, in short—according to Dostoevsky in a passage purged from the *Notes* by censors but implied by negative example—is transcendence over the "laws of nature" (i.e., Newtonian physics) and the exercise of free will to strive for an ideal predicated on love and compassion. In the final analysis, Dostoevsky stresses the responsibility of the individual for the moral direction of his or her will. He advocates not unbridled individualism but the requirements of "conscious" humanity to develop awareness of moral conscience and to learn its function in the liberation of spirit.

In sum, Christianity for Dostoevsky is a return to spontaneity in the full power of consciousness, a voluntary renunciation of the will, where, Dostoevsky writes, "development stops, the ideal is attained...there is a *future life*."[103] Later, in the mid-1870s, regarding the Second Coming, he would write, "the world will be reborn *suddenly*, by a miracle,"[104] and "[Vladimir] Solovyov and I believe in real, literal, personal resurrection, and believe that it will take place on earth."[105] On the other hand, Dostoevsky's understanding of the supremacy of the personality over society makes Solovyov's total unity, for him, impossible.[106]

In the projected article, civilization is where "personal consciousness negates the accepted patriarchal laws of the masses." This fragmentation is a "diseased" condition, for it exhibits loss of faith in God and cultural malaise, loss of "spontaneous sensations" that are "the source of living life."[107]

The final stage, Christianity, is a return to spontaneity and the mass, but now with full understanding of the ideal, "in the full power of consciousness and development": "Man returns to the mass, to spontaneous life, consequently to a natural condition, but how? Not by obeying authority but, on the contrary, in the highest degree voluntarily and consciously. It is clear that this highest voluntariness is at the same time the highest renunciation of one's will. My will consists in not having will, for the ideal is beautiful."[108]

As Scanlan writes, "history for Dostoevsky is a process leading up to and culminating in the establishment of the ideal community of mutual love."[109]

In the final analysis, we must bear in mind that Dostoevsky's understanding of the position of the modern self is twofold. He lived and wrote at a time when the modern age had apparently revealed that the true reality is a vast, alien universe—a disenchanted cosmology. It is emancipated from superstition and obscurantism but is mechanical and deterministic. The birth of the modern sensibility also brought with it a titanic power struggle between self and intellect that occasioned a radical shift in the cultural world view, placing science and religion in opposition. Emancipatory and disruptive, but affirming a transcendent sacred dimension of existence, this inward revolution constitutes a holistic vision of self, in which reason and empiricism are balanced by inward receptivity, imagination, beauty, passion, faith, and spiritual aspiration.[110] Dostoevsky's world view often puts the two modern outlooks into opposition, but the major point converges on their culmination in the modern self's quest for authenticity.

We might find this convergence illustrated by the sort of "collective Self" shared by the inhabitants of the Edenic star in Dostoevsky's 1877 story "The Dream of a Ridiculous Man," visited by the protagonist before it is splintered by his "progressive" ideas. His instigation of modern instrumental reasoning (based on calculated advantage rather than love) divides its inhabitants against one another. Dostoevsky's utopia is not grounded in the progress of human reason or rational control of natural forces, says Peace, "but on the retention of innocent primal feelings; for him the Golden Age is not in the future but in the past, and its image derives not from a construction of science but from a work of art."[111] A call to authenticity along these lines is also found in other parts of the *Diary*, which I discuss in the following chapters.

Duality-in-Unity
Another way of viewing Dostoevsky's dialectics is to see them in the light of ideas he inspired in a later group of thinkers who acknowledged their indebtedness to Dostoevsky, namely the Vekhi group. The end of the nineteenth and the early twentieth centuries saw a flourishing of culture and a revival of Russian art and poetry, but also a Russian religious renaissance of sorts led by Vladimir Solovyov and members of the Vekhi,[112] composed of Nikolai Berdiaev, Sergei Bulgakov, Semyon Frank, and others. The Vekhi were concerned with the moral regeneration of the individual as well as of society, believing that one couldn't happen without the other. Nineteenth-century revolutionaries of a socialist cast were their ideological opponents, caught in the "mystique of revolution," believing they needed only to topple the regime and establish a new social-political order (i.e., Russian socialism) in order to produce a better society—"that human beings are determined by their social environment, that consciousness reflects the influence of social-political structures, and that change in these structures causes change in human consciousness." Human consciousness could change for the better merely by doing away with the oppressive regime and remoulding social conditions. This view was common even among liberals who wanted progressive reform rather than violent revolution. The liberals believed it was possible to achieve gradual improvement and a better society through political, economic, and legal reforms.[113] Not so, said the Vekhi thinkers to both the socialists and the liberals. The Vekhis argued instead for the need for moral and spiritual rebirth. They stressed the priority of moral values and achievement of inner freedom, especially the freedom of the individual to cultivate and manifest the higher inner self. The revolutionaries were intensifying class hatred as a means of effecting social change, but the Vekhi wondered how hatred could bring about an increase in love, positive social

change, and a higher type of society. Without inner freedoms, attempts to change other aspects of the social and political environment could have no effect.[114] Still, manifesting the higher inner self requires integration of the dual natures, the plurality, of the modern self. Russian thinkers who were inspired by Dostoevsky referred to this as "duality-in-unity."

Like the Vekhi group's, Dostoevsky's ideal is a universal Christlike love. Dostoevsky illustrated this ideal, and its embodiment in universal Christian brotherhood, through his own versions of psychological realism and vision narrative. I discuss the metaphysics of Dostoevsky's vision narrative at a later point but close this section by considering the conceptual and metaphysical "leap" from duality to unity, or rather the integration of duality and unity, in a concept the Vekhi group shared with and derived in part from Dostoevsky. Working toward the fulfillment of a Schellingian view of the mission of art, Dostoevsky formed his poetics around the idealist—some would say mystical—view that the unknowable cannot become knowable through discursive reason alone, but rather requires the mystical union of opposites, an antinomic (dialogic) truth, a special type of union in the Russian tradition, called *dvuedinstvo* (duality-in-unity or duality-in-oneness). A principle indigenous to Christian Orthodoxy, duality-in-unity exemplifies the dual nature of Christ, at once his full divinity and full humanity. During the Russian religious renaissance of the early twentieth century, the idea of duality-in-unity inspired the concepts of Godmanhood [*bogochelovechestvo*], Sophia (divine wisdom and the connecting principle between spirit and matter), and theurgy, as well as other related concepts of *dvuedinstvo*.[115]

Ksana Blank's recent work sees Dostoevsky's exposition of conflicting truths not as a case of inexorable contradiction and paradox but as a kind of integral unity. Blank reiterates that Ivan Karamazov's mind, operating in Aristotelian binaries, cannot accept the contradictory truth of Orthodox Church doctrine that holds that everyone is inherently good, but everyone is at the same time inherently guilty. These two statements, to him, constitute a plain contradiction. Zosima sees that if the contradictions cannot be resolved in Ivan "in a positive way," they will never be resolved "in the negative way" either. Zosima exemplifies an alternative approach, in which one must not search for a way out of the apparently contradictory truth but accept the entire contradictory picture as somehow valid and true.[116]

Thus, for Blank, "at the core of Dostoevskij's philosophy and theology lies a concept according to which the Truth (*Istina*) is antinomical: it contains both a thesis and its antithesis without expectation of synthesis," while Russian religious thinkers such as Pavel Florensky, Sergei Bulgakov,

Nikolai Berdiaev, Semyon Frank, and Vladimir Lossky "help us to understand that Dostoevskij's dialogism, made famous in its secular guise by Bakhtin, has a theological underpinning," and "Dostoevskij's exposition of conflicting truths should therefore be seen not as a case of irresolvable contradiction or paradox but as an organic wholeness."[117]

Noting as well that duality-in-unity resembles the yin and yang of Chinese philosophy, Blank offers a new model for approaching Dostoevsky's Christian world view: "It actualizes itself as an alternation of two mirror-like processes: a downward motion causing schism, division, and rupture, and the upward striving toward a restoration of wholeness. The ever-changing equilibrium of these two motions makes Dostoevsky's universe antideterministic."[118]

Blank's caveat, with respect to Dostoevsky's dialectics, is that although there is no suggestion that Dostoevsky was influenced by Heraclitus, Lao Tzu, or others that she mentions, he did not "invent" his dialectic—instead he "discerned the functioning of its laws in the natural world and the world of ideas and clothed them in artistic garb. Traces of this dialectic appear in various literary sources belonging to quite different traditions, among them biblical, folk Russian, Chinese, ancient Greek, and medieval French."[119]

While the twenty-first-century mind is skeptical of absolute philosophies, and Dostoevsky himself scorned normalizing formulas, one can discern, nevertheless, as Blank does in her literary study of Dostoevskian dialectics, "a general pattern that is important for understanding Dostoevsky's religious philosophy as well as the paths he plotted for his characters."[120] Blank uses the yin-yang diagram (tai chi) to illustrate the functioning of Dostoevsky's dialectics. Although Dostoevsky was not especially familiar with Asian philosophy, "the Chinese model of change helps us see that contradictions as Dostoevsky presents them are not random, arbitrary or perverse, but internally structured and balanced."[121] She examines Dostoevsky's writing in the light of the dynamic reciprocity of thesis and antithesis, and their resultant dialectical whole.

I have summarized Dostoevskian dialectics in order to conclude this chapter on the divided self in Dostoevsky. In the next two chapters, I delve more deeply into a related aspect of his writing that I consider to be the feature of next-greatest importance for Dostoevsky's archetypal poetics: the *underground*. The underground in Dostoevsky represents the unconscious region of the psyche, and as such it is the seat of those aspects of self that emerge as archetypes. In the following chapter my task is to chart the territory of the unconscious in its unique concretization in the vocabulary and imagery of the Dostoevskian underground.

CHAPTER THREE

Dostoevsky's Underground

That's all there is to it, gentlemen: better not to do anything! Better to have conscious inertia! So then, long live the underground!
　　　　　　　　　　　　　　　　　　　　—*Notes from Underground*

Since the stars have fallen from heaven and our highest symbols have paled, a secret life holds sway in the unconscious.
　　　　　　—Carl Jung, *The Archetypes and the Collective Unconscious*

Dostoevsky understood probably better than most what could make life so ugly and tragic, when one feels it ought to be delightful and exalting. Indeed, he recognized this awareness in his own art. He considered one of his greatest achievements to be the discovery of the "underground," which had been overlooked by other Russian artists but became a literary trademark of sorts for Dostoevsky in his own lifetime: "'Underground, underground, *poet of the underground*,'" he once noted, with self-conscious irony. "Our feuilletonists have been repeating [it] over and over again, as if this were something derogatory to me." Then he continues in earnest, "Silly fools, it is my glory, for that's where the truth lies."[1]

What, then, in Dostoevsky's conception, is the *underground*?

Elsewhere in the passage quoted above, he states plainly, "The reason for the underground is the destruction of our belief in certain general principles. '*Nothing is sacred.*'"[2] I argue that Dostoevsky's underground is a broader concept than this statement alone suggests, though the remark addresses an important aspect of it and therefore is a good place to start. The remark and the underground itself have been interpreted in multiple ways. Ward, for one, sums up the implied issues in "the peculiar dissonant quality" of Dostoevsky's art, which stems from the "disease of disorder" contracted from the West. A generation of thinkers in Russia who had been "uprooted from the soil" [*bespochvenniki*] provided a living example of the consequences of turning away from native Russian traditions, from the people, and from the Russian *narod*. Uprootedness, disintegration of the family, alienation, ennui, and other social phenomena contributed to the general "loss of a common idea of the meaning of human existence."[3] I concur that Russian Westernism and the loss of whole meaning lies at the root of the problem for Dostoevsky.

I will return to Dostoevsky's concern, expressed in his remark that "nothing is sacred." However, recognizing that dreams, subliminal states of awareness, and other impulses of the unconscious mind are mainstays in Dostoevsky's dramatic prose, I turn first to other dimensions of the problem. I argue that the ruling metaphor of the subterranean or *underground* represents the elements of the unconscious as much as it does uprootedness and loss of wholeness. Moreover, I argue that Dostoevsky's underground is an analogy for the unconscious, or, better, a generative plane for the meeting of the conscious and unconscious minds to catalyze personal transformation. As such, the underground serves as the stage on which essential Dostoevskian archetypes act. In several examples below of the imagery associated with the underground principle in Dostoevsky, I mean to emphasize that the underground is the force of catalysis, the nexus where unconscious forces of the psyche meet the conscious mind, causing friction that erupts into thoughts, clusters of ideas, specific actions, and patterns of behaviour. These patterns that emerge are the archetypes themselves. They can be a collection of attributes, a set of ideas, a mental outlook, or an ideology.

The unconscious is manifested in concrete metaphors and symbols in Dostoevsky, as disparate as spiders and insects, water and feet, its deep-seated complexes and hidden drives expressed in more general ways as carnal passions, aggression and violence, egotism, pride, and other motives. All are rooted in the interminable flux and flow of the unconscious. How they surface is the drama enacted in Dostoevsky's works as the tension of opposites, the clash of ideas, or, at the extreme, the tearing asunder of the soul. But ultimately Dostoevsky's underground is also the generative plane of awareness, the bedrock, if you will, the archetypal ground of transformation, where the archetypes reside and express themselves in the journey of the self. Through trials, initiation, knowledge, and awareness, and the full transformative process of death and resurrection, the self is born and the hero's journey completed (until the next cycle). With these textual dynamics, which I describe over the course of the next three chapters, Dostoevsky's works come to form a codex of the self through its formative process, its cycles of crisis and resolution, and finally the revelations of rebirth and eternal life that potentially bring the self its mysterious sense of oneness and union with God.

To begin with the concrete symbols noted above, Veresaev observes that the reptiles, tarantulas, and "scores of spiders" in Dostoevsky's writings, like the cold and gloom of inanimate nature, "crawl into the human soul" to separate and divide it from the world of light and life.[4] Spiders, blood, and insect imagery recur many times throughout his works, often in relation to sensual lust. In *Notes from Underground*, for example, Dostoevsky refers to Cleopatra in Pushkin's "Egyptian Nights," in which she demands of her lovers the price of their execution in the morning. She represents the female of some species of spiders and insects that devour their mates after copulation. This is but one of many examples of Dostoevsky's use of insects to epitomize the sensual lust or lasciviousness [*sladostrastie*] of some of his heroes and heroines.

Spiders and insects are likewise symbolic, in Belknap's analysis, of some Karamazov family traits. Fyodor Pavlovich is described as "most perverted, and often cruel in his lechery: like a vicious insect." Dmitri elaborates: "I want to tell you now about the insects, about the ones which God endowed with lechery. 'To the insects, lechery.' I, brother, am that very insect, and that was said of me particularly; and all we Karamazovs are the same. In you too, an angel, lives this insect, and gives birth to storms in your blood. These are storms because lechery is a storm, and greater than a storm. Beauty is a dire and fearsome thing."[5] Fearsome, he continues, because it is indefinable [*neopredelimaia*], proving that God gave only riddles to humanity. In this same passage Dmitri refers to the inseparable link between the polar ideals of Sodom and the Madonna: "Here the shores meet. Here all contradictions live together."[6] On this point, Veresaev conjectures that the deeper the separation and more monstrous the contradictions between people, the brighter and sharper the passion.[7] Thus, we encounter similar imagery regarding blood and spiders when Dmitri considers the rape of Katya. He confesses that his emotions and motivation were as if a vicious spider had bitten his heart. To him, she was beautiful because she was noble, in the grandeur of her magnificent sacrifice for her father, while he was as vile and ignoble as a bedbug. "This thought, this spider-thought so gripped my heart that it almost bled from the feeling of it. It seemed that there could be no more struggling, but simply the behavior of a bedbug, of a vicious tarantula, without the slightest pity."[8] In all, insects and the lecherous cruelty, blood, and violence they represent, form a cluster, constituting one of the principle components of what I discuss in Chapter 4 as the Dostoevskian archetype, *Karamazovism*.

Spiders are used as an underground metaphor in other circumstances as well. In *Crime and Punishment* Svidrigailov taunts Raskolnikov with his vision of eternity as a mundane, spider-infested hell: "What if in the future life there are only spiders or something of that sort?" he suddenly said. "We always imagine eternity to be an idea beyond our conception, something vast, vast! But why must it be vast? Instead of all that, imagine to yourself that it's one little room, something like a country bath house, all dingy and grimy, spiders filling every corner, and that's all eternity. I sometimes think that's what it is."[9]

In response to Raskolnikov's cry of indignation at the injustice of the vision, Svidrigailov exclaims that perhaps it is even just, and that if it were in his power, he would have it exactly so.

Conversely, in *The Idiot*, as part of the rationale that explains his intended suicide, Ippolit Terentiev expresses horror at the tarantula as an expression of the force of nature: "I have sometimes felt as if I am seeing, in some strange, impossible form, an infinite force, a dark, dumb, and mute being. I remember it was like someone had taken me by the hand, holding a candle, and shown me some enormous and repulsive tarantula, assuring me that this was that same dark, mute, and all-powerful creature, while laughing at my indignation."[10] He refuses, he says, to submit to a dark force taking the form of a tarantula.[11] It represents for him the inexorable causality imposed by the laws of nature. Dmitri's lecherous insects, Svidrigailov's idea of a spider-infested hell, and Ippolit's dread and contempt of the dark, mute, tarantula-like force are concrete expressions of the archetypal underground. They are the symbolic forms as well as the psychic energy and physical forces—in other words the *motivations* behind forces that drive the individuals to act. They represent a formative stage of the self as its unconscious (the underground) comes into contact with the conscious mind. They are the discoveries and epiphanies that take place as a result of the process of transformation. Thus the archetype is both the *transformation itself* and the *dynamics* that occasion it.

In order to gain a more complete perspective on these dynamics of transformation, I need to set Dostoevsky's conception of the underground in the context of several ideas and trends in Western philosophy and psychology, after which I return to a deeper discussion of the inception and development of the principle of the underground in specific works by Dostoevsky.

The Archetypal Unconscious
Beverly Weisblatt puts the problem in Jungian terms:

> Jung…saw that the alchemist, in recognizing the value of unconscious material, was laying the basis for a deeper and more encompassing understanding of human experience. In the same way, Dostoevsky understood the warring and irrational forces at the depths of human nature to be the fundament and source of the spiritual in humankind. Dostoevsky's depiction of humanity's depths carries the message that it is these unwanted aspects of human nature—despair, madness, and evil—that must also be recognized as constitutive of and essential to the development of consciousness and, ultimately and paradoxically, the possibility for good.[12]

Dostoevsky and Jung shared an array of common sources and contexts out of which their thinking on the life of the unconscious mind and archetypal patterning could have arisen. They include German Romanticism and *Naturphilosophie*, which met in a compelling combination for both writers in the work of House of Saxony court physician, physiologist, painter and writer Carl Gustav Carus. Carus is the most direct link between Dostoevsky and Jung. Jung mentions Carus throughout his life, especially his *Psyche: Zur Entwicklungsgeschichte der Seele* (1846), a book in which Dostoevsky was also very interested. The psychology of the unconscious developed by Carus resonated strongly, in fact, with Dostoevsky, as documented by Frank, Rice, Gibian, and others.[13]

Dostoevsky's interest in *Psyche* proves his attraction to ideas that posit moral idealism as the transcendental end of reason, in the Kantian sense. At the time, Dostoevsky had been eager to find connections between the physiological and psychological within the realm of the spirit and moral consciousness. He eagerly sought out the book written by Carus, who practised modern science and philosophy on the foundations of idealism and a religious world view, and who emphasized the power of the irrational and the unconscious in both the human psyche and the natural material world. Carus considered the latter to be endowed with a spirit differing from the psyche only in degrees of consciousness and self-consciousness.[14] He took it as a first principle that the conscious mind operates in a sensitive balance with the unconscious, and moreover that the divine idea resides in the unconscious. The role of unconscious life in directing our physical and spiritual well-being is therefore a major tenet of *Psyche*, including the guiding role of spirit over the unconscious psychic forces and their manifestations in human physiology. In the tradition of Schelling's *Naturphilosophie*, Carus saw nature and human life as originating from a Divine Idea, and the individual soul as sharing in the divine creative principle and therefore having immortality.[15] Detecting its potential to pique Dostoevsky's interest, Rice describes the book as "the biological application of Hegelian ideas," and "an eclectic blend of science and poetic speculation, with an increasingly heady admixture of occult musings which always retained a certain magnetic appeal for Fyodor Mikhailovich."[16]

Dostoevsky knew of Carus before his exile, and there is reason to believe he was familiar with *Psyche* as he was writing *The Double* in 1845.[17] A renewed interest in Carus is documented by Baron von Wrangel, writing from Semipalatinsk in 1854 of his and Dostoevsky's plan to translate *Psyche*. While in Siberian exile in Semipalatinsk, Dostoevsky had been keen to study the philosophical and psychological aspects of spiritual life. He wrote to his brother with a request to send him the Koran, Kant's *Critique of Pure Reason*, and Hegel's *Philosophy of History*.[18] In these interests, Jones sees an indication of Dostoevsky's willingness to reinterpret the religious traditions he grew up with in the terms suggested by modern idealism: "Such evidence, combined with what we know of Dostoevsky's intellectual interests after his return to metropolitan Russia, suggests that he was keen to place Christianity in a wider context and to explore ways in which modern idealist philosophy had enabled his contemporaries to reevaluate the religious tradition without entirely abandoning it."[19]

Gibian regards Carus's views on the unconscious roots of disease to be exemplified in Raskolnikov, noting in particular the rebellion of Raskolnikov's subconscious against his whole way of life.[20] His illness is an infection both psychological and physiological in nature, spread throughout his body and mind. For healing, he needs repentance—a total remedy for his unconscious ills through spiritual redemption. By the same token, Elder Zosima in *The Brothers Karamazov*, in giving counsel to pilgrims, heals through uncovering the underlying causes of their ailments—in each case a spiritual defect rather than a physical symptom. He advises total repentance, an end to shame, and openness to love. In Dostoevsky's works doctors are generally seen as futile with their prescribed remedies; the profession fails to comprehend underlying causes. Golyadkin's visit to Dr. Rutenspitz in *The Double* illustrates this very fact: the medical profession lacked the means to diagnose the unconscious roots of a problem that is an infirmity more of spirit than of physical health. On the other hand, the true healers such as Zosima, Tikhon, Sonia, Myshkin, and Alyosha accord with Carus in their application of remedies of sympathy, love, and solidarity with humankind.[21]

Carus was an important source for Jung as well. The latter wrote, "The psychology of the unconscious that began with C.G. Carus took up the trail that had been lost by the alchemists. This happened, remarkably enough, at a moment in history when the apparitions of the alchemists had found their highest poetic expression in Goethe's *Faust*. At the time Carus wrote, he certainly could not have guessed that he was building the philosophical bridge to an empirical psychology of the future."[22] Carus was also an inspiration for Jung's theory of the collective unconscious:

> The hypothesis of a collective unconscious belongs to the class of ideas that people at first find strange but soon come to possess and use as familiar conceptions. This has been the case with the concept of the unconscious in general. After the philosophical idea of the unconscious, in the form presented chiefly by Carus and von Hartmann, had gone down under the overwhelming wave of materialism and empiricism, leaving hardly a ripple behind it, it gradually reappeared in the scientific domain of medical psychology.[23]

In sum, Dostoevsky's interest in Carus is evidence that Dostoevsky considered, as Jung did later, that an intangible but consequential foundation of reality might be present in the unconscious human psyche. Furthermore, as I have been saying, Dostoevsky's kaleidoscopic narratives of the unconscious crystallize into archetypes, with the underground principle acting as a formative agent. Dostoevsky's work on revisions to *The Double* and, ultimately, his abandonment of that work in favour of composing *Notes from Underground*, demonstrate the first major movement of that progression.

From Revision of *The Double* to *Notes from Underground*

As noted in my introduction, when Dostoevsky referred to the protagonist of his second short novel, *The Double*, as "my first underground type" nearly three decades after its publication in 1846,[24] he neglected to describe the parallels he drew between the hero Yakov Petrovich Golyadkin and the Underground Man, his "anti-hero" of the confessional monologue *Notes from Underground* (1864). The oblique reference is all the more intriguing in light of the fact that Dostoevsky's notes for a planned revision of *The Double* between 1860 and 1864 coincided with his work on *Notes from Underground* and show evidence of having contributed to the latter work's conception. Dostoevsky's notes for revision of *The Double* indicate that the author had thought of stressing the protagonist's ambivalent inclination to join the materialist and atheistic progressive left, which had gained great momentum through the 1850s and early 1860s in Russia. Advocates of this progressive camp are the main target of the Underground Man's vitriolic sallies against rational, utilitarian, social humanism.

Two notebooks, one from 1860–1862 and the other from 1862–1864, contain drafts that centre on particular themes and ideas for *The Double* that reflected the new cultural zeitgeist. The original novella explores the internal moral and psychological struggle of its main character as he tries to justify unscrupulous motives for advancing his service career in the Russian bureaucracy. His life is on the verge of destruction due to the sudden appearance of a doppelgänger, a literal facsimile of himself. This double, ostensibly a psychic projection of those parts of the protagonist's ego that moral conscience will not permit him to accept, attempts to destroy the protagonist's good name and claim his position in public life and the social circle in which he aspires to succeed.

In Dostoevsky's notes for revision of the work, proposals involving new episodes and new interactions between characters are augmented by psychological observations from the author, which are coloured with views that reflect political, social, and religious problems that had emerged since the novella's first publication in 1846.[25] In particular, the so-called "accursed questions" [*prokliatye voprosi*] that were appearing in the press—on the natural sciences, atheism, and nihilism—show some of Dostoevsky's attitudes toward the progressive ideas of his day. For example, the notes' thrice-mentioned "hydrogen and oxygen" is connected to the proposition "there is no longer a Supreme Being," and similarly to the freedom, anarchy, and irresponsibility that might result from eliminating the society "fathers." "What will happen to the ministry and to his superiors?" the notes ask. "*The dream.* Everything has been abolished. People are free. They all *beat one another* openly on the street. *They provide for themselves* (save their kopeks)."[26] There are obvious parallels here with Raskolnikov's dreams in Chapter V of *Crime and Punishment*, when Mikolka and other peasants beat a decrepit horse to death, and also with Raskolnikov's as well as Ivan Karamazov's ominous warnings of moral degeneration and chaos when "everything is permitted" [*vse pozvoleno*].

In rewriting *The Double*, Dostoevsky would have added a more discernible political dimension to the book. In the first notebook, the two Golyadkins dream together of becoming a revolutionary hero: "Dreams of becoming Napoleon, Pericles, the marshal of the Russian revolt. Liberalism and revolution restoring Louis XVI with tears and obeying him (out of goodness)." In the second notebook, contemporary political and social issues loom even larger. Clearly, Dostoevsky planned to depict Golyadkin as interested in the ideas of utilitarian materialism and social revolution that proliferated in Russia in the 1860s. What is more, Golyadkin is associated with the Petrashevsky Circle—an underground group of dissident intellectuals, association with which became the reason for Dostoevsky's arrest and exile in 1849. The author even introduces scenes that take place at Petrashevsky's and hark back to the 40s and his own life.

That Dostoevsky worked on a second version of the novel, a retelling and elucidation of the ideological thrust of the work, is tantalizing in its possibilities, unrealized though they were. Although a significant revision of *The Double* was never fully achieved, it may be argued that Dostoevsky's thinking in the late 1850s and early 60s about the issues he raised in *The Double* led directly to his conception of other, more fully developed works that shared some of the same themes. It is especially revealing that Dostoevsky's work on revising *The Double* coincided with his writing of *Notes from Underground*, and ceased shortly after the latter's publication. This work would produce a far more profound effect on readers and critics and was destined to achieve much greater status in the writer's oeuvre than the earlier piece would ever attain. Since Golyadkin himself shows a very limited understanding of his own internal conflict, one might suggest that Dostoevsky's great breakthrough in form of the 1860s may have been the creation of a character—the Underground Man—who possesses greater self-understanding and greater sophistication in his argument against the hypothetical ideological opponents he addresses in his protracted monologue.

Fortunately, conceptual links can be seen between Dostoevsky's work on *The Double* in the 1840s and *Notes from Underground* in the early 1860s. From the earlier work he incorporated key elements into the later—which is the first work, according to Frank, in which the author "attempted to portray the consequences for the human personality of the attempt to put into practice—but with a full awareness of *all* their implications—the ideas of the progressive and radical ideologies of the 1840s and 1860s; and one can observe him constantly trying to define his own position in relation to such doctrines."[27] This challenge to radical ideologies, one must recognize, is only vaguely grasped by the author at the time of his first composing *The Double*, and it comes into focus only after years of grappling with the wide spectrum of implications that stem from the principles he had begun to outline in the mid-1840s. Nevertheless, it is hard to underestimate the vital importance of Golyadkin as a prototype for some of Dostoevsky's more sophisticated character creations, from the Underground Man to Raskolnikov, Nikolai Stavrogin, and Ivan Karamazov. In

Frank's summation, "The character-type discovered in the 1840s, and used to further the progressive social ideals of the Natural School, becomes in the later Dostoevsky a weapon against radical ideology."[28]

In my view, we have in the Underground Man an indication of who the earlier protagonist ultimately becomes. The difference between the two heroes is that the Underground Man seeks self-knowledge, while Golyadkin is not conscious of doing so. In dualistic terms, the "underground" of his notes is the counter-ideal, the negation of idealism itself. It is the overdetermined, rational, material reality that undermines the subjective compulsion to strive for the unattainable. Thus, the divide between egoism and idealism is most acutely felt in the underground—the Underground Man knows the "good" but does not believe in the possibility of achieving it.[29] He rejects idealism outright, embracing egoism as the only viable frame of self-definition. Yet his underground cynicism still carries the potential, by negative example, to call out for the transcendent ideal for which the higher self strives.

It is widely known that a passage was cut from *Notes from Underground* by censors, in which a religious solution of the Christ ideal was presented. The Christ ideal is itself a duality, which Dostoevsky defined explicitly in his notebooks of 1863–1864 when he wrote, "a person strives for an ideal counter to his nature."[30] Awareness of this duality is the way to wholeness, for duality brings knowledge of the "idea," which creates from itself the ideal. In the end, it is the knowing and striving for the ideal that matters. Dostoevsky goes on in the notebooks to describe this striving as "The law of the development of the personality and the achievement of the ultimate goal, to which a person is bound."[31] Rebellious wilfulness complicates the effort, but "terrestrial equilibrium" intervenes to strike a balance: "When a person has not carried out the law of striving for the ideal, i.e., has not brought it about through love and sacrifice of his 'I,' to people or to another being...he feels suffering and has named that state sin."[32] This is an example of the reconciliation of opposites that seems, for a moment, to satisfy the writer's lifelong quest to deconstruct idealism. Dualities can find balance and reconciliation in the reasoning mind; yet, as Dostoevsky's novels attest, the idealism that stabilizes them is no panacea for personal, religious, or social harmony. For instance, Golyadkin sometimes allows himself to wish for reconciliation with his doppelgänger antagonist, whereby a "friendship" might be born.[33] But this tack is always undermined by the irrational shadow self (which I examine later on), who, as the Underground Man attests, acts out of the wilful impulse to freedom and self-assertion, which does not always accord with one's own "enlightened self-interest."

The underground type, as I've said, is what Dostoevsky called his first great literary innovation. Although he saw it as a social-cultural type, I call it an archetype because it rises beyond the social to collect the perceptions, psychological makeup, and ideas of the self in relation to its world outlook. Its process of development involves contact with the generative plane of the unconscious. Dostoevsky's first specimen of the underground type in *The Double* lacks the mental sophistication to ruminate over the contradiction between the ideal and the actual, but instead experiences it as a cognitive–emotional rupture. While the redaction published in 1866 differed little from the original publication, Dostoevsky's extant notes for revision show plans for a considerable reworking of the text that brings key issues and themes to light. The updated hero from underground in *Notes from Underground* displays a greater conscious understanding of his ethical dilemmas. At the same time, his awareness of their agonizing complexity emphasizes the still impassable divide between the rational, reasoning mind and the passionate force of the ego.

In the end, Golyadkin and the Underground Man share the fundamental ontological disease that stems from their feverish longing for spontaneous, direct, and purposeful action, clearly defined and understood—which is the constant need of every individual, as Dostoevsky described it in his 1847 article, "A Petersburg Chronicle" (shortly after *The Double* was first published). The inability of Golyadkin and the Underground Man to do "good" and satisfy their inner longing is the result of inertia that keeps them bound to the materialist philosophy and ignorant of the soul's heritage and the complex makeup of the human psyche. In Golyadkin's case, he tries to conform to the system but cannot accept it in his moral conscience, and the effect of his inability to reconcile his social aspirations with his moral conscience is so severe that it causes a rupture of consciousness. Trying to assert his free will and independence, he submits to determinism and inertia by misunderstanding his vital force and directing it toward selfish aims. This is the root cause of his confusion and suffering, as well as his penchant for fantasy and escape.

The Underground Man has a keener sense of both political consciousness and, as I have noted, self-awareness—an overdeveloped sense, which he terms "heightened consciousness" [*usilennoe soznanie*][34]—yet his self-consciousness is less moral self-awareness than the cyclical ruminations of a hyper-rational mind that give way to paralysis, ennui, and spleen. In Part I, Chapter 5, he queries, "Where are my primary causes on which I can rest, where are the foundations? Where can I find them? I exercise myself in thought, and, consequently, with me every primary cause immediately drags after it another still more primary one, and so on into infinity. Such precisely is the essence of all consciousness and thought."[35] The infirmity of finding no primary causes on which to rely leads him to the startling conclusion that consciousness is a disease. Like Golyadkin, the Underground Man is plagued by inertia that allows him to express core oppositions to the norms and values of his contemporary society only while despairing that innate yearnings for higher purpose cannot be alleviated by ruminations of the rational mind.

Feminine Archetypes: Mother, Madonna, and Femme Fatale
In Dostoevsky, and in the language of archetypes generally speaking, the feminine principle is linked to the underground in important ways. Jung defines the principle feminine archetype as the *anima*—specifically, the feminine psychological tendencies in the male psyche, functionally opposite to the *animus*, or the male principle in the female psyche. For present purposes I focus only on the anima, since, by Jung's definition, it functions as a connection to the unconscious, as a guide to the inner world, and as a mediator between ego and higher Self.[36] As such, it is relevent to my discussion of Dostoevsky's heroes and heroines in ways related to self-awareness and transformation.

According to Jung, the anima has four stages of development: Eve, representing instinctual and biological relations; Helen, signifying relations of a romantic, aesthetic, and sexual nature; the Virgin Mary, "a figure who raises love (*eros*) to the heights of spiritual devotion"; and Sapientia, "wisdom transcending even the most holy and pure."[37] While the logical mind is incapable of discerning truths hidden in the unconscious, the anima can help to bring them to the surface. Anima contains the possibility of achieving wholeness by putting the male mind in tune with right inner values, opening the way to more profound inner depths. It initiates him into a higher, more spiritual form of life, as Beatrice does, for example, in Dante's *Paradiso*.[38]

Like all archetypes, the anima is dual in effect. Jung develops this dimension of the concept in his writings on the mother archetype. He formulates the ambivalence of "the loving and terrible mother," defining such essential aspects of the mother archetype as her cherishing and nourishing goodness, orgiastic emotionality, and her Stygian depths:

> The qualities associated with [the mother archetype] are maternal solicitude and sympathy; the magic authority of the female; the wisdom and spiritual exaltation that transcend reason; any helpful instinct or impulse; all that is benign, all that cherishes and sustains, that fosters growth and fertility. The place of magic transformation

and rebirth, together with the underworld and its inhabitants, are presided over by the mother. On the negative side the mother archetype may connote anything that devours, seduces, and poisons, that is terrifying and inescapable like fate.[39]

The feminine archetype is thus both nurturing and destroying. It embodies the dual current of the energy of the underground, the perennial cycle of death and nativity. In the Russian context, the mother archetype is more than a personal symbol, it is an emblem of the national ethos.

In *Mother Russia: The Feminine Myth in Russian Culture*, Joanna Hubbs investigates the centuries-long tradition of folklore and myth that has placed Mother Earth (*Matushka Zemlia*) at the centre of Russian national consciousness and folk culture. The image emphasizes the land's fertility and the sacredness of the soil. Both the nurturing and destructive aspects of the anima archetype are represented. "Mother Moist Earth" is the good mother, but also the destroyer, who both gives and takes away. In this respect, Russia as earth mother is a peasant conceit: "For the peasant the earth is home, and as such defines the boundaries of life, labor, and community by binding her children to the round of the seasons. *Matushka Rus'* (Little Mother Russia) is simply the historical name of the land which the peasants perceived as 'married' to *Batiushka Tsar'* (Little Father Tsar)."[40]

Russian intellectuals of the nineteenth century, no longer living close to the soil, have a more complex relationship to the archetype. The intelligentsia conceived of the maternal land as a lost paradise of collectivity and communion:

Compelled to define the limits of self-expression against the backdrop of a suffering motherland crushed by autocracy, Russian writers and thinkers assumed the role of the true champions of Mother Russia. She represented for them the image of an all-enveloping Matrioshka [Russian nesting doll], whose children lived within her confines and depended upon their bond with her for function and identity in the spiritual as well as the physical sense.[41]

Mother Earth and Mother Russia, furthermore, both express creative power and its limits:

As the fertile earth, she gave birth to folklore, ritual, dance, and song, described as Dionysiac in their emotional range, variety, and abundance. Russia as motherland has been the source and object of much art, literature, and speculative thought. But as the Russia who calls for self-sacrificing champions, she also represents suffering and constraint. Her dual nature as the fount of creativity and its limit assumes metaphysical as well as social and psychological dimensions, raising the question of the proper relationship of the individual to the whole.[42]

The mother archetype, particularly in its national ethos, was therefore a vital component of Russian literature of the nineteenth century. In simple terms, the intelligentsia saw it as their mission to save the Russian *narod*. The tension, however, between the nurturing and suffering mother, soul of the nation, and the Westernized intellectual was strongly pronounced. An iconic example is Tatiana vis-à-vis Onegin in Pushkin's *Eugene Onegin*. Hubbs compares Tatiana to "Isis awaiting her mate," and Onegin to Napoleon, "whose persona Pushkin uses to illustrate the evils of Russian despotism as well as the Western ideology of the self." Further, she writes, "Pushkin presents his reader with the idle and alienated aristocrat; the *narod* he will not 'save' is embodied in the persona of a gentry girl, to whom the poet gives the name of Tatiana, a synonym for Mother Earth in peasant lore..." Onegin is the alienated modern individual, under the sway of the "Western disease." Meanwhile Tatiana, "named for the earth, is made to embody all that is spontaneous and close to the rhythms of the soil. She is 'whole,' *tsel'naia*, depicted by Pushkin as a zoomorphic goddess."[43]

These complexities of the feminine archetype as a literary trope vis-à-vis the Westernized Russian hero were inherited by Dostoevsky from Pushkin. In his famous speech commemorating the poet, Dostoevsky identifies the archetypal qualities of Tatiana, described here by Hubbs:

> In his "Pushkin Speech" (1880), Dostoevsky points out that Onegin lives as an exile and a wanderer in the very heart of his native land. Tatiana, on the other hand, is the embodiment of Russia. As Kore, the daughter, she has the power to reunite him with Mother Russia through marriage: "Here is contact with her own...people, with their sanctities." The tragedy of Onegin and Tatiana is that "she passed through his life unrecognized by him and unappreciated." Yet Russian woman, Dostoevsky tells us, the guardian of life-affirming and altruistic values, was a "great power" leading to the "principal and most salutary regeneration of Russian society," because she drew her strength from the "sacramental" soil, the source of rebirth. But her qualities of gentleness were spurned and ignored; she was a "martyr for the Russian man"—like Tatiana and like the motherland, her analogue.[44]

Moving now to specific representations of the female archetypes in Dostoevsky, it should be easy to see that Dostoevsky emphasizes, much like Pushkin did, women's life-affirming powers and close contact with the people and the Russian soil. In their essay "Dostoevsky's Heroines," Richard Avramenko and Jingcai Ying contend that while women are a vital component of Dostoevsky's vision of salvation, his female characters have been overlooked as a source of Christian compassion and self-sacrificial love (in Orthodox Russia, the chief bulwark against Western secularism, materialism, rationalism, and individualism). They analyze the roles of three heroines of *The Possessed*, each of whom exemplifies the kind compassion Sonya Marmeladova shows Raskolnikov, telling him, "We are going to suffer together, we will bear the cross together!"[45]

> It is in the Russian woman—especially the Russian peasant woman—that Dostoevsky sees the hope for the salvation of Russia and her ill sons. As a Russian Slavophile and Christian, he wants to defend both the Russian folk-belief in Mother Earth and the Orthodox faith in a more general sense. For him, the Russian peasant woman possesses both, which makes her the ideal healer for the Russian man's Western disease. As Nicolai Berdyaev puts it, the Westernized Russian man "has departed from the feminine principle" and "renounced his mother-earth...." He has lost his moral compass, continuously overstepping all moral boundaries (e.g., Raskolnikov in *Crime and Punishment*) and lusts for every sensual pleasure (e.g., Stavrogin in *The Possessed*). In the face of the Russian man's degeneration, the Russian woman preserves the "life-affirming and altruistic values" inherited from Mother Earth, the sacred soil that remains the regenerative source for all Russians.... To Dostoevsky, the Russian peasant woman might be the only way back to Mother Earth for the fallen Russian men.[46]

The best example comes again from Hubbs, who finds that Dostoevsky presents us with another Tatiana in the wounded and crippled Maria Lebiadkina, who marries Stavrogin in *The Devils*:

> The "simple-minded" cripple whose name, Lebiadkin, refers to the swan, is the abandoned and reviled wife of the intellectual Nicholas Stavrogin (whose name means "cross" and "horn," suggesting images of Christ and the devil). Like Onegin, he suffers from an anomie which has its source in the "disease" of westernization, with its stress on individualism. Maria, on the other hand, is a "traditional" Russian

woman.... Maria embodies Russia's *dvoeverie*: She is Vasilisa the Wise Maiden, the swan-*rusalka* who tells fortunes. She is Kore, but she is also Demeter, Mother Moist Earth of the peasantry, searching for her true tsar to deliver her from barrenness and oppression. She is, in short, the icon of Mother Russia abandoned and matryred [*sic*] by those self-willed intellectuals who claim to be her champions and yet, like petty autocrats, despise her.... In *The Possessed*, Dostoevsky warns the educated class that as self-professed defenders of *Matushka Rus'* they must, like Ilya Muromets, return to Mother Earth to regain a meaningful identity and invincible strength, else they will lead her to a cataclysm, which will engulf them, as well.[47]

If Maria Lebiadkina, like Tatiana, represents the wise Mother Russia/Mother Earth, we must not forget that the archetype has a dual aspect, which Dostoevsky (characteristically) exploits to the full. It is impossible in the space of the present study to treat the entire array of mythological symbolic meanings involved in the feminine archetypes as they appear in Dostoevsky's works. I comment instead on but a few of its manifestations while referring to two characters who represent the polar opposites within the archetype: the figure of womanhood emblematized in the Russian Madonna as portrayed by the prostitute Liza in *Notes from Underground*, and, at the opposite end, the femme fatale embodied in Nastasya Filippovna of *The Idiot*, who represents the terrible and inescapable Stygian force of destiny.

Researchers have investigated Dostoevsky's descriptions of ideal feminine beauty in the Western images of the Madonna and in Russian Orthodox iconography.[48] A major difference between them is that the Russian conception of Madonna stresses Mary's motherhood rather than her immaculate conception; she is recognized and commonly referred to in Russian as Mother of God (*Bogoroditsa*) rather than the Virgin Mary. Consequently, intercession is an important theme in Russian Orthodoxy, as Russian religious art foregrounds the Mother of God's protective embrace of the Christ child, symbolizing her nourishing and redemptive love.[49] Liza's relationship to the Underground Man reflects this aspect of the Russian Orthodox myth of the Madonna and child. She is not an object of physical or even ideal beauty, nor is her prostitution representative of sin and immorality; rather, she is presented as a selfless or self-sacrificing individual, whose love and compassion transcends human suffering. Liza's compassion and sympathetic nature is revealed by the description of her eyes, which resemble those of the *Bogoroditsa* in Russian iconography.[50] Even while subject to the Underground Man's crude manipulations, she perceives his personal torment and counters it with her own capacity for love and self-sacrifice. Behrendt writes, "His manipulations are a part of a cycle in which he attempts to inflict upon her all of the suffering that was previously inflicted upon him by others. He assumes that she will fulfill an archetypal, feminine role associated with the myth in which the Madonna, in perpetual sorrow, prays and weeps for the sins of the world."[51]

Through efforts to scorn and demoralize her, the Underground Man goads Liza with imagery of her inevitable death and burial in a watery grave, with no children or family to mourn her, and no chance of rebirth, "however she might knock on the lid of her coffin." Behrendt interprets his motives as an attempt "to destroy in her any possible hope for a figurative immortality through the memories of her children. The underground man expects Liza to respond to the basic issues associated with womanhood and with the ancient regard for the cycles of death, decay, and regeneration."[52] He fantasizes about becoming her salvation through his perverse game of humiliation, but finds himself on the receiving end of her greater compassion. In his own words, "What happened was this: Liza, insulted and crushed by me, understood a great deal more than I imagined. She understood from all this what a woman understands first of all, if she feels genuine love, that is, that I was myself unhappy.... Then she suddenly rushed to me, threw her arms around me and burst into tears."[53] Liza's gesture echoes the religious symbolism of the love and protection of the Madonna's motherly embrace. The Underground Man acknowledges that their roles in the power struggle have been reversed; defeated as he is, he recognizes the implicit moral lesson: "To a woman all reformation, all salvation from any sort of ruin, and all moral renewal is included in love and can only show itself in that form."[54]

Liza is a Russian Madonna figure vis-à-vis the Underground Man, much as Sonia Marmeladova is to Raskolnikov in *Crime and Punishment*. Sonia brings life back to the murderer Raskolnikov after his descent to the depths of moral depravity by showing him compassion, reading the Gospels with him, and offering to share his suffering. In this act, the archetype is not only a nurturing and protective mother, but also a vessel to share the light of higher consciousness. This sharing allows Raskolnikov to begin his penance and moral–spiritual regeneration; but this, the author tells us in the epilogue, is the topic of a different novel, the story of the hero's gradual rebirth and crossing over from one world to another.[55]

At the other extreme is the personification of the negative value of the anima archetype, its shadow expression, the archetypal fatal feminine or femme fatale. Known also to mythology as the Greek Sirens and German Lorelei, she represents the powerful subconscious depths, the force of destiny of the underground. Russian and pagan Slavic folklore have a parallel in the Rusalka—water nymphs who lure men with the promise of love and maternal warmth, only to bewitch and drown them.

Cusmerenco argues that Nastasya (Anastasia) Filippovna is an embodiment of this archetype of the fatal woman.[56] A tragic figure, she is motivated by a destructive force: "*the will for power* mainly shown in the space of *fatal love* equals the *need for destruction* and...even *self-destruction*." Her transformation into a victimized and hostile woman is due to her guardian Totsky having taken advantage of her innocence, raising her from orphanhood and forcing her to be his mistress, thus causing her "unfortunate inner metamorphosis."[57] Her choices in love are subsequently fatal and destructive: in Nastasya Filippovna, "the need for revenge equals the will for self-destruction." Fatal women such as she "need worthy opponents to justify and fuel their irresistible need to fight and destroy."[58]

The name Anastasia, from its Greek etymology, means "resurrection." With the destructive force that rules her, Nastasya Filippovna's descent to the underground—the descent to Hades in the hero myth—is the prefiguration of the seed of transformation, the germinating authentic self and regeneration of the living spirit. I discuss the idea of earth symbolism further in Chapter 5, in particular the themes of death and resurrection, as in the Eleusinian Mysteries enacted by Dmitri Karamazov. Though her name suggests resurrection, Nastasya Filippovna decides "to destroy her destiny so her symbolical rebirth will fail."[59] She is motivated from within by an urge to fight as if it is her implacable purpose. Cusmerenco calls the inner force the *underground*: "Thus, we are able to understand why Nastasya Filippovna, as an embodiment of this archetype of the *fatal woman*, prefers, that is she chooses from the very start, not Myshkin, who had just proposed and confessed his love, but Rogozhin, a dangerous man due to his instinctual, unpredictable and brutal behaviour, dominated by the *underground*, as in a sickening delirium, by an obsession stronger than him."[60] Avramenko and Ying observe, furthermore, that "In this context, men they choose to share their life with and who actually help them to fulfil their destiny of *fatal* women may be regarded as victims of their power of seduction. They mainly correspond to their continuous need to fight and they are rather turned into opponents, than lovers or husbands by these women."[61]

These are but a few of the female archetypes in Dostoevsky that mirror the feminine image in Christian mythology and other Russian contexts. They emphasize both aspects of the anima via the connection of the Madonna to the earth and earthiness: her qualities of nourishment and protection symbolize the fertility of the soil, perpetuating the worship of Mother Earth in Russian thought. The Russian conception of *Bogoro-*

ditsa invokes the ancient symbolism of the archetypal Earth Mother, or the Greek primordial earth goddess Gaia. In George Fedotov's summation, the Russian earth is equated with "eternal womanhood...mother not virgin, fertile not pure; and black for the best Russian soil is black."[62] Much to the same effect is the conclusion by Avramenko and Ying: "The women who will save Russia can never be Westernized, like Nastasya Filippovna in the *Idiot*. Russia's saviors can only be Russians in touch with both Mother Earth and the Mother of God."[63]

The Law of Personality and the Law of Love
Dostoevsky's treatment of the problem of modernity confronts the conflict between pre-modern enchantment and modern disengagement, as discussed in sections above. I explain in Chapter 1 how the primary conflict of Dostoevsky's stories and novels arises from the modern subject's identification with the *apparent self* of the conditioned ego. Less commonly, awareness of *authentic self* emerges, which overcomes and transcends the apparent self. To add to my earlier discussion, what do I mean by the terms *apparent self* and *authentic self*, and what do they have to do with Dostoevsky's underground?

By *apparent self* I mean self as an object of consciousness, as it is perceived and defined by the perceiving subject's conditioned reasoning. Its pedigree can be traced in time and in the contexts that formed it. For the modern stance that accepts the hegemony of instrumental reason created a self of disengaged reason, a product of the rational mind's self-scrutinizing behaviour. Trust in the rational faculties alone to arrive at certain truth created an apparent self that is *disengaged* from autonomous personhood that trusts in its origination in, and absolute unity with, divine essence. I look at it this way: the polyphony of Dostoevsky's novels, generally speaking, helps him represent the disseminated voices of the many, which diverge in the thinking and reasoning of the modern mind as competing ideologies. All of them are mere objects of consciousness, however, which distract the perceiving subject from knowledge of the *authentic self* that never diverges from the One.[64]

Before Dostoevsky, the Romantics established a new world view out of their critique of disengaged reason: the rational mind has to open to our own deepest feelings and instincts, allowing the recovery of authentic self through transcendent arts, liberty of spirit, spiritual epiphany, and utopian vision—all of which evolve in an eternally unfolding expression of the Absolute. Authentic self unifies individuals because it knows not diversity but only the All. In the Romantic view, humans need to heal the division within them that disengaged reason created by setting thinking in opposition to feeling or instinct and intuition.

Ignorance of the illusory separation or atomization of the apparent self is what keeps many of Dostoevsky's characters imprisoned in the underground. In Dostoevsky this is the inert spiritual void and the spectre of nihilistic materialism—symptoms of modernity he treated as directly related to the problem of excessive self-reflection. The Underground Man claims that he has "heightened consciousness," yet his conscious self-absorption is the motive force behind his perverse logic and contrary acts of self-assertion. He is aware that each impulse within him is accompanied by an impulse or attitude that is its absolute opposite.[65] Any effort to satisfy one set of needs activates the conflicting components of his personality.

Donna Orwin has shown that Dostoevsky implicitly blames the Underground Man's reading of Western literature and philosophy for creating the gulf between natural spontaneity and his self-reflective torments. Beyond the content of what he reads, the consequential influence is a change in his very psyche enhanced by the act of reading itself.[66] Generally speaking, the Underground Man's enhanced conscious mind represents the crisis of modernity that forced Dostoevsky to recognize the limitations of rational thought and resist the systematizing utilitarian and materialist philosophies inherited by Russia from the modern West. The Underground Man, who "knows the good but cannot do it because he does not believe in [general laws]," brags of the merit of his *lack of personality*, by which he means "that in this newly modern, bookish Russian, self-consciousness and analysis weaken all impulses so that the soul is influenced and shaped by the dialectic of consciousness itself.... Each mood succeeds the previous one as its opposite and as a reaction to it." He is proud of this, "because it is an attribute of mind, and of all his parts he is proudest of his mind. The mind of the Underground Man grinds up any feeling that might rise in him and suggests its opposite, which in turn is subjected to the dialectic of the mind again."[67] What is more, he is proud of the *intensity* of his simulated experience: "As for me, I have never done anything but push to extremes in my life what you yourselves would dare to push only halfway; in the process you call your cowardice wisdom and so console yourselves with lies. So that I am perhaps more alive than you."[68]

Orwin argues, furthermore, that self-consciousness is a distinguishing trait of the Russian literary tradition. For instance, the excessive self-consciousness in Turgenev's *Diary of a Superfluous Man* (1850) is modern man as he first appears in a Russian setting.[69] The self-conscious "I" destroys the possibility of spontaneity, and therefore empties the individual of content. In an earlier example, I've mentioned that Dostoevsky created the consummate dreamer in "White Nights"—the *mechtatel'*, who embodied a persona disconnected from his social reality. I'll add that Dostoevsky also observed in a letter to his brother Mikhail, shortly after writing *The Double*, that the compulsion to escape into an inner life of fantasy was the dangerous result of an individual's unsuccessful integration into society:

> It is true that the dissonance and the imbalance which society presents to us is a terrible thing. The *internal* must be balanced with the *external*. For, lacking external experiences, those of the inward life will gain the upper hand, and that is most dangerous. The nerves and the fancy then take up too much room, as it were, in our consciousness. Because of our lack of experience every external happening seems colossal and frightens us. We begin to fear life.[70]

It might be said that excessive conscious life achieved at the expense of attunement with the inner life is modernity's most prominent symptom, and it is what gives modern subjectivity its complexity. Insofar as the modern self is one of Dostoevsky's chief concerns, as I have argued here and in the previous chapters, it stands to reason that his conception of personality (*lichnost'*) is complex.

Dostoevsky's world view, which is never monological, identifies two loci of possible selves on a vertical axis: *identification with the ego or apparent self*, powered by rational agency and boundless will and supported by self-sufficient humanism; and *identification with the transcendent self*, which requires *transformation* of the self beyond its natural life to connect to a preternatural ground of being that supports authentic self. The first, apparent self, involves a buffering of the self, a stance of separateness from external forces, and rather a view of the external world as a mechanistic universe that relies on the rational agent to give it order and meaning. The second, the self of transcendence or authentic self, involves an implicit order and meaning, and a godhead with whom the self aspires to be in unity. This requires a conceptual leap into the realm of the numinous.

These understandings of the nature of self can be demonstrated in the light of several principles that Dostoevsky explicitly defined in some of his published works, notebooks, and diaries. In "Winter Notes on Summer Impressions," an essay of 1863, following his critique of the venerated morality of self-interest promoted in the West, Dostoevsky advances his thesis on egoism—"the personal principle, the principle of isolation, of intense self-preservation, of self-solicitousness, of the self-determination of one's own ego, of opposing this ego to all of nature and all other people as a separate, autonomous principle completely equal and equivalent to everything outside itself."[71] These qualities are exemplified by the Underground Man's above-mentioned heightened consciousness. His fixation on his own reactions, motives, and behaviour is, as Scanlan puts it, "a state of obsessive, anguished introspection, quite different from the complacent single-mindedness of Rational Egoists such as Chernyshevsky's heroes, who were men and women of action." Because he is a free conscious being, his is an egoism of personal *will* (and its glorification) rather than of personal *interests*.[72] Freedom of the personal will is raised to the level of an absolute, so even absurd and self-destructive impulses are celebrated expressions of that unbounded wilfulness. In sum, "The normative stance of the Underground Man, far from coinciding with Dostoevsky's, illustrates the evils of a freedom unstructured by higher values; the Underground Man's egoism is the perversion of a distinctive and precious human capacity by exempting it from all spiritual authority. For Dostoevsky, human will transcends natural law but not moral law."[73] Thus the Underground Man's self-absorption is treated as a moral failing and spiritual void.

Dostoevsky speculated on this problem in the so-called "Masha entry" of his personal diary, on 16 April 1864.[74] The well-studied passage, composed as the writer stood before the body of his recently deceased wife, Maria Dmitrievna, demonstrates the major departure of his belief system from the Slavophile nation-centric point of view. It is remarkable for its poignant insight into the nature of self, including something Dostoevsky called the Law of Personality [*zakon lichnosti*]. Explicitly, he saw a fundamental paradox involving the integrity and dissolution of the self, since the self stands in the way of fulfilling the Christian imperative to love: "The law of personality on earth is binding," he writes. "The I is an obstacle."[75] Dostoevsky reasons that the entire history of human struggle is the strife of selfish assertion of the ego, but its development means striving for moral perfection. Ego is exemplified most powerfully by Dostoevsky in the unbridled egoism of the revolutionaries in *The Devils*. Scanlan summarizes it nicely:

> In Dostoevsky's ethical universe, if hatred is the opposite of love as a moral feeling, egoism is the immoral misdirection of love from its proper object—one's neighbor—to oneself, one's own benefit, will, and power.... Each [of the revolutionaries] is convinced that all must bow to him because he knows the truth. Shigalov proclaims: "There can be no resolution of the social equation but mine" (10:311); Pyotr Verkhovensky counters with the boast: "One person, one person alone in Russia has devised the first step and knows how to take it. I am that person!" (10:324). Each is interested in gaining power over society, in demonstrating the force of his will by imposing it on others. Kirillov declares that he worships his own will as the attribute of his "divinity" (10:472). Verkhovensky's harangue to the members

of his revolutionary cell after they have murdered the potential traitor Shatov is suffused with the arrogance of intellect and will that Dostoevsky despised in the revolutionary mentality.[76]

Yet the path toward wholeness ends in ego dissolution, and Dostoevsky ultimately contravenes the Law of Personality with an argument for the imperative to love. In "Winter Notes on Summer Impressions," the highest development of personality was the "voluntary, fully conscious, and completely unconstrained self-sacrifice of one's entire self for the benefit of all"; thus, "One must love." The giving of oneself, he insists, must not spring from the calculation of self-interest in any form.[77] In the "Masha entry," finally, the revelation of human unity follows the Law of Love, which requires "[giving oneself] over completely to each and all, undividedly and selflessly."[78] The greatest good, then, is annihilation of "self" in the sense of subjecting one's will to the Law of Love despite opposition from the Law of Personality.[79]

Even the underground characters exhibit an inkling of understanding this transformative notion. Near the end of his tirade, the Underground Man finally says (in paraphrase), "To hell with the underground, what I want is something else, something I thirst for, something impossible to find!"[80] Similarly, Velchaninov, the adulterer stalked by the cuckolded husband in *The Eternal Husband* (1870), exclaims, "Enough with underground psychology!"[81] These revealing statements pivot upon the mystery of the underground as it begins to untangle. In this and previous sections I have discussed the deceptive ego, which can be conceived of as the mask, the performed self, or, in Jungian terms, the *shadow* archetype. As characters conform to patterns of stories and symbols, their self-perceptions create ego identities as they self-identify with these crystallizations of images and language. The presence of a catalyst causes the ego's expression in patterned behaviours.

But there is also a point where the ego makes way for an expression of authenticity. This is the shock of recognition at the core of the archetype: how ego consciousness meets the superior guidance of the self. The trauma appears in a symbolic form but is distorted by the ego and repressed, so it is often not consciously recognized. In this analysis, the underground is the symptom—the desire for the real, the inexpressible.

For Jung, the unconscious provides "nourishing" contents to the conscious mind

> which maintain the vitality of consciousness by a continual influx of energy; for consciousness does not produce its energy by itself. What is capable of transformation is just this root of consciousness.... It potentially contains that "round" wholeness which consciousness

lacks.... This "round" thing is the great treasure that lies hidden in the cave of the unconscious, and its personification is the personal being who represents the higher unity of conscious and unconscious.... [It is] a psychic totality and at the same time a centre, neither of which coincides with the ego but includes it, just as a larger circle encloses a smaller one.

The energy from the unconscious produces the archetypal forms, since it "gives us the feeling that it is something alien, a non-ego," and therefore, "it is quite natural that it should be symbolized by an alien figure."[82] Thus the self *itself* can be said to be the product of the ego selves cast in their myriad archetypal dimensions.

In Jung, the living spirit is equated with the unconscious, the wellspring of the psyche. In Dostoevsky the unconscious contents have the potential to become this life-nourishing force as well. Dostoevsky developed an answer to the underground in a concept he called *zhivaia zhizn'*: literally, "living life," it might also be interpreted as "real," "true," or "vital" life. Veresaev contrasts Dostoevsky's underground with this idea of living, true, or vital life. Since the human need for order is an idea of the ultimate meaning of life, the "idea" (*ideiia* or *mysl'*) finds its outward expression in the concrete world, where it generates meaning and purpose. Thus, spontaneous, vital life is a way of living out one's daily life in accordance with this idea. The unity of common life is at once personal and social, private and public.[83] In primitive societies of the ancient world, everyone implicitly accepted the idea of life, "the collective idea of humanity, the masses, *everyone*" (viz., what Dostoevsky was saying about brotherhood and selflessness in "Winter Notes on Summer Impressions" and "Socialism and Christianity"). In his reading of Dostoevsky, Veresaev finds that the writer contends that we are now so unused to the unifying idea—the idea that brings meaning and purpose to individuals and to humanity as a whole—that we sometimes experience an aversion to it and to life itself. Quoting Versilov in Dostoevsky's *A Raw Youth*, "It has to be something so terribly simple, so staring-you-in-the-face clear, so ordinary and everyday, so simple, that we cannot even believe it's so simple, and naturally, we've been passing over it for many thousands of years, not noticing or recognizing it."[84] The goal for both the individual and the human collective, then, is ultimate unity—unattainable, however, in earthly life, because it relies on the disintegration of our ego selves. This implies that an ontological gulf separates worldly existence, marked by moral imperfection, from otherworldly, perfect, transfigured humanity.[85] Since the Law of Personality dominates earthly life, one struggles for an ideal counter to one's nature, done "in accordance with the same law of nature, in the name of the ultimate ideal of [one's] goal." The implication is that human "nature" is a composite of animal and spiritual nature. The Law of Personality and the Law of Love counter each other in a dualist moral dialectic. Life is development, struggle, and striving for the goal. Present-day man is transitional to the transfigured, selfless creature of the Christ ideal—the ultimate archetype of the attainment of the higher self. Progress is "self-enlightenment in the name of love of one another."[86] "Self-will" [*svoevolie*] is the chief inhibitor of that possibility, as is distinctly outlined in Dostoevsky's fiction. Scanlan concludes, "The use of human freedom to assert one's will independently of the law of love ... is to act egotistically: it makes the self the determinant and warrant of actions and in so doing disregards others.... Dostoevsky believed that true freedom consists not in egoistic self-expression but in moral self-mastery."[87]

Toward that end, Dostoevsky's fiction prioritizes the theme of personal transformation in the form of narratives of visionary experience, epiphany, and personal insight. In Chapter 5, I illustrate this theme with examples from selected works and notebooks in which the author comments at length on the reality of a transcendent self that is, as Prince Myshkin puts it, "full of reason and ultimate cause." Some of these narratives have been contextualized in myths of resurrection and other types of religious experience, which make for suitable comparisons with the esoteric principles of transmutation and inward illumination. But first, in the next chapter, I compare Dostoevsky's concept of the underground to the *shadow* archetype and to the alchemical principle of the Coincidence of Opposites.

CHAPTER FOUR

Dostoevsky and the Shadow

*One is harassed by the divine being that is the image
of the living self within the locked labyrinth of
one's own disoriented psyche.*

—Joseph Campbell, *The Hero with a Thousand Faces*

*Actions are sometimes performed in a masterly and most cunning way,
while the direction of the actions is deranged and dependent on various
morbid impressions—like in a dream.*

—*Crime and Punishment*

In the Introduction, I classify Dostoevsky as an artist who was interested in creating character types—in particular, types that express the whole yet remain uniquely individualized. He would say of the hero of his Jekyll-and-Hyde story *The Double* that, in spite of its critical failure, he had never created a more important type. As I describe in Chapter 3, he endeavoured to revise *The Double* twenty years after its original publication, but abandoned the project in favour of a new work—*Notes from Underground*—which centres on a new, more important and essential *type*. These efforts would result in his most successful expression of the type since he had first attempted to achieve it in his earliest literary experimentations.

Later, writing *The Brothers Karamazov*, Dostoevsky added further dimensions to his "underground." In the Introduction I describe how underground symbolism is enmeshed in the cluster of characteristics known as *Karamazovshchina*, or "Karamazovism," which models the expression and interaction of deep-seated complexes with links to the archetypal unconscious. By and large, Dostoevsky's major characters, beginning with Golyadkin, are ideas cast as lived experience, or living embodiments of core ideas dramatized amid the conflicts of modernity. They are not reducible to psychological phenomena, but rather, as a complex whole, they create multivalent patterns that map onto archetypal forms. In a word, archetypes are complex aggregates of qualities that interact and catalyze change. These need to be investigated further in order to deepen our understanding of Dostoevsky's brand of psychological realism, which, as I've been arguing, is endowed with the dimension of depth psychology brought to it by archetypes.

The present chapter presses further into my analysis of the unconscious self as presented by Dostoevsky, specifically the manner in which the unconscious self is confronted by the conscious self. Here I draw on the Jungian archetype of the *shadow*. As noted earlier, Jung defines archetypes as patterns of thought or behaviour that take expression as symbolic imagery present in the individual unconscious and shared in past collective experience. The shadow is a prominent archetype in his system, since Jung defined it as "one example of an 'unconscious personality' which possesses a certain measure of autonomy." Its critical importance is stressed by the fact that "the shadow is often projected onto others. Examination of those attributes which a man most condemns in other people (greed, intolerance, disregard for others, etc.) usually shows that, unacknowledged, he himself possesses them."[1]

While some have mistakenly viewed it as entirely negative, Jung considered the shadow to be a suppressed yet vital part of the self: "If the repressed tendencies, the shadow as I call them, were obviously evil, there would be no problem whatever. But the shadow is merely somewhat inferior, primitive, unadapted, and awkward; not wholly bad. It even contains childish and primitive qualities which would in a way vitalize and embellish human existence, but convention forbids!"[2] I argue that it is possible to isolate and analyze the shadow characteristics of some of Dostoevsky's major characters and determine how they function in his texts in relation to compositional structure, themes, symbols, and other motifs. In addition, given that expressions of the deep-rooted complexes of the psyche in the texts are polar, just as archetypes are frequently dual, I investigate the correspondences between tropes of duality in Dostoevsky and the esoteric principle of the complementarity of opposites.

'Karamazovism'

Earlier I described how Dostoevsky took his method of character typology furthest, to its most sophisticated iteration, in his last novel, where he defines a new category: *Karamazovshchina*, or, roughly, "Karamazovism." To reiterate, the term arises during the court case at the culmination of *The Brothers Karamazov*, when Rakitin refers to the "muddled Karamazov way, which no one can understand or make any sense of." In his classic study, *The Structure of* The Brothers Karamazov, Belknap speaks of inherent relationships, "clusters of attributes" within which characteristics and their opposites are inherent in one structural system. Qualities and traits form clusters, the most prominent of which is the Karamazovan nature.

Without using the Jungian terminology, Belknap discusses the "structure of inherent relationships," describing structures that closely resemble archetypes and archetypal patterns.[3] A cluster of attributes, "some of which crystallize into symbols," gather into a whole and shape the reader's experience. Among the examples provided are money-grubbing, abandonment of loyalties, and lechery (licentiousness). But the novel is not, as Belknap is careful to point out, an allegory. Alyosha is not the embodiment of Christianity, nor is Ivan of socialism, as some have theorized. There is a hierarchical distribution of attributes, so that characters may occupy multiple rungs, for instance, on the ladder of sensuality. In fact, the "ladder of Karamazovism" is referred to by Alyosha; thus, Belknap employs the principle of hierarchy implied by the ladder to order the structure of inherent relationships arranged around certain dominant types.[4]

In Belknap's analysis, other clusters are co-extensive with Karamazovism and overlap with one another; their inherent relationships shape the reader's experience. A cluster, for instance, connects the Devil, the buffoon, the *nadryv*, and divine grace. On the Devil, for example:

> A greater or less involvement in self-annihilation, non-being, falsehood, cruelty, mystery, laughter, and distastefulness links Ivan, Smerdjakov, Lise, the Grand Inquisitor, Rakitin, and Fëdor to one another and to the figure of the Devil, with his schematic sub-embodiments, Zosima's mysterious visitor, Karp, and the vicious little demons. Some of these people and these attributes have other connections as well. Ivan is a Karamazov, and self-annihilation is an element of Karamazovism, for example, but the massing of associations generates a presence which is more specifically diabolic.[5]

In fact, Dostoevsky frequently employs the Devil as an archetype. Its heritage in Russian folklore and literature are discussed in Chapter 2. In the examples cited above and others found elsewhere in Dostoevsky's works (most notably Ivan Karamazov's famous confrontation with an apparition of the Devil in Book XI, Chapter 9, of *The Brothers Karamazov*), the devil archetype dramatizes the confrontation of suppressed aspects of the psyche, a confrontation that ultimately catalyzes transformative change.

Furthermore, according to Belknap, the "tragic aspect" and the "necessary absurdity" of buffoonery resemble the "indispensable minus" of the Devil, "without whom nothing might have existed. His is the metaphysical rejection of God's world, and its order, while buffoonery is the practical, everyday rejection of it, *in the name of the self, ordering the world according to one's own patterns*, but rejecting the reasonable, the socially acceptable, the religiously acceptable externals, and lapsing into the self-perpetuating shame caught in its self-dramatization."[6] Buffoons, like devils, are staple characters in Dostoevsky. As noted, they relate to the patterning of the self—you might say an affirmation and consolidation of the apparent self. Besides Fyodor Pavlovich and Maksimov in *The Brothers Karamazov*, other prominent examples are the eponymous hero of "Polzunkov," Lebedev in *The Idiot*, and Captain Lebyadkin in *The Devils*. In each case, the "self-dramatization" of buffoonery may be seen as the enactment of the apparent self in the form of an archetype; further, the archetype expresses a concealed dynamic involving shame, resentment, and the perceived injustice of being slighted by the world and rejected by God.

A third aspect of the cluster is *nadryv*, a Russian word used throughout the text of *The Brothers Karamazov* to refer to types of catalyst—outbursts of passion, irrational impulses, emotional catharses—that frequently seize Dostoevsky's characters. Belknap indicates the derivation of the noun *nadryv* from the Russian verbal root *rvat'*, meaning to "rend," "tear," "burst," or "split." It implies a heightening of emotion, a "paroxysm," or "anguish." The adjective derived from it is "heart-rending." Bordering on the diabolic, it can trigger self-annihilation, and matches the irrationality expressed in buffoonery.[7] Belknap summarizes a few of its occurrences:

> Just as buffoonery was a twisted response to poverty and blows received, so the *nadryv* is a twisted response to wealth and benefits received, or at least offered. Katerina Ivanovna's love for Mitja is connected with the money he lent her, and reaches the level of the *nadryv* when her affluence lets her return the money and entrust further money to Mitja. In the same way, the *nadryv* at Snegirëv's occurs when Alëša comes to offer money, and centers upon the gratitude for the money, which necessitates its abrupt refusal. In this sense,

the *nadryv* is the exact opposite of buffoonery, involving pride, riches, dignity, and a pressing fear of being base while the buffoon embodies humiliation, poverty, shame, and pursuit of baseness. The buffoon makes himself laughable in order to make others so. The *nadryv* causes a person to hurt himself in order to hurt others, or, perversely, to hurt others in order to hurt himself. These oppositions do not obscure the fact that *nadryv* and buffoonery have much in common. Both embody perversity, willfulness, self-consciousness, self-dramatization, and absurdity.[8]

Belknap's final element of the cluster is divine grace. He cites the recollections of Alyosha, Zosima, and Markel, in which they refer to the mystical presence of grace. Slanting sunlight is a prominent image that represents grace; other motifs are mother and child, tears, prayer, kneeling, clarity, silence, remoteness in memory, candles and incense (holy fire), blessings, and embraces.[9] In Zosima's account of grace, the elder acknowledges that he "knowingly received the seed of God's word in [his] heart." The elder's statement echoes the epigraph of the novel: "Verily, verily I say unto you, except a grain of wheat die, falling upon the ground, it remains alone, but if it die, then it bringeth forth much fruit."[10] Belknap explains the interaction of Karamazovism with grace:

> Like Karamazovism, grace is made into a force which can have a specific effect upon a man. Alëša is said to have placed his faith in God instead of socialism, "perhaps because he was affected by the slanting beams of the setting sum [sic] before the image to which his hysterical mother had extended him." But unlike Karamazovism, which is described as an inertial force, grace operates through the responses which it evokes from others, as in the passage just cited, or in the "answering love" Christ awakened in Seville, or when Zosima went before the believers: "They threw themselves before him, crying, kissing his feet, kissing the earth on which he stood, wailing; the peasant women stretching out their children, and leading up sick hysterical women." In the same paragraph, many of Zosima's other attributes are mentioned, including "power and glory," knowledge of secrets revealed in a man's face, ability to make "the darkest face turn into a happy one," greatest love for the greatest sinners, apparently miraculous cures, and the status as a "keeper of divine truth in the eyes of the people." This capacity to inspire answering love belongs not only to Zosima and Christ, but to Alëša.[11]

In sum, Belknap's clusters of attributes model a framework that can be useful for examining more of Dostoevsky's dynamic character types. As I continue to examine those types below, I investigate the complementarity of opposites as a dimension that defines them, indicating additional parallels with archetypal forms.

The Coincidence of Opposites
Dostoevsky's works gain much of their dramatic force by consistently following a principle of the complex of inexorable opposites. Known for representing psychological and philosophical contrasts, Dostoevsky juxtaposes characters as well, each of whom embodies a complex of ideas: the characters meet in a dialectic of dual forms, whether juxtaposed to one another or in the experience of dual forces and dual beliefs within each of them individually. Such is the structure of *The Double* with respect to the meeting of Golyadkin Sr. and Golyadkin Jr. Going further, here I consider whether we find evidence in these juxtapositions that Dostoevsky the artist had an explicit interest in dramatizing the clash of opposites that catalyzes change and transformation.

Dostoevsky's most direct precursor in this respect is undoubtedly Nikolai Gogol. In his book about Gogol, in the chapter "The Psychology of Gogol's Creative Work," Russian psychoanalytic school founder Ivan Ermakov explains how most observers perceive in Gogol an inner and outer disharmony of contradiction (*protivorechivost'*) and duality (*dvoistvennost'*):

> We have already seen that his humorous descriptions were hostile to and in conflict with his sentimental and religious constructions of the fantastic and romanticism, to which he was inclined. "One has to wonder—Kotliarevskii said—that, such being his soul's orientation, Gogol could so often forget about himself, ironize when he wanted to ruminate and talk about any ordinary trivia and banality, as his soul meanwhile clung to the sublime and eternal."[12]

It can be safely said that Dostoevsky gained a good measure of the principles of contradiction and duality from Gogol's narrative style; likewise the inner nature of Gogol's vision, the sublime and eternal to which his soul allegedly clung, is met in equal or greater proportions in Dostoevsky. I am not interested in seeking out the psychological complexes that gave rise to this tendency, as Ermakov and other psychoanalysts have been, nor do I inquire whether the principles of contradiction and duality are rooted in Dostoevsky's relationship with his father or other family members. Others have speculated at length on that question. I am concerned instead with the writer's propensity to use his characters as avenues for expression of the modern subject in narrative fiction, and expression of their contradictory impulses, showing their very humanity in the inner division itself.

On that point Veresaev takes the pessimistic view: "The aggravating disunity of spirit and the body, the feebleness of the connection between them, makes Dostoyevsky's characters completely incapable of striving toward bright, whole passion."[13] The Underground Man says that in his underground dreams, he has never imagined love that does not struggle, starting always with hatred and ending with some degree of moral subjugation, conquest, or enslavement. But then he could never imagine what to do with the subjugated object. True, says Veresaev, what would Dmitri Karamazov and Grushenka do? Or Stavrogin and Liza? Rogozhin and Nastasya Filippovna? "If the way is not opened to suicide or murder, then there is only one alternative—vulgarity."[14]

Taking a different view, Russian philosopher Nikolai Berdiaev hearkened to medieval forms of mysticism to attribute this feature of Dostoevsky's fiction to the principle of the complementarity of opposites, a precept of Western esotericism: "His conception of the world was in the highest degree dynamic, and we must look at it in that way; the internal contradictions of his work will then vanish, and it will verify the principle of *coincidentia oppositorum*."[15] This Latin phrase attributed to fifteenth-century German theologian and mystic Nicholas of Cusa, means the "coincidence of opposites," indicating a complementarity of polar forms that combine in a sacred union. This idea may be traced to the sixth-century Neoplatonist Dionysius the Areopagite, who elaborated the dichotomy of positive (cataphatic) and negative (apophatic) theology in Christian dialectics; forms of it can be traced further back, to Heraclitus and even more ancient sources. Inherent to Hermeticism, Neoplatonism, Gnosticism, and other mystical traditions, the perennial tradition of the coincidence of opposites holds that the knowable and unknowable represent complimentary realms.[16]

Jung studied the principle in the symbols and practices of medieval alchemy. In his work *Mysterium Coniunctionis*, he defines the "Sacred Marriage of opposites" (*mysterium coniunctionis*, or simply *coniunctio*), which he claims is the mystical principle of transformation. The principle holds that the creative tension of opposites symbolizes the unconscious psyche coming to the light of awareness in the conscious mind. In living terms, the process coincides with the manifestation of archetypal patterns. One of the proofs of the validity of the *coniunctio* for Jung was that he found when he observed his patients that certain archetypal motifs of alchemy appeared in the dreams of individuals who had no knowledge of the alchemical symbols and cosmology.[17]

The *coniunctio*, to be exact, refers to opposites that either confront one another in enmity or attract one another in love.[18] They form a dualism or polarity. The polarity is often arranged in a *quaternio* as the opposites cross and produce an emblem of the four elements and symbols of the sublunary world. They precipitate the confrontation of the unconscious and conscious minds, a confrontation that catalyzes fear of the unconscious, which nevertheless needs to be manifested in spite of the fear: "Man's descent to the water is needed in order to evoke the miracle of its coming to life. But the breath of the spirit rushing over the dark water is uncanny like everything whose cause we do not know—since it is not ourselves. It hints at an unseen presence, a numen…it lives of itself."[19]

In Chapter 3 I note the inseparable link that Dmitri Karamazov identifies between the polar ideals of Sodom and the Madonna: "Here the shores meet. Here all contradictions live together."[20] In the same outpouring, Dmitri claims that he plunges "head down, feet up, into the abyss." Later he adds that this indicates his "thirst for life." Thirst for life is a quality claimed, in addition, by Ivan, Fyodor Pavlovich, and Alyosha. Nevertheless, as Belknap demonstrates, the unquenchable Karamazovan thirst for life coexists with suicidal tendencies in the brothers: for Dmitri, the "one putrid insect he must kill" is himself; at another time he draws a sword, declaring, "do you understand how one can kill one's self from certain ecstasies"; and his brother Ivan once says, "at 30 I shall probably cast the cup aside." Nor can we overlook Smerdiakov's suicide, committed in spite of his having stated that he dreaded death.[21] Most other Karamazov attributes coexist with their opposites: substantial pride versus vileness with regard to money and loyalty; lechery versus intellectual hunger; childlike halfwittedness versus the spirit of rebellion, mutiny, or revolt. Here we see evidence that the complementarity of opposites pervades all of the Karamazov features, indeed stands as its founding structural principle. Dostoevsky gives explicit attention to this point in the prosecutor Ippolit Kirillovich's speech at Dmitri's trial:

> As a rule in life, with two opposites, we must seek the truth in the middle; in the present case, this is literally not so. Most probably in the first case he was genuinely noble, and in the second case just as genuinely base. Why? Just because we wide, Karamazov natures…are able to contain all conceivable opposites and to contemplate at once the two abysses, the abyss above us, the abyss of the highest ideals, and the abyss below us, the abyss of the lowest, most fetid downfall.[22]

The Prosecutor gives the "wide Karamazov nature" its widest summation here, offering the most direct and definitive statement of *Karamazovshchina* in the novel. Belknap concludes that Karamazovism thus "becomes not only a cluster of attributes coupled in tension and arranged hierarchically, but also an inclusiveness which permits the existence of such a cluster of incompatibles in a single man." More than a mere collection of attributes, moreover, Karamazovism is made out to be a *force in the world*. Alyosha laments, "My brothers are ruining themselves...my father too. And they're ruining others along with themselves. Here is the 'earthy Karamazov force,' as Father Paisij recently phrased it—earthly, violent, in the rough.... I only know that I myself am a Karamazov."[23] I venture that Alyosha means by this that he recognizes that the Karamazov nature is a dual force that contains a shadow side and, moreover, that he recognizes the shadow archetype in himself. Yet he is closer to awareness of the higher self, I contend, because he strives to know the shadow in himself and others. I substantiate this regarding later instances of Alyosha's transformation through visionary narrative, which I discuss in the next chapter. But first, my comparison takes a closer look at the notion of the complementarity of opposites in Jung's conception.

Jung's work has been compared to Dostoevsky's in detail in Weisblatt's insightful and articulate master's thesis mentioned earlier, "The Numinous on Russian Soil: A Depth Psychological Interpretation of Religious Experience in The Brothers Karamazov." According to Weisblatt, Jung determined that alchemy emerged in European culture in response to the loss of relevancy of traditional symbols of Christianity. Jung described the work of the alchemists in psychological terms, using the concept of "active imagination." Says Weisblatt, noting that alchemy involves the *coniunctio oppositorum* or Sacred Marriage of opposites, forming symbolic manifestations of the individuation process, Jung saw in the alchemical symbol of the king an archetype of regeneration. Jung also interpreted the *filius sapientiae*, or Christ's birth, as well as the assimilation of the Christ image within the individual, as the incarnation of God and the transformation of consciousness. Weisblatt argues that, according to Jung, a range of Christian images or concepts, such as the Trinity, originated in and were realized in personal religious or visionary experiences, based on the parallels he observed between Christian and alchemical symbolism. Turning to Dostoevsky, Weisblatt applies Jung's analysis, wherein symbols of both alchemy and Christianity evoke archetypes of renewal and individuation, to *The Brothers Karamazov*:

> Alchemical imagery becomes incorporated into the story's narrative of the death of the elder Zosima when his corpse's putrefaction causes a scandal among his brethren. This event becomes a test and a moral

crisis for Alyosha, which, however, finds its resolution in a numinous dream, which he has while sitting vigil in Zosima's chambers during a reading of the Gospel over his casket. Alyosha's dream of the marriage feast at Cana provides an example of the spontaneous emergence of *coniunctio* symbolism in response to psychological crisis and demonstrates, in congruence with Jung's... conception of the experience of the medieval alchemists, its healing and transformative effect on the dreamer.[24]

Weisblatt's application of Jung's comparison of Christianity and alchemy to the scandal caused by the stench of Elder Zosima's decomposing corpse illustrates the utility of my archetypal approach to understanding Dostoevsky's struggle with the conflict between modernity and spirituality. She notes that the monks who identify the mortal Zosima "with the archetypal God-man he has come to represent" confuse external reality with psychic processes and events, connecting human conflicts and dilemmas with "the enduring conflict between religion and scientific rationalism of matter versus spirit." Situating Zosima's death and bodily decomposition within "a larger mythic process... allows for an interpretation of its psychological significance as an archetypal event. The incident thus takes on symbolic significance in much the same manner as the king's death and decomposition was imaginatively experienced by the alchemists."[25]

Here Weisblatt analyzes Jung's account of the parable from the *Allegoria Merlini* involving the king's sacrifice to renew the subjects' spirit. Quoting Jung, Weisblatt notes that this event brings back the "spirit of the chaotic waters of the beginning, before the second day of Creation, before the separation of the opposites and hence before the advent of consciousness." Jung then connects the parable to the contrast between the historical Christ and the figure around whom a religion was formed: "The real Christ vanished behind projections and emotions that swarmed about him.... He became the collective figure whom the unconscious of his contemporaries expected to appear." Similarly, Weisblatt argues,

> Zosima functions as the collective figure for his brethren's projections and desires, who expect in him a manifestation of what Jung calls the "cosmic saviour, the mediating God–man"... In the same way as Christ the historical figure, Zosima constellates the archetype of the Self within his followers, and his figure becomes the "victim of the universal longing for light"... but where Christ "opened men's eyes to revelation precisely because he was, from everlasting, God, and therefore unhistorical"... Zosima, the mortal, must engender doubt.[26]

Adding to her Jungian analysis of Dostoevsky, Weisblatt then examines the symbolic significance of the odour of death in both the alchemical and Christian traditions. Jung finds that alchemy involves, in particular, the "stench of graves" and "the perfume of flowers, the latter being a symbol of resurgent life. In ecclesiastical allegory and in the lives of the saints a sweet smell is one of the manifestations of the Holy Ghost." In the case of Zosima's corpse, though, we see the symbolism inverted: "putrefaction becomes the sign of life renewed. Zosima's death and the deterioration of his corpse...thus come to represent the paradox his followers each must resolve within himself."[27]

Zosima's putrefaction, Weisblatt argues, becomes a riddle because it combines, as if through alchemy, evil, and death on one hand with goodness and life on the other. She argues that Dostoevsky uses this episode to relocate faith from "external signs of God's grace" to the human individual. Zosima's "bodily decay, the sign of his humanity, indicates that, as in the myth of Christ's resurrection, the miracle is to be found elsewhere. Like Christ's death, the events surrounding Zosima's death indicate that the source of renewal is ultimately within each individual, in the change of consciousness resulting from the confrontation of the ego with the Self." The decomposing corpse therefore represents "the ego, that archetypal factor that, together with the body and spirit, defines the mortal man. The central psychological component here is the event of the ego's forfeiture, which must occur in order for a wider consciousness to emerge.... The lesson Zosima teaches, even in death, is that grace is arrived at through loss, and apotheosis lies in forfeiture. In the apprehension of personal dissolution, the one recognizes one's place in the cycle of life."[28]

Weisblatt explores these themes further in analyzing the dream Alyosha has while he holds vigil over Zosima's dead body. The dream, she argues, brings into modern times the religious figure that reconciles the opposites dramatized in Zosima's corpse, with Alyosha playing the role of "the spiritual pilgrim and intermediary who is actively engaged with secular humanity. In allegorical terms, Alyosha signifies the final phase of the *coniunctio*, the emergence of the new conscious dominant in the birth of the divine son."[29] In other words, the spirit reawakens through the dream, thus symbolically reintegrating the personality as theorized in Jung's thought. Weisblatt observes that the "concurrence of such spontaneous imagery as the wedding couple, Christ at the feast, the transformation of water to wine, and the image of the sun—symbols which are, for the most part, overtly Christian, come straight out of the alchemical opus, and are shown to have, in the Jungian sense, a psychologically healing and transformative effect on Alyosha."[30]

My adaptation of the Jungian notion of archetypes echoes Weisblatt's treatment of Alyosha's dream, in which "the imagery and drama of the *coniunctio* archetype become imaginatively reconfigured in a way that makes it specifically meaningful to Alyosha."[31] Again arguing that Jung's comparison of alchemy and Christian symbolism helps to make sense of the message Dostoevsky means to transmit through the dream sequence, Weisblatt maintains that,

> As in the alchemical process, the Christian and alchemical symbolism in Alyosha's dream function both to bring about *and* to describe to him, or make real, the healing processes at work within him.... The conjunction of the pair of opposites that make up the phenomenology of the Self... symbolizes the integration of the personality. As the central element of the dream... the marriage feast thus communicates that this dream is dealing with Alyosha's struggle to resolve his inner doubts and conflicts over worldliness and spirituality and the resolution of that conflict in his attainment of greater self-knowledge and emergent consciousness.[32]

Thus does Alyosha see the *coniunctio* as simultaneously divine and mortal, giving the human event of marriage Christ's imprimatur. The wedding couple represent not merely the ego's submission "to the transpersonal Self but also the descent of the spirit to the earthly." In this way the events of the dream enable Alyosha to accept his life outside of the monastery as a fitting site for achieving the spiritual healing he sought within it. When Alyosha asks, "Was it really in order to provide wine for the weddings of the poor that he came down to earth?" he acknowledges that Christ's role in turning water into wine for the wedding is, as Weisblatt puts it, to bring "to life the union of body and soul, and this, as Alyosha experiences it in the dream, appears to be Christ's purpose."[33]

Weisblatt concludes her discussion of Alyosha's dream by noting that when Christ turns the water into wine the elder Zosima himself appears at the wedding feast, and it is he who invites Alyosha to join the celebration: "One could say that at this moment, the ego has been invited to join with the Self and that the *coniunctio*, the marriage couple, now invites Alyosha as subject or ego to join the celebration and commune in joy with the Self," enabling Alyosha "to internalize the image of God or apprehend its symbolic truth." This moment of epiphany or transcendence parallels "the Christian image of Christ's resurrection and the birth of the *filius sapientiae*, and can thus be seen to further signify the miracle of spiritual rebirth." This experience is reinforced when the dreamt figure of Zosima draws Alyosha's attention to the sun, which serves as yet another symbol of the divine source of life, a new symbol of the awakened consciousness that the dream makes available to Alyosha. Thus Alyosha experiences an apotheosis that parallels that of Jung's king, one that in Jung's terms represents the "world-creating significance of the consciousness manifested in man," enabling Alyosha to recognize "the God within."[34] I explore the implications of Alyosha's epiphany and the role of vision narrative more specifically in the next chapter.

Intelligentsia: Illness and Apocalypse
Illness in the intelligentsia is another theme in Dostoevsky that mines the issues of self-identity and the potentially catastrophic forces of the psyche. Dostoevsky draws many of his characters from the Russian intelligentsia—the class to which Dostoevsky belonged—many of whom, at the same time as they preach Western liberal ideas, are associated with forms of illness, madness, chaos, and destruction. Frank maintains, for example, that there is a connection between the ideological intoxication of characters from the Russian intelligentsia and mental illness. Dostoevsky's characters of the 1840s who were ill were broken down from trying to sustain the struggle of asserting themselves in a crushing social environment.[35] Earlier, while suffering from the onset of his own nervous disease, Dostoevsky had been extremely susceptible, at the time of the first flowering of his artistic and social consciousness, to the ideas of French utopian socialism (which I referred to earlier) and had become an eager member not only of Petrashevsky's circle but also of a secret, inner conspiratorial group led by Nikolai Speshnev that had had more concrete aims for social agitation and advocated the overthrow of tsarism. "I was guilty," Dostoevsky later confessed in a letter of March 23, 1856, to General E.I. Totleben:

> I recognize it fully. I was convicted of having had the intention (but only that) of acting against the government; I was condemned legally and justly; a long tribulation, torturing and cruel, sobered me up and changed my ideas in many ways. But then—then I was blind, believed in theories and utopias.... Previously, I had been ill for two years running, with a strange, moral sickness. I was a hypochondriac. There were even times when I lost my reason. I was excessively irritable, impressionable to the point of sickness, and with the ability to deform the most ordinary facts and give them another aspect and dimension. But I felt that, even though this sickness exercised a strong and evil influence on my fate, it would have been a very pitiful and even humiliating justification. Yes, and I wasn't even very well aware of it at that time.[36]

He would later describe similar obsessions—to the point of possession—of radical members of the intelligentsia in his characters whose rationality and atheism develop into a perverse sort of mental and moral illness. In *Crime and Punishment* and *The Devils*, this quintessential type from the Russian intelligentsia aspires to revolutionary aims of social and moral revolt justified on the basis of his rational-materialist socio-political and philosophical beliefs. In *The Brothers Karamazov*, he aspires to parricide.

Illness is a common attribute of another type of character as well, associated in at least one case with the condition from which the author himself suffered. Pairing his own nervous susceptibility with the possession by rationality and atheism he saw in his peers and co-conspirators, Dostoevsky, after long, trying years suffering both from his worsening nervous disease and attacks of epilepsy, and from the taxing years he spent in prison and exile, began to conceive of a new type of character, one whose Christian humility in the face of human suffering and degradation gave him the ability to transcend the tribulations of life and live after the model of the image of Christ. Dostoevsky described the mystic harmony felt by the hero of *The Idiot*, Prince Myshkin, in the moments before an epileptic seizure, which are strikingly similar to the author's descriptions of his own pre-seizure state of mind that he reported in letters. I discuss the significance of Myshkin's vision-like experience at some length in the next chapter.

In Chapter 3 I cite Gibian's view that Raskolnikov's illness is an infection both psychological and physiological in nature, spread throughout his body and mind. For healing, he needs repentance—a total remedy for the unconscious through spiritual redemption. That involves a return to roots, to the faith traditions of the Russian *narod*, for the core conflict is related to Dostoevsky's ideas regarding the Russian people vis-à-vis the uprootedness of the Russian intelligentsia. He perceived the latter as lacking a ruling idea. Gartered with European liberalism, scientific socialism, and atheism, the Russian intelligentsia had become unmoored. This he counterpoised with the national folk identity (what Belinsky called *narodnost'*) and a more mystical sense of the Russian *narod*, whom Dostoevsky believed he had come to understand intimately during his years of exile living and working shoulder-to-shoulder with peasant convicts in Siberia. In particular, he came to know that the identity of the people was related to their conception of God.[37]

Over and above illness, apocalyptic imagery is strongly related to the intelligentsia vis-à-vis the people in Dostoevsky. Gary Saul Morson contends that imminent apocalypse is the most prevalent theme of *Diary of a Writer*. Social "fragmentation," "dissociation," and "isolation" have reached an extreme, and the "final battle" is near.[38] The image of self in

"The Dream of a Ridiculous Man," for instance, is part utopian vision, part millennial Christian eschatology. A modern Russian progressive, the Ridiculous Man cannot comprehend how the inhabitants of the utopian planet he visits can know so much without the benefits of modern science. He has knowledge they do not have, so how can he help telling them? Over the course of a millennium, which sweeps by, leaving him with only an impression of the whole, his "knowledge" corrupts them like a trichina strain (similar to Raskolnikov's dream in *Crime and Punishment*). It is as if microscopic creatures "infect" the people with an endowment of reason and will. Those infected at once become possessed and insane, but never before had they considered themselves so wise and so unassailably correct about everything.[39] Whole towns and nations go mad. The inhabitants begin to lie and to love sensuality over beauty. Their languages are dispersed. Jealousy, cruelty, shame, and honour enter their experience and social fabric. They number science, humanism, brotherhood, justice, and corporeal punishment among their accomplishments. They hardly remember and do not want to believe that they once were happy, free beings; but they "want" to be innocent and happy again, so they build temples to this desire and pray to their idea, all the while believing only in its impossibility. They have science and will discover truth—so they believe. Finally, they love themselves above others. They are jealous and try to belittle others, yet they live in voluntary slavery to one another as a core belief develops: let everyone continue to love themselves the most but agree not to harm anyone else. Thus they are meant to live together in peaceful concord, but instead fight to the death over the idea itself.[40]

Not only is the whole tenor of this passage apocalyptic, certain details are also clearly drawn from Revelation, in particular the outbreaks of pestilence, famine, and fire.[41] Leatherbarrow contends that the two most apocalyptic of Dostoevsky's works, though, are *The Idiot* and *The Devils*:

> Both possess a distinctive, urgent, almost hysterical tone not matched by Dostoevsky's other great novels. In "Crime and Punishment" one feels that the spiritual disease that afflicts Raskolnikov has not yet spread to everyone in the novel, and the work ends with a promise of reconciliation, not the threat of Armageddon. "The Brothers Karamazov" too ends with a promise, as Alesha and the children meet over little Iljusha's grave and pledge loyalty to his memory. But "The Idiot" and "The Devils" end with the eruption of that death and violence which has threatened throughout both novels. In "The Idiot" the murder of Nastasja Filippovna precipitates the return of Myshkin to darkness, and the hope contained in Stepan Trofimovich's last

pilgrimage, which concludes "The Devils," is not enough to offset the orgy of murder and suicide that accompanies it.[42]

Besides those characters already mentioned, Ivan Karamazov is the foremost example of the Russian *intelligent* who views the world as a Western rational materialist, but who nevertheless is a complex character who both confronts the irrational and recognizes (unlike the Underground Man) the limitations of his own rational mind and ego self. He finds himself inside a beguiling paradox:

> Listen to me: I took only little children [for my example], to make it more clear. About the rest of human tears, which soak the earth from its cortex to its center, I don't say a word, I narrowed my topic on purpose. I am a bedbug and I admit in all humility that I can't understand anything about why it's all set up the way it is. People themselves are to blame: they were given paradise, they wanted freedom and they stole fire from heaven knowing perfectly well that they'd become miserable, so there's no being sorry for them. Oh, I know, my miserable, earthly Euclidean mind knows what suffering is, that no one is at fault, that all things come out of one another plain and simple, that everything flows and evens out—but this is all just Euclidean nonsense, I know that too, don't I? And I can't agree to live by these terms, can I![43]

Apart from political contexts, I explain these associations with the intelligentsia as an application of Dostoevsky's interest in the tendency to project one's self-vision onto the movements of history. By that I mean that the anxiety of the self, with its perception and fear of the unconscious psyche, comes to express the self-narrative in symbolic, archetypal forms. The imminent transformation that threatens to annihilate it is projected onto history as the expectation of apocalypse. Such a projection contrasts with authentic self seen as redemptive vision or revelation of ultimate truth.

Inertia and the Decomposition of Consciousness

To understand the problem of illness and apocalypse in the intelligentsia, I turn now to Dostoevsky's view of the nature of the rational mind as a property of the material world. His conceptualization of the operation of reason serves as something of an antecedent to his diagnosis of the plight of those who struggle with the opposition between reason and feeling. This sets up a problem for Dostoevsky, because inertia plays such a large role in the material world of nature.

In Chapter 3 I note that Dostoevsky identified the rejection of the sacred as one of the sources of the underground mentality. People are prevented from imitating Christ by the so-called Law of Personality, and this is the chief cause of sin and suffering. I connect the problem of inertia to human dismay over the contradiction between an innate sense of inner freedom and external subjection to necessity. The socialists wanted to free humanity by improving material conditions and creating a civic utopia. But for Dostoevsky, if human nature is determined by physical laws, then free will is superfluous. The socialists believed in an atheistic, materialist philosophy—all humanity had to do to thrive was discover the laws of nature. But Dostoevsky insisted that their aims, driven by mechanization and the law of inertia, were resistant to change, subject to the Law of Personality, and could lead only to evil and death. Life, on the contrary, is the *annihilation of inertia*; it transcends the laws of nature and Newtonian physics. The law of spirit delivers humanity from material necessity, and faith in the resurrected Christ liberates us from subjugation to nature. Thus, one must strive toward an ideal (Christ-like love) that is inherently contrary to one's nature. Ultimately, humanity's divine origins guarantee us freedom of will, but one must participate in one's own salvation by struggling against natural law.[44] Without faith in one's soul and its immortality, as Dostoevsky attests in the short polemic "Unsubstantiated Claims," existence is unnatural and unbearable. "In a word, the idea of immortality is life itself, it is living life, its ultimate formula and principal source of truth and the right consciousness for humanity."[45]

Koehler ties these themes to the short story "A Gentle Creature" (1876) in a study of Dostoevsky's use of the word *kosnost'*, with which, in his last words, the narrator rails against the laws of nature: "Insensibility [*kosnost'*]. Oh, nature! People are alone in the world. That's what is so dreadful.... Everything is dead. Dead men are everywhere. There are only people in the world, and all around them is silence—that's what the earth is!"[46]

"*Kosnost'*" translates variously as "insensibility," "stagnation," "inertia," "indolence," "sluggishness," or "narrow-mindedness." Koehler notes that, in addition to such purportedly literal translations, scholars have given the word other interpretations: D.V. Grishin identifies it with loneliness; L.M. Rosenblium with indifference toward the existence of society and even the universe. In this connection Rosenblium remarks: "'It is difficult to overcome kosnost' in the surrounding world, but it is even more difficult to overcome it in oneself.'"[47]

Koehler discovers that *kosnost'* appears most often in situations linked with the "implacable laws of nature" and associated with annihilation and death. For example, Dostoevsky uses the term in *A Raw Youth* when the protagonist Arkady Dolgoruky addresses some young radicals: "Nothing is clear in your society, gentlemen. You are denying God, you deny heroic deeds; what deaf, blind, dull *kosnost'* could compel me to act in this way if it is more advantageous to me to act in another?" As Koehler explains, Arkady then rejects the "code" of the young radicals and their rationality, as well as society and the world, which links him to the Underground Man and the narrator of "A Gentle Creature": "But in Arkadii Dolgorukii's rejection he casts implicit blame on the socialist ideal, declaring that he does not care what happens in the future if he is 'not to get either love, nor future life, nor recognition of my feat.' He is frustrated by the idea of a future that offers 'barracks and phalansteries' instead of love and immortality and, like the Underground Man, he rejects this future."[48]

In *The Idiot*, Ippolit Terent'ev rails against the inexorable forces of inertia that seem to be drawing him toward his impending death, which he calls a "death sentence." Ippolit rebels against the "dark and dumb fate" that was to "crush him like a fly." Koehler continues, "The realization of the irrevocability of these laws hits him with special force as he contemplates Holbein's 'Christ in the Tomb' in Rogozhin's gloomy dwelling. Ippolit begins to doubt the possibility of resurrection: If 'death is so horrible and the laws of nature so powerful, how can they be overcome?' Nature appears to him in the guise of a 'monstrous, implacable, dumb beast' and then as 'an enormous machine of the newest construction which insensibly took hold of, crushed, and swallowed dumb and insensible, a great and priceless Being.'"[49]

Ippolit's fear and loathing in the face of pitiless nature compares to the insect imagery I discuss with regard to Karamazovism earlier in this chapter, and to spiders and other images in Dostoevsky that I present in Chapter 3 as symbols of the underground. All might be thought of as synonyms of *kosnost'*.

Dostoevsky uses the word elsewhere in his case against the materialists. Reflecting on the death of his first wife, testing his thoughts in a personal diary entry (the so-called "Masha entry" I discuss in Chapter 3), the grieving husband arrives at the idea of immortality, concluding, "The teaching of materialists—universal *kosnost'* and the mechanism of matter—means death." The "true philosophy," by contrast, is "the destruction of stagnation [*kosnost'*], that is: Thought, that is... God and eternal life."[50]

"Bobok" is another tale where *kosnost'* is the ruling force, a macabre tale of the decomposition of consciousness.[51] In tone and atmosphere it takes Dostoevsky back to his roots—gothic horror, the supernatural, and his own uniquely ironic, slightly absurd brand of fantastic realism. The narrator starts by speaking of ideal form versus realism; he is disturbed that an artist has drawn his portrait, and advertised, "Go and see this face—morbid, on the verge of insanity." The narrator takes offence, complaining that in print, everything ought to be noble; what is needed are ideals, while today's artists lack general ideas, so they make do with phenomena, showing warts and all. "And they call that realism," he complains.[52]

In the tale that follows, the narrator visits a graveyard, where he witnesses the conversation of corpses in their graves. The biochemical basis of their capacity to think and communicate after death is explained by the resident philosopher Platon Nikolaevich (Platon is Russian for *Plato*), who reveals that, during an interlude of two to three months, before consciousness fully recedes, there is still time to consider one's intentions and motives, and repent for one's sin in life.[53] However, the narrator finds that the beings he overhears conversing in their graves prefer to enjoy themselves while they can rather than repent; they even make a pact to reveal all and be ashamed of nothing. Perturbed, the narrator perceives it as a "stench of the soul," as these decomposing conscious entities engage in pandering, lust, insults, intrigue, and slander. "We stand equally in our sins [*vo gresekh*] before the Lord's judgment," declares the one character who refuses to partake in the shameless flaunting of vices. "In our sins [*vo gresekh*]!" another replies, mocking the righteous man's use of the Old Church Slavonic form of the word "sins"—"Don't you even dare to speak to me!"[54]

The rejection of faith and mockery of the Christian belief in the immortality of the soul is dramatized as a grotesque distortion of the truth. Here, where the dead souls treat their minds and selves as they did in life—as material entities—their consciousness is literally decomposing. The narrator had heard an unsettling sound when he entered the cemetery: "*bobok! bobok!*" He now learns of the two-to-three-month period of post-mortem socializing, after which the individuals began fading away, emitting the feeble gurgling sound "*bobok*" as they go.

Finally, Veresaev uses the word *kosnost'* in an argument stressing the unbelief of Dostoevsky's principle characters: "Dostoevsky's religion, in any case...is an infirmary for the tired, an almshouse for the infirm. The god of this religion is only a crutch which the hopelessly crippled man grabs for. He grasps, tries to get up and lean on it, but the crutch then breaks. And all around—only the grim, bleak desert, and over it reigns the cold 'mute silence of inertia [*kosnost'*].'"[55] Veresaev is correct in his assessment insofar as it applies to Dostoevsky's *intelligenty*—to those ruled by ideology, their minds mechanical, lifeless, and inert—or to the examples of Ippolit, the chattering corpses in "Bobok," and the examples provided above. I do not believe their lifelessness is emblematic of Dostoevsky's religion, however; nor is it in any respect the end of his philosophy.

Not the pessimist some may perceive him to be, Dostoevsky presents alternatives to inertia, madness, and apocalypse. One alternative is tied to the native Russian traditions that Dostoevsky valorized, which I discuss presently. Another, the topic of Chapter 5, refers to the related but more universal theme of transformation.

Dostoevsky and the 'Russian Idea'
Dostoevsky was a nationalist thinker who professed that full realization of the kingdom of Christ on earth is more likely in Orthodox Russia than anywhere else. The Law of Personality, he claimed, was less dominant there.[56] In the *Diary*, he grounds his idealism in the character of the Russian people, writing, "In the Russian individual there is no European-like angularness."[57] Moreover, Dostoevsky believed there was a universal instinct in the Russian character, an ingrained sympathy with all of humanity. The so-called "Russian idea" [*russkaia ideia*], which he shared with other thinkers but understood in a way uniquely his own, is both a ruling principle of national identity and a principle of universal, panhuman [*obshchechelovecheskaia*] unification. A form of Russian messianism further developed after Dostoevsky by the (previously mentioned) pre-revolutionary Russian philosopher Nikolai Berdiaev and the philosopher-mystic Vladimir Solovyov, the Russian idea epitomizes the social-political legacy for which the writer is known. Dostoevsky espoused it to advocate for a Russian-sourced panhuman unification: "the Russian idea will be a synthesis of all the ideas through which Europe has developed," he believed.[58] The idea maintains, in a nutshell, that the Russian people had the capacity to deliver others from evil and lead them to harmony and unity; thus it was the mission of Russia to implement the Russian idea of universal panhuman unification.[59] Ward summarizes: "In the synthesis of European and Russian cultures, in the return of the intelligentsia to its primordial traditions, in the healing of moral and social corruption, Dostoevsky saw the 'Russian solution to the problem': a new conception of existence based on the moral principles of Christian brotherhood and self-sacrifice."[60]

In *The Agony of the Russian Idea*, Tim McDaniel enumerates the complex, sometimes contradictory dimensions of the idea, specifying that its core tenet was that Russia had a superior path to modernity, "a kind of antibody to modernity, incubated in Europe but grown much more potent in its Russian environment."[61] On this basis, the idea emphasizes the "spiritual wealth of Russia" vis-à-vis materialism of the West. Furthermore, Russians have a unique capacity for redemptive suffering, a point which is particularly germane to Dostoevsky: "This theme of redemption through suffering is absolutely fundamental to Russian culture, and central to a great many views of Russian distinctiveness. For Dostoyevsky, 'the main and most fundamental spiritual quest of the Russian people is their craving for suffering.'"[62] Other aspects of the Russian idea include a view of Russia as having a higher form of community, a native-born model of egalitarianism in the peasant commune, and a paternalistic conception of government.[63]

As early as 1860 Dostoevsky's stated goal in undertaking the publication of his journal *Vremia* was to lay a path from educated society to the *narod*, and from the *narod* to the intelligentsia. "It should be an exhortation," he wrote.[64] But it was his later ideological writings in *Diary of a Writer* that would earn him the mantle of prophetic chronicler of the Russian soil. National identity and its modern crisis are major themes throughout the *Diary*. One prominent treatment of the theme comes in "One of Today's Falsehoods," Dostoevsky's last article in the 1873 edition, in which he writes about the recovery of his roots in the ethical values of the *narod* and its spirit. Beyond that, his famous speech at the unveiling of the Pushkin monument in Moscow in 1880 is his most direct formulation of the creed. In Martin Malia's summary, "Dostoevsky's power of insight into the lower depths and the higher yearnings of the human soul was peculiarly Russian, born at once of the Russian people's intimate acquaintance with suffering and of their unusual vitality of character."[65]

There are obvious problems with the Russian idea. In McDaniel's view, the idea is defined negatively—an opposition to and rejection of the West. It has been seen by others as a form of Great Russian chauvinism, imperialism, nationalist prejudice, or worse, a justification of totalitarianism. The *Diary of a Writer*, *The Idiot*, *The Devils*, and *The Brothers Karamazov* each contain passages that could be considered expressions of religious nationalism. Elder Zosima refers to the salvation of the Russian earth and its folk, the "God-bearing" people. Russians preserve the image of Christ, Orthodox Rus' will one day come to be, and God will save Russia.[66] For these and other nationalist biases, Dostoevsky has been found to be inconsistent and incoherent in his religious views. Critics have called his narrow nationalism chauvinistic. The notion of a Russian Christ and the Russian folk as "God-bearing people" has been called patently absurd, remote from Russian Orthodoxy, and heretically ethnocentric. It has even been said that his narrow nationalism "ran counter to the universalist aspiration contained in Christianity." After all, doesn't Dostoevsky's religious nationalism contradict his own ideal of universal Christian brotherhood, about which he is so emphatic in his doctrine of the Law of Love?[67]

Cassedy explains this seeming contradiction in terms of its contextual cultural bias. In the famous Pushkin speech, Dostoevsky preached the gospel of Russia as the great force of reconciliation and brotherhood. But, Cassedy argues, the speech is more about the supposed universalism of the Russian character than about the universal church.[68] Moreover, as Cassedy proves, in Dostoevsky's universe belief is contextual, belief is expressed in antinomies, and belief is ideal (the titles of three of Cassedy's chapters). Furthermore, Zosima's creed is remote from Russian Orthodoxy, representing not only a type of nature mysticism, but a heretically ethnocentric belief condemned in an Orthodox Church Council in 1872.[69]

While Dostoevsky's messianic nationalism is problematic, I am chiefly concerned here with the textual dialectic that makes up his vision of self. Is there an implicit universal principle in his writing of which Dostoevsky could have been only liminally aware? If the Russian nationalist prejudice of his vision is a cultural bias, then couldn't that be said of other contexts too, besides the soil in which the *pochvennik*'s ideas had taken root?[70]

Recall that Dostoevsky believed that Peter the Great had corrupted the Russian intelligentsia with European culture, distancing it from the *narod*. The gulf between the gentry and the Russian people had become so great and impassable that Dostoevsky referred to it as a "schism." Thus Westernism owed to Peter I its "restriction to an upper-class minority uprooted from the living Russian traditions."[71] This created the condition of *obosoblenie*: fragmentation of the human "I" and disengagement from traditional moral values held by the *narod*.[72] Russians came to sense a discrepancy between their actual and ideal selves, which they wrongly identified with European culture.[73]

In Dostoevsky's opinion, Peter's turn to the West was utilitarian, based on military and administrative expedients. Catherine's was vanity, and the Russian Enlightenment under Catherine was a façade, although it was so adroitly contrived that Europe was fooled temporarily. "Peter was anxious to learn from Europe; Catherine was more anxious that Europe should think well of Russia, and especially of her."[74]

The Decembrist generation, too, left a legacy of profound gulfs between the Westernized gentry and the people as well as between the gentry and the monarchy. Although he admired the Decembrists' selfless dedication and energy, Dostoevsky suspected that their plan to establish a liberal constitutional regime would have been a failure because they would have freed the serfs without their land, and thus would not have enlisted the support of the people.[75] Moreover, the Decembrist era was a critical juncture in the evolution of the intelligentsia and its estrangement from the people: "The attitude of the Decembrists toward the Russian people differed little from that of their fathers during the final consolidation of serfdom under Catherine.... The 'grandfathers' had been divorced from the people by social and economic circumstances; the 'fathers' were becoming divorced from the people by the *force of ideas* as well as by the force of external circumstances (and were thus becoming an 'intelligentsia')."[76]

One notes that Dostoevsky's grandfather and uncle had been Orthodox priests, and that he grew up in "a pious Russian family" and was exposed to the Gospel "almost from the cradle," as he wrote in an 1873 number of the *Diary*. One compares this upbringing, as Dostoevsky was wont to do, with that of other writers among his contemporaries, such as Herzen, Tolstoy, and Turgenev, and finds a sharp contrast, as theirs was almost entirely Western and secular. His early childhood was spent in Moscow, which he considered the spiritual centre of Russia, and he made annual trips to the Holy Trinity Monastery. In a letter of 24 March 1870 he declares, "I am an expert in this world, and I have known the Russian monastery from childhood."[77] Moreover, his friendship with Solovyov and their visit to the Optina Pustyn monastery together in June of 1878 coincides with the beginning of the writing of *The Brothers Karamazov*. There is reason to believe that Dostoevsky based Zosima on Father Ambrose, with whom he met and conversed there,[78] and some have speculated that the hero Alyosha was inspired by Solovyov.[79]

In spite of these monastic inclinations, however, Dostoevsky also had, as I discuss in earlier chapters, a secular Western education from early childhood. In youth he read Anne Radcliffe, Voltaire, Friedrich Schiller, Sir Walter Scott, Hugo, Balzac, George Sand, Homer, Shakespeare, Hoffman, Byron, Racine, and Corneille, as well as many Russian authors who could be counted among the advocates of Russian Westernism. In some cases he saw them as texts with admirable moral force. From the great novels of Scott, for example, he recalls gaining a moral bolstering of sorts: "At twelve I read right through Walter Scott during the summer holidays.... I got from it many fine and noble impressions, which gave my soul much power of resistance against others which were seductive, violent, and corrupting."[80]

Researchers including Hudspith, Carpi, Tikhomirov and Fridlender have investigated the ethical and philosophical implications of Dostoevsky's Russian idea.[81] Vassena investigates the persuasive strategies Dostoevsky used in his journals to convey the essence of his idea to readers. For example, in *The Brothers Karamazov* Liza Khokhlakova plans to compile a journal to showcase the "moral life of the people."[82] Dostoevsky was aiming not to teach the *narod*, Vassena argues, but to be in tune with it, to win the confidence of the people, and to induce them to read by giving them what they wanted. This magnetic quality is one of the structural principles of his art: to startle, to intrigue, to sensationalize (as I discuss in Chapter 2, with regard to *zanimatel'nost'*).⁸³ More than that, Dostoevsky's motives may have been coming from within his own searching art.

A witness once reported that Dostoevsky engaged in vigorous discussion with Father Ambrose at the Optina Pustyn Monastery. Rather than "obediently and with fitting humility paying attention to the edifying discourses of the elder and monk, [Dostoevsky] spoke more than [Father Ambrose] did, became excited, heatedly raised objections, developed and explained the meaning of the words pronounced by the elder..."⁸⁴ This odd behaviour, which seems disrespectful to someone of Father Ambrose's position, might be explained by the fact that Dostoevsky was planning his next novel and wanted to interrogate the discourse of the church and its traditions in preparation for the conflicts he would present in the scenes he wrote for *The Brothers Karamazov*. At any rate, Dostoevsky's skepticism and religious doubts are well documented. He seems to have made them the driving force of his art as much as they had been the source of his own apotheosis of faith. Near the end of his life, in his notebook of 1881, he would profess that his "Hosanna" had been "forged in a large furnace of doubt."⁸⁵ Ivanits finds that Dostoevsky,

> by his own admission...was tormented all his life by the question of God's existence.⁸⁶ Dostoevsky struggled to believe in Christ and in the Christian essence of the Russian people, but at times his striving and the dark face of Russian reality were uneasy bedfellows.... The Dostoevsky who steps forth as an overt champion of the people in *The Diary of a Writer* may seem quite different from the wily artist of the great novels. Imagery relating to his fictional *narod* can be double-edged and one must approach it with caution. Dostoevsky uses motifs from popular lore for characters that represent positive spiritual ideas (Sonia Marmeladova, Alesha Karamazov, and Father Zosima). But his art also abounds in travesties of the supposed holy, and some of the same patterns and images that appear in depictions of Sonia, Alesha, and Zosima accompany such counterfeit saints as Semen Yakovlevich, a fool for Christ in *The Devils*, and the monk Ferapont in *The Brothers Karamazov*.⁸⁷

Ivanits offers opportunities to tie Dostoevsky's spiritual ideas to archetype theory, although it is certain, in the first place, that Dostoevsky's aesthetics are rooted in Christian aesthetics. In Dostoevsky's understanding, as Robert Louis Jackson describes it, Ideal Beauty cannot be separated from its embodiment in Christ. Thus the word comes to life only in the artistic image. So the problem of conveying truth in art is solved only by creating a suitable artistic form.⁸⁸ Dostoevsky defines this as *khudozhestvennost'* (artistry): "the most convincing, unquestionable, and understandable means of representation by images"; and "the novelist's ability to express his thought in the heroes and the images of a novel so clearly that the reader, reading the novel, could understand the author's thought exactly as the author had conceived of it."[89]

Dostoevsky biographer Yuri Seleznev confirms this reading: "Dostoevsky saw in literature not just a means for the implementation of certain ideas—no, he believed in the artistic word as an independent force, spiritually transforming human nature, and creating an ideal of beauty in the minds of the people." Moreover, that ideal needed no inventing. In Dostoevsky's own words, "If in the *narod* there is a preserved ideal of beauty and there is a need for it, that means there is also a need for health and norms, and consequently, in that same [ideal] is guaranteed the highest development of the people."[90] Therefore, he argues, one needs to struggle not for art to present certain ideas, but for art to be real, original. The ideal exists in nature, and the artist need only reveal it in its development. Moreover, on the question of artistry, in the 1861 article "Book-learning and Literacy," Dostoevsky writes, "The author of the book, if he is a clever person, will have to take into account both logic and all these practical and psychological considerations. But they must be hidden as far as possible. It would be even better if these principles were hidden also from the author himself and operated inside him naively and even unconsciously."[91]

In "The Golden Age in [Your] Pocket," the diarist declares that the power is in each one of us to be his or her honest and sincere self, with a perfection and beauty not to be outshone by the greatest expressions of beauty and perfection in Homer, Dante, Shakespeare, or Schiller, not to mention wiser than Voltaire and more feeling than Rousseau. But it is hidden so long that it is no longer believed.[92] By contrast, in part 3 of the January 1876 entry, "Something about Devils," he writes a hypothesis predicting what would happen if the discoveries of science were to be revealed by devils all at once like Promethean fire from heaven. Would a life satisfied by material well-being and the elimination of environmental hazards make man a perfect species without vice or moral imperfection? On the contrary, he reasons, people would find that they have no freedom of spirit, will, or personality [*net svobody dukha, net voli i lichnosti*], that the very face of their humanity would have disappeared [*ischez chelovecheskii lik*], that they had becomes slaves or cattle. They would see that their lives had been traded for stones turned to bread (anticipating the Legend of the Grand Inquisitor), see that there is no joy in inactivity, no love without sacrificing oneself for another, and that happiness is not in happiness, but in the act of achieving it.[93]

In a later piece from February of that year, "About the Fact That We Are All Good People," the topic changes to the innate goodness in the Russian character, a willingness to make peace even with one's faults and vices, a desire for good that precedes egoism [*prezhde vsiakogo egoisma*], and above all, a belief in living by an idea, an ideal, while personal, earthly blessings come after. High society and the folk share the same ideals, valuing their faith above everything that is of the world and fleeting. Even if there is an element of depravity in the people, even a scoundrel knows he is a scoundrel, and knows that there is a higher ideal that he shares with his countrymen. The contemporary youth who love their paradoxes mistake them for truth, and they who are willing to sacrifice their lives and destiny for them will find that those paradoxes will vanish, but their purity of heart will not.[94]

In "On Love for the Russian People," Dostoevsky muses that if the Russian people have wallowed in depravity for most of their history, they have still preserved their human image and its great beauty. The author begs: "Judge the Russian people not by the abominations they frequently commit, but by the great and blessed things which they, in their very abominations, continuously exclaim."[95] A Russian who loves the Russian *narod* and a true friend of humanity cannot help but forgive them their filth and wantonness, and can find within them the diamond in the rough. As an illustration he offers the story "The Peasant Marei," prefaced with the terrible brutality among inmates he had witnessed in prison. This he interpolates within the story, culled from a wonderful recollection from childhood about the spontaneous, kind, and selfless humanity of a Russian peasant who had comforted him as a boy when he was frightened by a sound he imagined to be the cry of a wolf.

The artistic force of the *Diary of a Writer* ultimately makes for a powerful exegesis of the Russian nation's collective history of coming into its own, a discovery of its inherent character and national identity, the "Russian idea" that the Russian intelligentsia had been in search of since the days of the Decembrists, Chaadaev, Belinsky, and Herzen. Yet Russian intellectuals love the Russian people only as they want them to be, Dostoevsky writes in the conclusion to "The Peasant Marei." That is, the intelligentsia's grasp of the *narod* depends on their theories. That society considers itself an ideal for the *narod* is a false aim. Are not the people an ideal for us, he pleads, and we merely prodigal children who must return to bow before them and discover everything, the perennial thought and image, *from them*?[96]

On the other hand, Dostoevsky's ersatz faith in the goodness of the Russian people here and expressed throughout the *Diary* is unsatisfying. Dostoevsky was never one to settle for tidy solutions or monologic truth. Reading his novels, one knows there has to be more to the story.

CHAPTER FIVE

Myths of Transformation

Like happy families, the myths and the worlds redeemed are all alike.
— Joseph Campbell, *The Hero with a Thousand Faces*

No one who has undergone the process of assimilating the unconscious will deny that it gripped his very vitals and changed him.
— C.G. Jung, *Two Essays on Analytical Psychology*

I argue in the previous chapter that the Karamazov brothers and a number of other characters exemplify Dostoevsky's use of the shadow archetype to dramatize change and integration of the whole self. This particular dynamic becomes important as Dostoevsky sets the shadow against the distinctly other, higher, transcendent self, which I have been calling the *authentic self*. That confrontation is the catalyst for a transformational process that gives the authentic self the chance to embody and incorporate the archetypal patterns. In the present chapter I bring to bear the insight afforded by certain Russian and cross-cultural cycles of myth, such as the Russian folk tale, classical myths of death and renewal, and the universal myth of the hero's journey. I show that patterns that recur in tales and myth such as these underlie prominent stories and motifs in Dostoevsky, demanding comparison with them. The keys that might unlock the "mystery of man," which the young Dostoevsky had vowed to discover, became, for the mature writer, doors to a transformative vision.

In spite of the predominance of polyphony and the many forms of duality to be found in Dostoevsky's works, which I describe throughout this volume, I aim to show now that the Dostoevskian universe pivots on the immanence of unity. Normally, his characters' existential dilemmas are rooted in the reality they experience, which might be seen in the writing as fractured segments of self. Several of the heroes I describe resemble ideological patterns that are scattered among multiple personas. However, the merger of faith and reason in a higher fusion is also a productive formula, often in the same works. As I discuss below, Dostoevsky treats the self as an inalienable entity that escapes the duality that permeates the structure of modern Western humanism, moving closer to a perennialist view of immanent unity with the transcendent Godhead or ground of being. But first I pause to survey more of the traditions that give rise to the expression of duality and unity in archetypal forms, particularly in folktales and mythology. In the next several sections I discuss some of the crossovers between them and examine their implications for Dostoevsky's fiction.

Russian Folktales and the Question of Genre
Russian folk tales have been examined from a number of scholarly angles, following structural, psychological, feminist, sociological, and political approaches. An authority on the structural approach, Vladimir Propp, published *Morphology of the Folktale* in 1928. In a later book, *Historical Roots of the Wonder Tale* (1946, based on Propp's 1939 doctoral dissertation), he argued that the structure of the wonder tale reflects its origins in initiation and funeral rites. His last work, based on a series of lectures he gave in the 1960s at Leningrad State University, was published posthumously as *The Russian Folktale*. In all his work, Propp uses a historical-anthropological framework. His structuralist–morphological approach to folk tales is interdisciplinary and international. Interested in the rise and evolutionary process of folklore and folklore studies, Propp provides a detailed history of folklore studies in Russia as well as Western Europe, covering scholars studying, in particular, English, French, and German folk tales.[1] He bases his study of Russian folk tales in particular on the large collection of tales edited and published in eight volumes by Aleksandr Afanasyev, which was reprinted several times in the nineteenth century (first between 1855 and 1864)—a collection Propp calls both "purely scholarly" in its goals, far surpassing the Grimm Brothers in that respect, and "one of the best loved and most popular books for Russian readers."[2]

While studying Russian folk narratives, Propp emphasizes his own comparative, interdisciplinary method, noting that peoples across the world have their own folk tales, but that plots that are common internationally offer evidence that they are interconnected. The folk tale's ubiquity "is just as striking as its immortality." He does not try to explain it, instead suggesting that the main justification for this conclusion is that, unlike other forms of literature, everyone understands folk tales. They contain eternal, unfading values. "The folktale symbolizes the unity of peoples, who understand one another in their tales." Nevertheless, Propp also says Russians should first and foremost study Russian folk tales—it is their duty, for each group of people has its own national plots and distinctive features.[3]

In his research, Propp recognized repetitive patterns and functions in large bodies of folk tales, which he preferred to call *wonder tales*. In *Morphology of the Folktale* he established thirty-one functions of the wonder tale. Later, in *Historical Roots of the Wonder Tale*, he traces the origins of the functions and genre of the wonder tale to rituals, customs, and myths of primitive peoples. He compares Russian tales to classical myths and tales from other traditions. However, he does not idealize the people, as Zipes writes in the preface to the 2012 translation of *The Russian Folktale*, but is "interested in belief systems and initiation rites that contributed to the formation of narrative structures, and he tried to trace these through history."[4]

When it comes to myth, however, Propp discusses how the folk tale's relationship to myth is problematic. He does not unreservedly accept the thesis of the mythological school of folklore studies, which asserts the invariable descent of the folk tale from myth. Although they exhibit resemblances in their compositional schemes, myths and folktales are not of the same order. Although myths are not always presented as reality, they are acknowledged as descriptions of a higher-order reality. They are usually connected with cults. "When the gods appear in human consciousness and human culture, myth becomes a story about deities or semideities":[5]

> Cults were intended to act upon deities so they would help people. The difference between myths and folktales is thus a difference of social function. "The myth, having lost its social significance, becomes a folktale." Myth is a story of religious order; the folktale is aesthetic. Myth is an earlier formation; the folktale is a later one. In this way, myth and folktale are distinguished not so much in themselves but in how people approach them. This means that folkloristics is a science not just of plots, texts, but also of the role of plots in the social lives of peoples.[6]

Propp was careful to distinguish between folk tales and myth, and insisted that they not be considered the same genre. Myths and folk tales may coincide in their plots, composition, and fundamental motifs, but here is their essential difference: a myth is a sacred story that people believe to be true, whereas a folktale is a tale that is *not* presented as reality.[7] Propp provides the example of the myth of Orpheus: "The Greeks believed in the existence of the underworld, believed in the god Hades and the goddess Persephone.... The myth of Orpheus and Eurydice was sacred truth for them."[8]

Propp contends that even by his own time, however, classical mythology was little known to Russia.[9] Nevertheless his earlier book, *Historical Roots of the Wonder Tale*, is devoted to the question of the genre's ancient origin. Propp ties the wonder tale's *master narrative* not to classical mythology but to its origins in rituals of initiation or death in the primitive religion and material culture of the deep East Slavic past.[10] The plot, he says, may be older than the genre and may have *roots* in myths of the past. "Primitive people did not have fairytales. They had only myths. Individual motifs, episodes, or events may reflect ancient concepts that existed before the creation of the folktale. The folktale did not yet exist, but those concepts, those images, those fantastic or real events that it tells about, could have had a place in formations that preceded the folktale or even in reality."[11]

In fact, as Forrester tells us in her introduction, "Propp assumes that there used to be a single underlying narrative of initiation, based in the life of a forest culture at the stage of hunting and gathering and early (garden) agriculture, and that the outlines of the initiation ritual had blurred in the wonder tales that evolved from primitive myths."[12] Forrester concedes that these theoretical assumptions may appear to be antiquated nineteenth-century scholarship, not to mention disappointingly Eurocentric. They are also evidence of a Marxist vision of societal development via historical materialism.[13] While there is undoubtedly an overtone of Marxism—required of someone publishing in the Soviet Union at Propp's time—Propp's research, in fact, has something in common with Jung's in that it is both nationalist and comparative. Forrester rightly calls Propp's reconstructive impulse a response to the loss of Russian traditional culture and the destruction of peasant life during the Soviet period. It balances the idea that the past can be reconstructed as an idea or ideal against the danger that oral tales and rural culture will pass away in the face of modernization.[14]

Here I must reiterate that Dostoevsky was also responding to modernization and the advent of socialism in Russia. His brand of Russian nationalism involved a reconstruction of an *idea* of the past, of ideals of Russian folk culture, in its moral character and traditions. Further to my discussion of the Russian idea above, Dostoevsky's mission is not so much to revive the oral tales and rural culture as to invoke the *idea* of the Russian people, their faith, and their archetypal complexity of character.

Propp studied German mythology and its incorporation by the Brothers Grimm, but he criticizes the religious bias in the studies made by the Grimm brothers. It was to re-establish and promote Old German pagan religion, Propp says, that Jacob Grimm published his data related to the pagan cults of the ancient Germans in *German Mythology*. "His fundamental source was the relics of those cults, and the folktale occupied an important place among them. Individual chapters speak of various aspects of the cult. Thus there are chapters devoted to the gods (Wotan, Donner), giants, trees, animals, the sky, the stars, day and night, and so on. The folktale's penetration by various elements of the original faith becomes apparent, although the study as a whole was not undertaken on behalf of the folktale."[15]

The Russian folklorist Fedor Buslaev, in Propp's opinion, outshone the Grimms. Proceeding from their methods and assumptions, his work is superior because "Buslaev understands the properly folkloric character of folk creativity. The folk, for him, is not only an idea; it is a concrete historical given. In this regard Buslaev far surpasses the Grimms. He treasures folk creativity not because it reflects moral ideas in allegorical or symbolic form but because he sees in it 'the foundation of the moral physiognomy' of the people." The past interested Buslaev because "it is precisely in the deep past that the people's moral face took shape. Anyone who wants to understand his own people must understand that people's past."[16]

Dostoevsky's view was similar. But Buslaev believed that the moral face of the people must be studied as "dispassionately" as possible, to examine "everything Russian life has elaborated over the centuries and has taken organically for itself from what was imported from outside."[17] Dostoevsky, as we know, was more apt to dramatize the elements that make up the organic roots of the Russian nation and delve into the moral complexities of the *narod* with passionate engagement.

Ivanits studied Dostoevsky's use of folk sources and found his method eclectic: "Dostoevsky tends not to distinguish between Old Russian literature (especially apocrypha and saints' lives) and oral legends and songs as narratives that reflect the moral values of the people. On occasion he mingles folklore with biblical or hagiographic imagery in such a way as to create tension between their respective associations." An example is water used as a symbol in *Crime and Punishment*: "Biblical overtones connect it to 'living waters' of rebirth; but in popular notions water is the place where devils dwell, and from this perspective it is associated with suicide and darkness.... It is not possible to know what a reference or motif means [in Dostoevsky's work] until its function within its own text is assessed."[18]

When it comes to genre and classifications of the folk tales established by Afanasyev and adhered to more or less by Propp, the main focus of my concern, because of how it relates to structural motifs in Dostoevsky, is the wonder tale. It is the most "mythological" and fantastical of the folk tales—what Propp called "probably the most splendid variety of artistic folk prose."[19]

Propp enumerates and analyzes the formulaic structure of wonder tales, defined by their characteristic and generic traits. He finds a unity of composition in their structure among a variety of plots. Specifically, the typical elements of the wonder tale are: The Opening; Lack; the Hero (often either a seeker or a hero-victim); Gift Givers; Magical Helpers and Magical Objects; the Outcome; Complications, the Difficult Task; and Marriage and Crowning of the Hero.[20] Several of these elements play similar roles in Joseph Campbell's monomyth of the hero journey, which I examine below. Even though Propp distinguishes folk tales from myth, as I've described, he noted the likelihood of their common origin.

Furthermore, an adjacent genre of folk oral prose, distinct from folk tales, is the *legenda* (legend). It was used as a source by Dostoevsky, Gogol, Tolstoy, and other Russian writers. Unlike many folk tales of pre-Christian origin, this type of folk legend came from Byzantium, the fountainhead of Russian Orthodoxy. Its goal is not entertainment, but moralizing. An example of the *legenda* is the tale of two sinners. It features figures from the Old and New Testaments plus the addition of a grievous sinner whose exaggerated transgressions and punishment in the form of penance presented in symbolic forms of death and resurrection (such as having to water a burnt log until it sprouts and grows) are followed by moral salvation and cleansing. Also in this genre, people are sometimes taken alive to Hell or Heaven. Typically, the sinner is saved because he kills another even greater sinner, such as a serf who slays a cruel, merciless lord. The original sinner's sins, no matter how grievous, are forgotten; his penance is complete, the tree finally blossoms, and his soul is saved. Although this plot contradicts Christian ethics, it is born of the experience of the Russian folk, often victims of exploitation at the hands of cruel landowners.[21]

The folk tale's influence on the process of literary development is undisputed, but its influence is limited to certain periods of this growth. Propp has little to say about folk tales in the medieval period, when, he says, culture in both Russia and the West bore a clerical character. He passes over the chivalric literature of the medieval period, which took the place of folklore in the Middle Ages, but refers to Western Europe when a new art comes to be based on the pagan art of antiquity, along with the advent of a new secular literature in the epoch of humanism (roughly the fourteenth century through the Renaissance). Rather than the Christian medieval tradition, a new, secular narrative literature of realistic character grows up from the soil of national folklore. But, as Propp cautions, there are deep and principled differences between the poetics and aesthetics of folklore and literature.[22]

In Russia, secular literature develops later, in the seventeenth and eighteenth centuries, but the process is essentially the same. The word *skazka* (folk tale) dates from that time as well.[23] Adjacent to the folk tale are later "novelistic" or realistic everyday tales, with common plot types, and other related genres, such as seventeenth-century urban tales and moralistic tales. Furthermore, for the urban working class, the peasant *bylina* (epic song) complements the stories and subjects of secular literature for entertainment. However, the separate *bylina* genre shares less in plot with its traditional precursors than realistic narrative style does. Overall, the images and motifs as well as the style of early, anonymous Russian secular tales come from folk tales.

As noted above, Dostoevsky did not often borrow directly from folklore, and when he did his appropriation of folk motifs was eclectic. However, I argue that when he did we see a strong undercurrent of mythological prose, especially in Dostoevsky's later novels. I look now at the particular myths that he exploited to the fullest.

Myths of Death and Renewal

The folk occult had always been a part of Russian folk traditions. Ancient folk apprehensions saw the universe as alive and seething with a multitude of harmful powers [*nechistye sily*]. Folk religion is known for *dvoeverie*, its dual belief, melding Christianity with pagan beliefs and practices. In the latter part of the nineteenth century, occultism began to permeate upper- and middle-class Russian society, a manifestation of the spiritual hunger that generated the Russian religious renaissance. It evinced a response to the larger crisis of culture and consciousness as Europe tired of scientific empiricism and positivism.[24] In the introduction I discuss Dostoevsky and his works vis-à-vis mysticism and spiritualism. I have referred to some of the narratives and symbols of death and resurrection that match the archetypal patternings of Western esotericism. One such narrative that serves as an introduction to other forms of myth used by Dostoevsky that I examine in this chapter is Dmitri's reference to finding God underground, which we encounter in Book XI, Chapter 4, of *The Brothers Karamazov*.

Anticipating the years of penal servitude to which he will be sentenced for a murder he didn't commit, Dmitri speaks these cryptic lines to his brother Alyosha: "If they drive God from the earth, we'll meet Him underground! It is impossible for a convict to be without God—even more impossible than for a non-convict. And then we underground men will start singing, from the bowels of the earth, a tragic hymn to God, in whom there is joy! Hail to God and His joy! I love Him!"²⁵

In his curious avowal "If they drive God from the earth, we'll meet him underground!" Dmitri paraphrases (or misquotes?) a passage from Virgil (*The Aeneid* VII, 312): "Flectere si nequeo Sueros. Acheronta movebo" (If I cannot bend the gods above, then I will move the infernal regions).²⁶ In Ksana Blank's analysis, the Old Church Slavonic term *sretim* that Dmitri uses (translated simply as "we'll meet") gives the remark a distinctive biblical connotation; thus, his statement "if God is driven from the earth, we'll meet him underground" echoes the epigraph to *The Brothers Karamazov* about the grain of wheat that dies in order to be reborn.²⁷ Blank goes on to discuss Dmitri's allegorical descent to the underworld, with parallels to the Eleusinian Mysteries and the myth of Demeter. In so doing, "He shares with Alyosha his new conviction that an encounter with God is possible not only within 'higher spheres' but also in the 'lower depths.'"²⁸

The images and figures that arise from the unconscious—which, as I've argued, we can read in Dostoevsky's works as forces that catalyze change—are, in Jung's research, related to the mythical. Jung distinguishes two main groups of experience: that of the *transcendence* of life, and that of one's own *transformation*. In examples below, I aim to illustrate that the act of transformation of the *apparent self* and the inner awakening to the *authentic self*—a cycle repeated in world myths of death and rebirth (or resurrection)—is a foundational principle also of Dostoevsky's writing. The myth of death and renewal in Dostoevsky's works generally speaking is a narrative of transfiguration, which gives force to the moral and aesthetic ideal that necessitates and guides personal transformation. By examining the function of this particular myth in Dostoevsky we can view a dramatization of the archetypal process at work in his major fiction.

As we know, Dostoevsky's life experience brought him on more than one occasion to live through and metaphorically embody the transformative death-and-resurrection cycle. His own virtual death upon facing a firing squad on 22 December 1849 in Saint Petersburg, followed by his "resurrection" upon the sudden and unexpected reprieve from the tsar, prompted him to write to his brother, "Now, with this change in my life, I am being born again in a new form.... I shall be reborn in a better form."²⁹ He also saw his years in penal servitude and exile in Siberia as a gradual rebirth, and his release from prison was like "a second resurrection from the dead."³⁰ It is interesting that Dostoevsky had in his pre-exile fiction already rehearsed the sense of gratitude for life as a feeling of resurrection; Ordynov, protagonist of "The Landlady" (1847), for example, refers to such an emotion: "When you feel that the flesh is weak before such oppressive experiences that break all the threads of life, while at the same time you congratulate your whole life with resurrection and renewal."[31] However, notwithstanding this and a few other rare instances, such as the Vision on the Neva episode referred to in Chapter 2 in this volume, there are far more examples of the transformation or rebirth narrative found in Dostoevsky's post-exile works, especially the later ones.

Raskolnikov's change of heart and the beginning of his transformation in the epilogue of *Crime and Punishment*, in which the story of the raising of Lazarus plays a role, is Dostoevsky's first mature development of the narrative of death and resurrection. Later works take the narrative down several other streams. In Dostoevsky's notebooks for *The Idiot* we see his plan for Prince Myshkin to rehabilitate Nastasia Filippovna,[32] whose name, in its Greek origin, means "resurrection."[33] Narratives of the onset of transformative vision followed by resurrection and rebirth are prominent themes in *The Brothers Karamazov* and "The Dream of the Ridiculous Man," which I examine below. The transformative process indicated in each of these examples involves the death of the apparent self, with its temporal and culturally conditioned makeup, to allow for the emergence of the higher, authentic self, which becomes aware of being in unity with some form of eternal, divine essence. To some degree this pattern accords with the Orthodox tradition: the themes of spiritual awakening, moral rebirth, resurrection, and particularly the Easter myth of death and renewal assume particular prominence in Orthodoxy. The spiritual epiphanies of Myshkin, Makar Dolgoruky, Zosima's brother Markel, and Alyosha Karamazov also reflect the Orthodox emphasis on transfiguration.[34] Yet, as Jones argues, while they adhere to the Orthodox heritage, these themes in Dostoevsky are nourished more deeply by personal religious experiences than by doctrinal bases or sacramental rites.[35] Although Easter motifs in particular undergird the narrative and thematic structures of Dostoevsky's works, they are for the most part non-institutional. Jones adds that "resurrection" is a metaphor for spiritual rebirth in Dostoevsky, and that the death of Orthodoxy is itself a metaphor in Dostoevsky's works, meaning that its tradition as authoritative discourse had lost its force. Conflict between belief and unbelief in the modern age required that Orthodox tradition be set aside so that personal faith could blossom again, nourishing the shoots of a new faith. Religious experience as inwardly persuasive discourse takes its place.[36]

Freed of its Orthodox trappings, the myth of death and resurrection opens Dostoevsky's works to the narrative of personal transformation, giving them a consistency of meaning and purpose that is independent of doctrinal or institutional authority. I turn now to another type of myth, one analyzed at length by Joseph Campbell and that sheds light on the journeys of personal transformation experienced by several of Dostoevsky's most memorable characters. The *hero myth*, with its ancient origins, connects Dostoevsky's characterizations to a range of archetypal forms that help us to understand his characters' struggles to reconcile their aspirations with the often harsh realities of their lives and relationships.

The Hero Myth
The underground is a literary topos along the mythic journey of the hero that is common to creation myths, ancient epics, and some folk tales: the hero passes through the underground, or Hades (Hell), before undergoing initiation and a series of trials, accomplishing his purpose, reaping a reward, and reaching some form of higher unity. Combined with other stages of the hero's adventure, these compositional functions form a ubiquitous cycle of myths that Joseph Campbell called the *Monomyth*. Campbell studied the Monomyth across diverse cultures and civilizations, and found this pattern of archetypal myth to be indigenous to every cultural tradition he studied. The stages of the Monomyth include a summons or call to adventure, a crossing of the threshold, a descent to the underworld, the achievement of a boon or prize, and sometimes a form of knowledge, rebirth, resurrection, or ascent to heaven. The rebirth, and the cyclical repetition of the entire myth, expresses the achievement of unity or wholeness through transformation of the psyche. This transformation typically involves a unification or reconciliation of opposites, and achievement of the higher self.

Dostoevsky's characters model various phases of the process of the awakening of self-awareness, or the unity of conscious and unconscious minds that is found in the successive stages of the hero myth. As noted above, Dostoevsky often attributes religious experience not to *faith* but to a rationally defensible form of *direct experience*.[37] More than mysticism, it is a *participation mystique* that is frequently encountered in Dostoevsky's writing in terms discussed earlier, such as "living life" [*zhivaia zhizn'*][38] and "spontaneity" [*neposredstvennost'*].[39]

The Call
The first phase of the hero myth is the "call to adventure." Writes Campbell, "The call rings up the curtain, always, on a mystery of transfiguration—a rite, or moment, or spiritual passage, which, when complete, amounts to dying and a birth."[40] The call to adventure is announced by the Herald, a figure who appears suddenly as a guide, marking a new adventure. The hero is overcome with fascination with that figure. "Whether dream or myth, in these adventures there is an atmosphere of irresistible fascination about

the figure that appears suddenly as a guide, marking a new period, a new stage, in the biography."[41]

The Herald's summons may be to live or die, or it may be a call to illumination or the awakening of the higher self. It can be perceived as disgusting or be rejected, representing the unconscious deep. "That which has to be faced, and is somehow profoundly familiar to the unconscious—though unknown, surprising, and even frightening to the conscious personality—makes itself known; and what formerly was meaningful may become strangely emptied of value."[42] Examples of the Herald in Dostoevsky would include Golyadkin Junior in *The Double*, the pawnbroker Alyona Ivanovna in *Crime and Punishment*, and the little girl on the street in "The Dream of a Ridiculous Man."

There are consequences for the hero who refuses the call. Golyadkin and the Underground Man are examples of this type of hero. Refusal of the call, says Campbell, is regarded not in terms of an unremitting series of deaths and births but in terms of a refusal to give up what one sees as one's immutable personal interests. "[It is] as though a once present system of ideals, virtues, goals and advantages were to be fixed and made secure." Campbell describes how, in the myth, it is possible for the divinity itself to become the hero's terror: "If one is oneself one's God, then God himself, the will of God, the power that would destroy one's egocentric system, becomes a monster." In other words, "one is harassed, both day and night, by the divine being that is the image of the living self within the locked labyrinth of one's own disoriented psyche." An example of such a monster is the minotaur of King Minos of Crete: "King Minos retained the divine bull, when the sacrifice would have signified submission to the will of the god of his society; for he preferred what he conceived to be his economic advantage. Thus he failed to advance into the life-role that he had assumed—and we have seen with what calamitous effect."[43] This may be the situation of characters in Dostoevsky's later fiction such as Raskolnikov, Kirillov, and Stavrogin. Each exemplifies the ego that has become a god unto itself; hence the power of the egocentric system becomes a monster.

The minotaur is finally slain in the Athenian myth by the hero Theseus. Typically, the challenge is put to the hero who has not refused the call and is often given, at this point, unexpected assistance from a supernatural source. He then progresses to the stages of crossing the threshold, descending into the underworld, and receiving the reward or treasure. Like the archetypal imagery of the underground discussed in previous chapters, descent to the underground as part of the hero's journey is symbolic of discovery of the energy of the unconscious psyche and the process of bringing it to conscious light. There is some crossover in Raskolnikov, who, although consumed by the monster of his self-serving crimes, begins to experience the awakening, which comes about in further stages of the myth, albeit only tentatively, in the epilogue to the novel. Some later heroes, such as Prince Myshkin, the Ridiculous Man, and Alyosha Karamazov respond to the call and move on to subsequent phases of the myth.

Supernatural Aid

The hero is often aided by a benign power at this stage, in a supernatural form that sometimes guides and transports him. The Ridiculous Man is met in his dream by a spirit who transports him through time and space. Another benign supernatural power is represented by the people on the utopian planet to which he is brought, who aid him in grasping the fundamental truth, which he later brings to waking consciousness. Raskolnikov's guide and supernatural aid is Sonia Marmeladova. In this case, the story follows the myth of the hero who comes under the protection of the cosmic mother. Under her protection, the hero cannot be harmed; he is led, Campbell writes, as Theseus is led by the thread of Ariadne. She guides the hero safely through the adventure of the labyrinth. This is the same guiding power that runs through the work of Dante in the female figures of Beatrice and the Virgin. It also appears in Goethe's *Faust* successively as Gretchen, Helen of Troy, and the Virgin.[44]

Sonia brings Raskolnikov supernatural aid in the form of a Bible she reads with him and a copy of the Evangels, which she brings to him in prison. He had asked her for it, but: "He hadn't opened it yet, but one thought flashed inside him: 'Could it really be that her convictions are now my convictions? Her feelings and strivings at least...'" Thus begins his transition to another world.[45] In *Crime and Punishment*, as noted above, the rebirth comes late in the novel; a new life begins for Raskolnikov only in the Epilogue, when he is in prison camp, but it needs to be dearly earned with expiation and suffering ("ее надо дорого купить, заплатить за нее великим, будущим подвигом..."). "But here begins a new story," the narrator says, "a story of gradual renewal of a man, a story of his gradual rebirth, his gradual crossing-over from one world to another, acquaintance with a new, hitherto completely unknown reality. This could be the subject of a new tale—but the present one is finished."[46] Here I need to emphasize that the adjective *postepennoe* (gradual) is repeated three times. It is used in reference to a transition from one world to another, to a hitherto *unknown reality*.

Campbell cites examples of the supernatural helper and the characteristics it takes on when it appears in masculine form:

In fairy lore it may be some little fellow of the wood, some wizard, hermit, shepherd, or smith, who appears, to supply the amulet and advice that the hero will require. The higher mythologies develop the role in the great figure of the guide, the teacher, the ferryman, the conductor of souls to the afterworld. In classical myth this is Hermes–Mercury; in Egyptian, usually Thoth (the ibis god, the baboon god); in Christian, the Holy Ghost. Goethe presents the masculine guide in *Faust* as Mephistopheles—and not infrequently the dangerous aspect of the "mercurial" figure is stressed; for he is the lurer of the innocent soul into realms of trial. In Dante's vision the part is played by Virgil, who yields to Beatrice at the threshold of Paradise. Protective and dangerous, motherly and fatherly at the same time, the supernatural principle of guardianship and direction unites in itself all the ambiguities of the unconscious—thus signifying the support of our conscious personality by that other, larger system, but also the inscrutability of the guide that we are following, to the peril of all our rational ends. The hero to whom such a helper appears is typically one who has responded to the call.[47]

This is the situation, for instance, in which we find Alyosha Karamazov. The helper, in this case, is Elder Zosima, an initiatory priest of sorts, if we are going to compare him to Campbell's model, for "the call, in fact, was the first announcement of the approach of this initiatory priest."[48]

Crossing the Threshold
Central to the hero myth is the idea of the passage of the magical threshold—a transit into a sphere of rebirth. Campbell writes, "The familiar life horizon has been outgrown; the old concepts, ideals, and emotional patterns no longer fit; the time for the passing of a threshold is at hand."[49] The passage is often symbolized by the universal womb image of the belly of the whale: "The hero, instead of conquering or conciliating the power of the threshold, is swallowed into the unknown, and would appear to have died."[50] Thus, passage over the threshold is a form of self-annihilation. Instead of passing outward, beyond the confines of the visible world, the hero goes inward, to be born again.[51]

We can see the passage over the threshold in the moments that occur just before pivotal events in some of Dostoevsky's works. In *Crime and Punishment* there is a series of threshold guardians for Raskolnikov. When Raskolnikov takes the decision to act upon his theory and prepares to murder the pawnbroker, for example, his landlady is the first guardian, then the pawnbroker herself, as well as her younger sister Lizaveta, whom

Raskolnikov also murders. "The adventure is always and everywhere a passage beyond the veil of the known into the unknown; the powers that watch at the boundary are dangerous; to deal with them is risky; yet for anyone with competence and courage the danger fades."[52]

Kirillov, in *The Devils*, decides to act on his own theory to commit suicide and thereby become like God; the Ridiculous Man falls asleep and dreams that he pulls the trigger of the gun pointed at his own head. These and other instances of "crossing the line" in the experience of Dostoevsky's characters signal the point of departure, as the hero transitions from ordinary life to the realm of archetypal initiation.

Initiation
Having traversed the threshold, the hero moves over a dream landscape of curiously fluid, ambiguous forms, which concludes the separation or departure stage of the hero myth. This is the "belly of the whale" or "passage into the realm of night." It may be that the hero here discovers for the first time that there is a benign power everywhere supporting him in his superhuman passage.[53] Further stages hold the trials and victories of initiation, which include encounters and clashes with gods and goddesses. Here, Campbell refers to the Siberian Shamanic tradition: "And so it happens that if anyone—in whatever society—undertakes for himself the perilous journey into the darkness by descending, either intentionally or unintentionally, into the crooked lanes of his own spiritual labyrinth, he soon finds himself in a landscape of symbolic figures (any of which may swallow him) which is no less marvelous than the wild Siberian world of the *pudak* [obstacles encountered by the Shaman in his trance] and sacred mountains."[54]

Initiatory experience is a critical theme in Dostoevsky, and it links his view of the self to the pre-modern idea of ego transcendence. I have described how the dramatic force of Dostoevsky's writing plays out in a world where the underground is dominant. With the underground as a ruling idea and a governing narrative principle, Dostoevsky models archetypal patterning and meaning within the hero myth structure, as we witness the hero enduring the trials that contribute to his initiation and some form of rebirth.

Myths of initiation always refer to the rediscovery of the authentic self and its deeper purposes in some form or other. This is the "Great Work" (Ars Magna) of the Gnostic tradition, in which initiates unite in consciousness with God, to awaken, as Stephan Hoeller puts it, from "slumber in their material prison, their self-awareness stupefied by forces of materiality and mind."[55] There are many individuals among Dostoevsky's characters who "slumber in their material prisons": Gospodin Prokharchin, Svidrigailov, Luzhin, and Stavrogin, to name a few. Others who respond to the call, receive supernatural aid, undergo rebirth or resurrection, and connect to the sacred include the holy fool Prince Myshkin, the transformed dreamer the Ridiculous Man, the Orthodox elder Zosima and his brother Markel, and the novice Alyosha Karamazov.

Initiatory experience is the process through which the unconscious becomes conscious, usually sparked by a sudden illumination or insight, and often accompanied by symbolic or archetypal forms that guide the initiate. Transmutation (in alchemy, the philosopher's stone) represents self-awareness, inward awakening, spiritual rebirth, or visionary knowledge gained through initiatory experience. It is the healing and empowering connection to the sacred Divine Reality. Progressive awakenings contribute to the revelation that the perceived world of the apparent self is impermanent, and one sees through the illusion of physical, emotional, and mental bodies. Essence or true self is found "beyond *maya*."

It bears repeating that duality—and overcoming duality through the marriage of opposites—is a vital component of the ancient hero myth. According to Campbell, "The hero, whether god or goddess, man or woman, the figure in a myth or the dreamer of a dream, discovers and assimilates his opposite (his own unsuspected self) either by swallowing it or by being swallowed. One by one the resistances are broken. He must put aside his pride, his virtue, beauty, and life, and bow or submit to the absolutely intolerable. Then he finds that he and his opposite are not of differing species, but one flesh."[56] The accomplishment of this cycle and its apotheosis in the rebirth or awakening of the higher, or authentic self, is the final stage of the myth. I compare it here to several more examples from Dostoevsky.

Rebirth

In the hero myth, the rebirth unites the hero with his God, a process that involves moving beyond opposites. Campbell writes, "Mythology does not hold as its greatest hero the merely virtuous man. Virtue is but the pedagogical prelude to the culminating insight, which goes beyond all pairs of opposites. Virtue quells the self-centered ego and makes the transpersonal centeredness possible; but when that has been achieved, what then of the pain or pleasure, vice or virtue, either of our own ego or of any other?"[57]

Elder Zosima's spiritual life is the result of an inner awakening not unlike the culminating insight of the mythological hero. His "awakening" to the hidden reality is expressed through his perennialist-type "nature mysticism." A passionate youth who became entangled in a duel, Zosima himself had had a conversion experience and exhorted his companions:

"Nature is beautiful and sinless, and we, only we are godless and foolish, and we don't understand that life is paradise, for all it takes is our wanting to understand, and it will come at once in all its beauty, and we will embrace each other and weep.'"[58]

The life and teachings of Father Zosima as recounted in Alyosha Karamazov's "Biographical Notes" concerning his mentor provide the most detailed illustration among all of Dostoevsky's works of the authentic self lived in the present life to the full extent that is achievable, even if the non-dual realization of the ideal is reserved for the world beyond. Many of Zosima's teachings were inspired by his brother Markel, who, on his deathbed at age seventeen, remarked, "'Life is paradise, and we're all in paradise, but we refuse to see it. If we only wanted it, there would be paradise tomorrow on all the earth.'"[59] This idea is also expressed in Zosima's narrative of the Mysterious Visitor who confesses murder to him and informs him that he had intended to murder Zosima but for his epiphany that saved them both (Book VI, Chapter 2). The Visitor speaks a version of the underground narrative, of how individuals are isolated, how "all have separated themselves into units," and "everyone alienates themselves from others and hides." But the end of "even this frightful individual isolation will come," he avers, "and people will understand how unnaturally they have separated themselves from one another." Moreover, it will happen without fail that all will live harmoniously in brotherhood.[60]

Summarizing his philosophy on the whole, which he developed and had lived since his conversion experience years earlier, Zosima confirms that the roots of the self are in "the other world": "There is much on earth concealed from us, but to make up for it, we are given a precious, mystic sense of our living bond with the other world [*s mirom inym*], with the higher heavenly world [*s mirom gornim i vysshim*], and the roots of our thoughts and feelings are not here, but in other worlds. That is why the philosophers say that the essence of things cannot be conceived here on earth."[61]

Zosima's example and teachings inspire his disciple Alyosha Karamazov, the novice/hero who grapples with his Karamazovan nature even while dedicating himself to monastic life. He is happily doing so and becomes upset when Zosima advises him that his path lies outside the monastery and that he should spend more time in the secular world. The advice comes after the Karamazovs' visit to Zosima's cell, where Ivan insists, shockingly, that if people did not believe in an afterlife, there would be no reason to worry about morality, while in the same scene, as if to illustrate, Fyodor Pavlovich and Dmitri rudely argue in front of the elder over the love and jealousy both feel for Grushenka. Thus Zosima may have concluded that the other Karamazovs needed Alyosha. Alyosha is troubled by his family's scandalous dealings and later by his mentor's death. A moment of illumination visits him, however, during the vigil for Zosima, which changes everything for him and fills him with peace, compassion, and ultimate knowledge. Alyosha's vision of the wedding at Cana of Galilee (which I discuss in Chapter 4) provides the clearest, most succinct example of rebirth or transformation in a single moment of illumination. He had fallen into a reverie while listening to Father Paissy reading the Gospels over the coffin of the deceased elder when, upon waking, he feels

> as if threads from all these countless of God's worlds had all coincided within his soul at once, and it trembled all over, in the "contiguity with other worlds" [*soprikasaias' miram inym*]. He wanted to forgive all creatures for all things and to ask forgiveness, oh! not for himself, but for everyone, all creatures and all things, while "others ask the same of me" resounded again in his soul. But with each moment that passed he felt something palpable and tactile, as firm and unshakeable as the celestial vault, descending into his soul. It was as though some idea had seized and taken mastery over his mind—and now for the rest of his life and until the end of the ages. He had fallen to the earth a feeble youth, but now he had become a resolute warrior for the rest of his life and knew and felt this suddenly, at that same moment of his ecstasy. And never, never would he forget that moment for the rest of his life.[62]

Alyosha's transformation is instantaneous and complete. The qualities of the numinous moment of his spiritual epiphany include an awareness of wholeness, connection to other worlds, compassion, and selflessness, all of which coalesce in an "idea" that seizes the sovereignty of his intellect [*votsarialas' v ume ego*]. That idea, I venture, is awareness of the authentic self, which brings Alyosha confidence that he is connected to the divine Oneness. Like the Ridiculous Man, he is transformed by the discovery of truth and recognition of the higher self, which corresponds to the rebirth that greets the mythic hero at the conclusion of his journey.

In Western esotericism, indeed, illuminated knowledge leads to a second birth, elevating the secular to the religious. One way of looking at occult doctrines is as means of ordering the world and postulates of unifying principles. They go beneath or rise above material reality, involving intangible essences of mind, soul, and spirit.[63] These esoteric principles, and the symbols or archetypes they are known by, also refer to the unconscious coming into the conscious light of self-awareness.

The occult principle of "living nature" later coheres with *Naturphilosophie* and Schelling's cosmic pantheism—the idea that nature is subject to exile and will participate in salvation.[64] Living nature, moreover, is associated with Sophia, or Divine Wisdom, an essential component of Russian Orthodox theology.[65] Others have commented on similar principles in the nature mysticism of Zosima. This principle, furthermore, resembles the Dostoevskian concept of *zhivaia zhizn'* ("living life"), which I discuss in Chapter 3 and develop through the concepts of the archetypes of the shadow in Chapter 4 and of the hero myth here.

We saw in Chapter 4, led by Weisblatt's application of Jung's comparison of Christian symbolism to alchemical transformation, how forms similar to Jungian archetypes help to explain transformations in Dostoevsky's central characters. In his study of archetypal elements that inform hero myths, Jung maintained that the hero myth originated at a time when no one knew it as a "hero myth," when we did not consciously reflect on what we were saying. Thus, the hero archetype has existed since time immemorial.[66] An early iteration is the ancient mystery of the god-man, which has roots in the archetypal Osiris–Horus myth of ancient Egypt.[67] This specific hero myth centres on the sun god or god-man who descends to the underworld. As the god-man archetype informs the central hero myth of Christendom, Christ looms large in the works of Dostoevsky, and the god-man is an important archetype for him.

In Dostoevsky's later works we encounter several symbols of the unification of opposites, as I describe in Chapter 4 and, above, in my discussion of the hero myth. In the hero myth, the union and integration of opposites occur at the nexus of the hero's unification with the (or a) god and participation in the mystery of unity-in-multiplicity: "The two—the hero and his ultimate god, the seeker and the found—are thus understood as the outside and inside of a single, self-mirrored mystery, which is identical with the mystery of the manifest world. The great deed of the supreme hero is to come to the knowledge of this unity in multiplicity and then to make it known."[68] In Dostoevsky's works, unity with the god is an important idea that generates the archetype he called the "god-man" [*bogochelovek*].

For Dostoevsky, the most critical aspect of the awakening and enlightenment that the rebirth signifies is the Christological moral and aesthetic ideal of the god-man, and the sacred story of his resurrection. Jackson argues that the focal point of Dostoevsky's aesthetic ideal is the image of Christ: "Man, Dostoevsky insists, cannot reason his way to moral and spiritual truth. Truth—the ideal—must be felt. Christ, for Dostoevsky, is the 'ideal of humanity.'"[69] For Dostoevsky, faith in the Christ ideal in an embodied form is beauty, perfection, and transfiguration.

Now I move to my final topic, in which all the elements presented in this chapter converge: Dostoevsky's vision narrative as a transformation myth. To introduce my discussion of the myth of transformation and other examples of archetypal consciousness in Dostoevsky, I examine passages in which Dostoevsky's characters experience epiphanies of awareness and undergo transformation that involves the mystical union of opposites.

Self as Vision of 'Moments of Eternal Harmony'
The personal experience of "Truth" through ecstatic vision has been a mainstay of the Western novelistic tradition at least since Cervantes gave us Don Quixote's visions in the Cave of Montessino (Part II, Chapters xxii and xxiii). Vision narratives involve the healing of the rift between mind and nature, subject and object, which I've discussed as part of the crisis of modernity. Some of the most compelling expressions of religious content in Dostoevsky are these moments of elevation, insight, ecstatic vision, revelation, epiphany, or expanded consciousness that a small set of his characters experience, as I observe above. Among those whose visionary experiences give them a primordial connection to the sacred are Prince Myshkin, Father Zosima, Alyosha Karamazov, and the Ridiculous Man. Although commentary on these characters is usually framed by a Christian mythopoeic narrative, an alternative to a salvationist theory emphasizes the awakening of self-awareness, the unity of conscious and unconscious mind in the archetypal enactment of transformation. Typically, such events are focused catalysts of self-awareness related to the crisis of modernity, and they initiate personal transformation and sometimes the transcendence of the ego self. While revelatory truth remains a problematic motif in Dostoevsky, he creates in rare instances a vision narrative of non-dual transcendence, offering resolution of the conflicts that arise from the dualistic clash of archetypal forces and completing the rebirth cycle of the hero myth.

Kirillov describes to Shatov his experiencing a feeling like eternal harmony: "There are seconds, only five or six at a time, when you suddenly feel the presence of eternal harmony, perfect and complete. It is not earthly, not that it is heavenly, but that people in their earthly form cannot bear it. We would have to change physically or die." He concludes, "It's a feeling that is clear and incontrovertible."[70] Similarly, Myshkin claims that those moments are worth giving one's whole life for (in his case, referring to his pre-seizure ecstasy, which is similar to the experience of awakening he recounts in the story, not unlike Dostoevsky's own, of a condemned man presented with a reprieve).

Of all his characters, it is Prince Myshkin, Elder Zosima, and the Ridiculous Man to whom Dostoevsky gives the experience of inner illumination of authentic self its most direct expression. Myshkin's heightened spiritual sensitivity and his purity and goodness, which have an infectious impact on others around him, are often remarked upon as Christ-like qualities.[71] On the other hand, most researchers have not failed to recognize that Myshkin is a fallible individual, not a saint, much less a Russian Christ.[72] He is ultimately subject, like all others, to the Law of Personality. On the other hand, he provides a positive example of someone with intuitive awareness of his authentic self. His thoughts on the transcendent qualities of his pre-epileptic aura are often quoted because they illustrate the momentary experience of unitive consciousness in its fullest presentation by Dostoevsky. The narrator describes Myshkin's awareness at that point as follows:

> The sensation of life, of self-consciousness multiplied almost tenfold at these moments, flashing by like lightning. His mind and heart were illumined with extraordinary light; all his worries, all his doubts and anxieties were as if allayed at once, resolved in a kind of higher serenity, full of clear, harmonious joy and hope, full of reason and ultimate cause.[73]

Myshkin speaks of gleams and flashes of a higher perception [*samooshchushchenie*] and consciousness [*samosoznanie*] of "higher existence" [*vysshevo bytiia*]. There is a feeling of fullness, of proportion, of reconciliation and ecstatic fusion with the highest synthesis of life in which there could be no doubt.[74] The awakening of self-awareness to unitive consciousness is a sacred truth of apophatic Orthodox theology as well as the Western esoteric tradition. Inward illumination and a form of sudden change known as *metanoia* is integral to Orthodox Christianity, where it refers not only to repentance in a narrow sense but more broadly to a transformation that achieves spiritual knowledge.[75] Such an awakening is central to the apophasis of Plato and Dionysius the Areopagite, wherein illuminative transformation is seen as the visitation of divine Logos, occasioning the transcendence of the personality (the apparent self) and identification with the divinized self of higher cognition (the authentic self). Bearing in mind that the mystical philosophy of Platonism was available to Dostoevsky through Eastern Orthodoxy, it is possible that self-transformation was a native principle to Dostoevsky as a legacy of the effect of Neoplatonism on Russian Orthodoxy.[76]

Myshkin's mention of reason [*razum*] and ultimate cause [*okonchatel'naia prichina*] deserves notice. His vision suggests a numinous awareness of divine reason emanating from the supreme intelligence underlying all and catalyzing his spiritual transformation. This idea is evocative of divine Logos in the Hellenic tradition, wherein nature is permeated with divine rationality and final causes—a notion that was co-opted into medieval Christianity by Neoplatonic thinkers.[77] In this sense Myshkin is an initiate, albeit independently of the rites and rituals of the mystery religions. Initiatory experience in the esoteric tradition entails conscious deliberation of the idea of the sacred and awakening to a previously hidden or suppressed reality that is superordinate to the established secularism of the modern mind.

Inevitably, however, after experiencing the illumined moment, mundane life returns, in most cases, and along with it come the challenges of everyday life and interaction with others. This is true of Myshkin, who, researchers have noted, fails to save anyone, loses some measure of his integrity and compassion, and in fact makes matters worse for several of the protagonists in later parts of the novel.[78] Yet for some of Dostoevsky's characters, the experience of sudden enlightenment leaves a lasting impression and a sense that truth, once seen, transforms the individual permanently. This is the story of the Ridiculous Man.

In "The Dream of a Ridiculous Man," the dream brings the protagonist new life when he had planned to shoot himself: he has a vision of truth upon falling asleep with the gun in his hand. "They tease me now because after all, it was only a dream. But does it really matter if it was a dream or not if that dream showed me the Truth? After all if you discovered the truth and saw it, then you know it's the truth and there is no other, sleeping or awake."[79]

In his dream, the Ridiculous Man is taken by a dark force that transports him through time and space, but soon he meets the happy "children of the sun" of a new earth. He has never seen such beauty in people: "Their faces shone with intellect and a fullness of consciousness in peace, but these faces were happy; in their words and voices rang childlike joy."[80] The inhabitants of the utopian planet profess no religion. Yet they have no sin, and possess the consciousness of a superior wisdom. They do not worship or acknowledge deities, idols, or even rational principles. On the other hand, we know that Dostoevsky's ideal society would not be atheistic. On the planet, there is another kind of harmony. The people are guided by life absorbed in union with the "Purpose of the universe" [*edinenie s Tselym vselennoi*].[81] Their harmonious society is founded not on civic ideals but on intrinsic knowledge that comes from love. Bathed in and animated by its power, the extraterrestrial beings live harmoniously and commune with trees and animals. They communicate by means of love and have no individuated ego identities. Theirs is an integrated society that flows in natural organic rhythm; it is an integral life of brotherhood that they live, reflecting Dostoevsky's ideal, of which he wrote fervently in his later works.

The authentic self is shared by the inhabitants of the Edenic star in "The Dream of a Ridiculous Man" when they are visited by the title character, but after his arrival their collective authenticity is slowly dispersed by his "progressive" ideas. The instigation of modern instrumental reasoning (interpersonal relationships based on calculated advantage rather than love) pits them against one another. Like Zosima, the Ridiculous Man concludes as the result of his vision that, "In a single day, *in a single hour*—everything could be worked out instantly! The main thing is to love others as yourself"; if you do, he says, "you'll at once find a way to work it out."[82] The Ridiculous Man's encounter with "the Truth" in the dream vision thus prompts a new distillation of forces inside his imagination that entirely alters his apprehension of self and others.

This truth-in-vision is a unique sort of truth—a categorical "other." It is a kind of truth that is revealed but misunderstood and ridiculed. In waking reality, public reaction to the Ridiculous Man's utopian vision, which he shares with proselytizing vigour, is laughter and ridicule, while his attitude toward his fellow beings on the natural earth spans an emotional range that extends from despair and anguish at one end to compassion and love at the other. He is called ridiculous, and a madman, but what saddens him most is that those who ridicule him do not know the Truth, while he does: "I am ridiculous. They call me a madman now.... But I no longer mind—they are all dear to me now, even when they are laughing at me—indeed, something endears them to me particularly then. I would laugh with them—not at myself, that is, but because I love them—I would laugh if I did not feel so sad watching them. What saddens me is that they do not know the Truth, and I do. Oh, how hard it is to be the only one to know the Truth!"[83]

The issue for the Ridiculous Man is that the Truth he discovers is inaccessible to modern reason and therefore incommunicable to his contemporaries. The moral ground that concerns him is present on a spiritual plane that is supra-rational, a transcendent vision that defies articulation. The modern reasoning subject, by contrast, views transcendental metaphysics as ridiculous and incomprehensible. The prevailing post-Enlightenment attitude among the intelligentsia in Russia at this time is positivist. Religious attitudes are Kantian, wherein moral conscience itself is viewed as a faculty of reason. Thus, the discovery of truth by ecstatic vision is invalid by the standards of modern discursive practice.

The dream is pertinent to the discussion of religious insight in Dostoevsky, which frequently takes the form of such elevated moments as might be called epiphany or revelation. These events are a focused catalyst of self-awareness, related to the crisis of modernity, involving an experience of transcendence of the ego self. The Ridiculous Man believes he experienced ultimate truth in his dream vision. "I have seen the truth," he says, "it is not as though I invented it with my mind, but I saw it, saw it, and its *living image* has filled my soul forever. I saw it in such full wholeness, that I can't believe that it couldn't be in people."[84] In this sense, the text of "The Dream of the Ridiculous Man" is a kind of initiation. Its truths are not expository but revelatory. The reader is expected not only to listen to the words but to *realize* them, to make their truths an integral part of character, conduct, and consciousness.

The inhabitants of the Edenic star in "The Dream of a Ridiculous Man" are "children of the sun" whose original, unblemished self-awareness aligns with an authentic life of the spirit. How is it, then, that the Ridiculous Man corrupts them? This is his own rehearsal of the secularization and disenchantment of modernity. It aids in his coming to understand his own epiphany and return to the plane of everyday experience. He is the initiate of otherworldly knowledge, catalyzed by thought pictures of the self. The star dwellers are objects of imagination in his dream, in the way that the dreamer-initiate is a thought-picture builder, a creator of forms to engender the awakening of the authentic self.[85]

Furthermore, the Ridiculous Man's preaching about the importance of love invites comparison to Elder Zosima's oratory in *The Brothers Karamazov*, which Dostoevsky was writing at the same time he published "Dream." Zosima preaches, "Much on earth is hidden from us, but to make up for that we have been given a precious mystic sense of our living bond with the other world, with the higher heavenly world, and the roots of our thoughts and feelings are not here but in other worlds. That is why the philosophers say that we cannot apprehend the reality of things on earth."[86] More broadly, the ontology of vision narrative dates back to older traditions such as those I discuss above in connection with Western esotericism.[87] Morson contends that Dostoevsky drew on esoteric "wisdom" genres to form the basis of his modern philosophical thrillers. Thus one of the sources of the *Diary*'s coordination of political journalism with revelatory fictions is the alternation of argument with embedded myths and allegories in Plato's *Republic*.[88] The Allegory of the Cave (from Book 7) provides a master plot for later utopian genres: "An apparently foolish visionary, the only one awake," embarks upon an "epistemological parable" of "a journey to light and knowledge and a return to darkness and ignorance." In the final stage of the journey the hero returns "to liberate the other prisoners, who, regarding him as 'awkward and ridiculous,'... refuse his help."[89]

In all, the Ridiculous Man's and Elder Zosima's creed of engagement with the world and panhuman brotherhood offer significant evidence of heterodox or syncretic religion in Dostoevsky's fiction. It is not exactly Russian Orthodox doctrine. It is, however, tied to a critical idea connecting Dostoevsky's world view and ideology to his native Russia.

The great writer who dreamed of universal brotherhood finds universality in the living immanence of his vision, in a multi-faceted, ever-changing, and self-contradictory self—a self that is, ultimately, transformational.

CONCLUSION

Dostoevsky beyond Duality

We do not fully inhabit our selves: some vision of our self inhabits us. Where self was, ego now searches for it.

—Art Berman, *Preface to Modernism*

Throughout this book I have endeavoured to show that, for all their conflicting variety, Dostoevsky's major works converge on a compelling vision of personal transformation of the individual and give expression to that vision through archetypal narrative motifs. Frequently paradoxical, at turns unorthodox and heretical, Dostoevsky's vision neither mandates nor guarantees this radical shift of awareness; yet it intimates a nascent self-consciousness that naturally inclines toward its fulfillment in the individual's transcendent union with divine Logos. The problem of the modern self in Dostoevsky's major works is thus presented as an imperative of self-transformation via an archetypal process. The theory of archetypes I have applied to my analysis of Dostoevsky's works coheres with the integral vision that Dostoevsky encountered in German Romanticism and other syncretic philosophies, and shows that the focal point of Dostoevsky's critique of modernity is the primordial idea that the true self is revealed by the moral and aesthetic vision emanating from, and at one with, a transcendent order of being. The indeterminacy of the typical Dostoevskian text notwithstanding, its major schematic challenges the modern world view of nihilistic materialism by confirming the positive potential for true correspondence with divine essence.

I have argued that principles of ego transcendence and unitary consciousness are prominent themes in Dostoevsky's writing, which suggests that personal transformation was among his central artistic concerns. Without a doubt the plane of analysis that proved most productive for Dostoevsky involved the exploration of that which separates us from oneness with divine essence. Certainly personal transformation and moral regeneration are less frequently encountered within the scope of a Dostoevskian text than instances of deformed and suffering personalities; or they are alluded to only provisionally, as in Raskolnikov's moral and spiritual rehabilitation in the epilogue to *Crime and Punishment*. This feature owes especially to the cultural setting in which Dostoevsky lived, an age growing progressively more secular with each decade, defined by the triumphs of empirical science and challenges to pre-modern metaphysics that had become nearly unassailable. The flourishing of Western thought ensured that the modern self, with its procedural reason and self-serving bias, had become the only organizational model of personhood acknowledged by progressive thinkers. The apparent self of procedural reason had replaced the immaterial psyche with the material personal self. However hopelessly fractured and lacking in intrinsic unity that model might be, it formed the basis of modernity, with its insoluble contradictions and permanent state of crisis. For Dostoevsky, the threat to genuine awareness and expression of one's authentic self is especially grave in utopian socialism, a pernicious doctrine because it accounted only for the superficial, utilitarian needs of the apparent self. The cult of unity on a utilitarian, political level was a civic ideal that Dostoevsky vigorously contested, in the post-exile phase of his writing, in favour of genuine unity through personal transformation.

Especially in Dostoevsky's later works, self-transformation is met with increasing frequency in narratives of visionary experience—personal insight that takes the form of epiphanic, ecstatic, or revelatory experiences. These instances indicate the author's readiness to posit the reality of a plane of transcendent awareness, where the self rises above duality to align with what might be called primary consciousness.

In spite of modern cultural imperatives, then, the evidence revealed by textual analysis points to Dostoevsky's authentication of a nascent quality in the human psyche, one which is predisposed to seek illumination of the divine intellect. This psychic quest catalyzes the birth or awakening of the noumenal self that exists *in potentia* until it is revealed by the insight of numinous vision. I have therefore argued that one of Dostoevsky's chief artistic concerns was to revitalise the pre-modern vision of a transcendent, authentic, personal self, a self that achieves oneness with the divine presence.

Few if any of Dostoevsky's characters reach the apogee of higher unity in any form of integrated personality or enlightened union with God. Why that is so remains open to speculation, but it might be simply that it is not essential that they do. Such higher unity is, for Dostoevsky, a transcendent ideal, one that cannot be achieved in this life. Still, the immortality of the soul is a necessary condition of Dostoevsky's world view, even while in this world the underground is dominant. In advanced scenarios that involve archetypal figures of the underlying hero myth, immortality catalyzes transformation for some characters (Myshkin, Zosima, Alyosha, the Ridiculous Man), while for others it does not (the Underground Man, Svidrigailov, Stavrogin).

Unfortunately for Dostoevsky's doubting, conflicted characters, maintaining faith in God in the face of the problem of evil in a society that extols atheism and strict empiricism requires them also to maintain a delicate psychic balance. Veresaev reminds us that Svidrigailov in *Crime and Punishment* remarks that life without God is "slow suffering and death"; that Ippolit rejects God and all religion; that Ivan Karamazov wants to "return his ticket" to God; and that, in the first part of his dream, the Ridiculous Man harboured eternal spite for the punisher of his would-be sin of suicide.[1] On the other hand, Veresaev maintains that Dostoevsky's "unbelievers" are not, in actual fact, completely godless:

> Dostoevsky loves to portray unbelievers, but his unbelievers are very strange. For them, God is not just an empty word. They all see God, they just don't look at Him. In their proclamations of their faithlessness, in each of them bursts out a word or action, giving away their secret apprehensions. The atheist Raskolnikov suddenly informs [the police detective] Porfiry that he believes in God, that he even believes, literally, in the raising of Lazarus. The nihilist Ippolit says that he allows for the idea of eternal life. It's not that Ivan Karamazov "doesn't accept God, but only politely returns Him his ticket." The unbeliever Kirillov frequently lights a lamp before an icon, and Peter Verkhovensky says of him, "He believes in God more than the pope does." None of them are unbelievers at all. They have a deep longing for God, and God, for them, exists—He is right before them. But they can't bow to Him—they have too many questions for Him, to which there are no answers.[2]

Dostoevsky gives his ideal its fullest treatment in his last novel, which avoids the fantastic overtones of "The Dream of a Ridiculous Man." In Frank's words:

Even though Dostoevsky's works are suffused with a sense of the importance of mutual moral responsibility, nowhere is this theme stated more broadly than in *The Brothers Karamazov*, where each person is declared to be responsible for all. The bold conception of a future humankind that would literally be a huge, united and interdependent organism—a humankind in which any separation between individuals would no longer even be physically conceivable—may well have guided Dostoevsky toward his epochal formulation.[3]

Unity, then, is the ultimate goal of humanity—indeed, its destiny—as Dostoevsky envisions the ideal world. In his works the principle of duality, rather than merely being instantiated in an experience of internal conflict, can be viewed, as I've argued, in archetypal terms of the complementarity of opposites and thus of immanent, integral unity. Moreover, the creed of engagement with the world and universal brotherhood that is inherent to Dostoevsky's model of faith plays out in a *both–and* dialectic, which resembles the synthesis of opposites that informs the development of the Western understanding of the self and the archetypal process of its development. While it is customary to view the existential dilemmas of Dostoevsky's characters as insoluble contradictions of modernity—or if unity is seen only as a possible future Christian afterlife—the universal self shared in Dostoevsky's ideal of brotherhood may in fact be seen to overcome the dualist frame of the European heritage and find its longed-for unity in a mode that occupies a wider ground of tradition.

Many of the values of Western civilization stem from the Platonic principle that the universe is permeated with divine reason.[4] Traditions of Western esotericism such as Hermeticism and alchemy gave prominence to the tension of opposites and their underlying complementarity. Rediscovery and recovery of the authentic self is the "Great Work" of the perennialist tradition, grounded in Neoplatonism. An experience of rebirth or awakening is the noumenal event of seeing and recognizing the apparent self for what it is—a fiction, an illusion, the "veil of *maya*" (world of appearances).[5] While there is no direct evidence that Dostoevsky, like his contemporary L.N. Tolstoy, took an explicit interest in Plato,[6] the major principles of the idealist framework of Platonism may be discerned in Dostoevsky's artistic vision: knowledge of the divine is implicit in every soul; ultimate reality is not only ethical and rational but also aesthetic; beatific knowledge of the True and Good is accessible via transcendent human intellect; the universal passion to restore a former unity, overcome separation from the divine, and become one with it is the sublime form of Eros.[7] The Dostoevskian self can be viewed in light of the same precepts:

the illusory finite self is subordinate to the authentic self, with its moral and aesthetic knowledge of ultimate reality. The self's true essence is often catalyzed by an initiatory experience of visionary knowledge. With illumination comes the ability to perceive the divine, intelligent unity of design behind all apparent diversity.

In the final analysis, not only does Dostoevsky make it his mission to solve the mystery of man, as he stated in his letter of 1839, but he also joins the movement to reclaim the individual and *reaffirm* the mystery of existence—a movement that, once inspired, has propelled the transcendental strivings of many modernist artists and writers among Dostoevsky's successors in Russia, Europe, and the Western world. But the overwhelming question in Dostoevsky that has occupied philosophers and dialecticians the world over is this: How does one reconcile the true order of unity in reality with the apparent lack of unity in the world? With my reading of archetypes in Dostoevsky, I hope to have made a step toward an understanding of Dostoevsky's position on that question. I believe that for Dostoevsky, bridging the divide is a question of art. Even if the laws of history are unavailable or the final truths undiscoverable, archetypes often underlie the metaphorical nature of our common structures of knowledge. Tarnas observes, "The postmodern philosopher's recognition of the inherently metaphorical nature of philosophical and scientific statements (Feyerabend, Barbour, Rorty) has been both affirmed and more precisely articulated with the postmodern psychologist's insight into the archetypal categories of the unconscious that condition and structure human experience and cognition."[8] For Tarnas, history, class, culture, imagination, and the unconscious *all* propel the expression of archetypes. Even though Tarnas is expressing a view that grew in prominence after the time of Dostoevsky's writing, the same understanding can be applied, I argue, to Dostoevsky. This book has been a sketch of a theory of archetypes, taking into consideration the application of archetypes in critical analysis of Dostoevsky and the role of archetypes in Dostoevsky's own thinking. I have shown that archetypal patterning can be used to guide a close reading and textual analysis of Dostoevsky's works in the light of sources that played a large part in the ideological formation of his world view. Finally, the connection to a great variety of sources of archetypal patterning based in such generic traditions as myth and folk tales, diverse traditions of syncretic philosophy, and depth psychology leaves open the possibility to use archetypes in a variety of ways as an analytical tool for further research on Dostoevsky's works.

Notes

Notes to Introduction

1 Letter of 1 October 1859. *PSS* 28 Bk 1: 340. I examine Dostoevsky's efforts to revise *The Double* in Chapter 3. Citations of Dostoevsky's work by volume and pages number refer to G.M. Fridlender et al., eds., *Polnoe sobranie sochinenii v tridtsati tomakh* (Leningrad: Nauka, 1972–1990). Abbreviated throughout this volume as *PSS*.
2 *PSS* 1: 489.
3 *PSS* 26: 65.
4 "Такие лица, как сочинитель таких записок, не только могут, но даже должны существовать в нашем обществе, взяв в соображение те обстоятельства, при которых вообще складывалось наше общество." *PSS* 5: 99.
5 See Joseph Frank, *Dostoevsky: The Stir of Liberation, 1860–1865* (Princeton: Princeton University Press, 1986), 331; and Bernard J. Paris, *Dostoevsky's Greatest Characters: A New Approach to "Notes from Underground,"* Crime and Punishment, *and* The Brothers Karamazov (New York: Palgrave Macmillan, 2008), 3.
6 Victor Terras, *Handbook of Russian Literature* (New Haven, CT: Yale University Press, 1985), 356. Emphasis in original.
7 Mikhail Lermontov, *A Hero of Our Time,* trans. Vladimir Nabokov with Dmitri Nabokov (Garden City, NY: Doubleday Anchor, 1958), 2.
8 "Это—один из представителей еще доживающего поколения." *PSS* 5: 99.
9 Frank, *Stir of Liberation,* 331.
10 Ibid., 316.
11 *PSS* 26: 313; cited in Robert Bird, "Refiguring the Russian Type: Dostoevsky and the Limits of Realism," in Robert Louis Jackson, ed., *A New Word on* The Brothers Karamazov (Evanston, IL: Northwestern University Press, 2004), 28, note 7. Bem explains that Dostoevsky was critical of "the gruesome world of the Gogolian masquerade—whose participants were not real people but masks." *O Dostoevskom,* Vol. 2 (Prague, 1933); cited in Bird, "Refiguring the Russian Type," 19.
12 "…при бестолковой карамазовщине, в которой никто себя не мог ни понять, ни определить." *PSS* 15: 99.

13 "O karamazovshchine" and "Eshche o karamazovshchine." Gorky's occasion for writing was his sharp protest against the productions of *The Devils* and *The Brothers Karamazov* by the Moscow Art Theatre.
14 "Человек есть тайна. Ее надо разгадать, и ежели будешь ее разгадать всю жизнь, то не говори, что потерял время; я занимаюсь этой тайной, ибо хочу быть человеком." Letter of 16 August 1839. *PSS* 28 Bk 1: 63.
15 "«Надо изображать действительность как она есть»,—говорят они, тогда как такой действительности совсем нет, да и никогда на земле не бывало, потому что сущность вещей человеку недоступна, а воспринимает он природу так, как отражается она в его идее, пройдя через его чувства; стало быть, надо дать поболее ходу идее и не бояться идеального." "Po povodu vystavki," *Diary of a Writer*, March 1873, 9. *PSS* 21: 75.
16 See Robert H. Stacy, *Russian Literary Criticism: A Short History* (Syracuse, NY: Syracuse University Press, 1974), 87–88.
17 "Идеи летают в воздухе, но непременно по законам; идеи живут и распространяются по законам, слишком трудно для нас уловимым; идеи заразительны, и знаете ли вы, что в общем настроении жизни иная идея, иная забота или тоска, доступная лишь высокообразованному и развитому уму, может вдруг передаться почти малограмотному существу, грубому и ни об чем никогда не заботившемуся, и вдруг заразить его душу своим влиянием?" "Koe-chto o molodezhi," *Diary of a Writer*, December 1876, i, 4. *PSS* 24: 51.
18 Vyacheslav Ivanov, *Freedom and the Tragic Life* (Wolfeboro, NH: Longwood Academic, 1989).
19 Robert Louis Jackson, *Dostoevsky's Quest for Form: A Study of His Philosophy of Art* (New Haven and London: Yale University Press, 1966), 108.
20 See Yuri Lotman, "The Tradition Generated by *Onegin*," in *Russian Views of Pushkin's "Eugene Onegin,"* translated by Sona Stephan Hoisington (Bloomington and Indianapolis: Indiana UP, 1988), 176; cited in Bird, "Refiguring the Russian Type," 18.
21 *PSS* 14: 5.
22 Bird, "Refiguring the Russian Type," 17–18.
23 Richard Tarnas, *Cosmos and Psyche: Intimations of a New World View* (New York: Plume Books, 2007), 45.
24 Depth psychology, a psychoanalytic branch of psychology associated with the work of Carl Jung (1875–1961), explores the unconscious and its archetypes as part of the process of personality formation.
25 Laurie Bernstein, *Sonia's Daughter's: Prostitutes and Their Regulation in Imperial Russia* (Berkeley: University of California Press, 1995).
26 Kenneth Lantz, *The Dostoevsky Encyclopedia* (Westport, CT: Greenwood Publishing Group, 2004), 159.
27 Alexandra F. Rudicina, "Crime and Myth: The Archetypal Pattern of Rebirth in Three Novels of Dostoevsky," *PMLA* 87, no. 5 (October 1972), 1065–1074.
28 C.G. Jung, *The Undiscovered Self, Vol. 10, The Collected Works of C.G. Jung*, 2nd ed., trans. R.F.C. Hull, Bollingen Series XX (Princeton: Princeton Univer-

sity Press, 1970). Hereinafter I refer to Jung's *Collected Works* as CW, followed by year and either title or volume number.
29 See Jung, *The Archetypes and The Collective Unconscious*, CW Vol. 9, part 1, 1969.
30 See Jung, *Psychological Types*, CW Vol. 6, 1971, par. 789.
31 Tarnas, *Cosmos and Psyche*, 80.
32 Jung, CW 1969, 4.
33 Tarnas, *Cosmos and Psyche*, 82.
34 Ibid.
35 Ibid.
36 Ibid.
37 Ibid., 82–83.
38 C.G. Jung, *The Undiscovered Self* with *Symbols and the Interpretation of Dreams*, trans. and revised by R.F.C. Hull (Princeton, NJ, and Oxford: Princeton University Press, 2010), 39.
39 Northrop Frye, *Anatomy of Criticism: Four Essays* (Princeton, NJ: Princeton University Press, 1957), 365.
40 Richard Noll, *The Jung Cult: Origins of a Charismatic Movement* (Princeton, NJ: Princeton University Press, 1994), 41.
41 According to Lukács, says Noll, the *fin-de-siècle Lebensphilosophie* movement gave a "special type of objectivity" to mythology. "Mythology becomes a novel—and potentially dangerous—reference point for claims about the true nature of reality or of one's own subjective experience of life." Noll, *The Jung Cult*, 39. [*Lebensphilosophie*, which comes about after 1870, is an insight that opens inwardly.]
42 Jung, CW 1969, 5.
43 Ibid., 13.
44 Ibid., 76.
45 Ibid., 6.
46 Ibid., 69.
47 C.G. Jung et al., *Man and His Symbols* (Garden City, NY: Doubleday & Company, 1964), 67.
48 C.G. Jung, *Four Archetypes: Mother, Rebirth, Spirit, Trickster*, trans. R.F.C. Hull (Princeton, NJ: Princeton University Press, 1970), 5.
49 Ibid., 104.
50 Nicholas Berdyaev, *Dostoevsky*, trans. Donald Attwater (New York: Meridian Books, 1968), 13.
51 *PSS* 22: 127; 130. For a study of spiritualism in nineteenth-century Russian literature and society, see Ilya Vinitsky, *Ghostly Paradoxes: Modern Spiritualism and Russian Culture in the Age of Realism* (Toronto: University of Toronto Press), 2009.
52 *PSS* 14: 232.
53 James Scanlan, *Dostoevsky the Thinker* (Ithaca, NY, and London: Cornell University Press, 2002), 55.
54 Ibid., 50.

55 See Thomas Berry, "Dostoevsky and Spiritualism," *Dostoevsky Studies* 2 (1981): 45–46.
56 Ibid., 45–46.
57 Bernice Glatzer Rosenthal, ed., *The Occult in Russian and Soviet Culture* (Ithaca, NY: Cornell University Press, 1997), 11.
58 The books are *Experimental Researches on Spiritualism*, by R. Gera (1866); and *Spiritualism and Science: Experimental Researches on the Psychic Force*, by William Crookes (1872). See note to page 112, *PSS* 12: 293.
59 *Diary of a Writer*, April 1876; *PSS* 22: 127. Quoted in Berry, "Dostoevsky and Spiritualism," 44.
60 Berry, "Dostoevsky and Spiritualism," 43.
61 Joseph Frank, *Dostoevsky: The Seeds of Revolt, 1821–1849* (Princeton, NJ: Princeton University Press, 1976), 105. On the impact of philosophy on Dostoevsky more generally, see Frederick C. Copleston, "Dostoevsky and Philosophy" in *Philosophy in Russia from Herzen to Lenin and Berdyaev* (Notre Dame, IN: University of Notre Dame Press, 1986), 142–167. A related formative influence on Dostoevsky was the movement of Russian transcendentalists, which flourished in the 1830s and 40s. Also see Donna Orwin, *Consequences of Consciousness: Turgenev, Dostoevsky, and Tolstoy* (Stanford, CA: Stanford University Press, 2007), 28–33.
62 *PSS* 24: 254–256.
63 *PSS* 23: 130.
64 C.G. Jung, *Analytical Psychology: Its Theory and Practice* (London: Routledge and Kegan Paul, 1982), 44–45.
65 Ibid., 110.
66 Gary Lachman, *Jung the Mystic: The Esoteric Dimensions of Carl Jung's Life and Teachings* (New York: Jeremy P. Tarcher/Penguin, 2013), 117. Lachman's emphasis.
67 Noll, *The Jung Cult*, 18.
68 Ibid., 13.
69 Ibid., 14.
70 Lachman, *Jung the Mystic*, 7. See Sonu Shamdasani, *Cult Fictions: C.G. Jung and the Founding of Analytical Psychology* (New York and London: Routledge, 1998).
71 Lachman, *Jung the Mystic*, 6.

Notes to Chapter 1
1 Letter to Nikolai Ozmidov, *PSS* 30 Bk 1: 10–11; Dostoevsky's emphasis. See discussion in James P. Scanlan, *Dostoevsky the Thinker* (Ithaca, NY, and London: Cornell University Press), 32 and 45. Translation by Scanlan.
2 On Ermakov and the development of psychoanalysis in Russia, see Donald Young, "Ermakov and Psychoanalytic Criticism in Russia," *Slavic and East European Journal* 23.1 (Spring 1979): 72–86. Ermakov's essays are reproduced in I.D. Ermakov, *Psikhoanaliz literatury. Pushkin. Gogol'. Dostoevskii* (Moscow: Novoe literaturnoe obozrenie, 1999).

3 Otto Rank, *The Double: A Psychoanalytic Study* (Chapel Hill: University of North Carolina Press, 1971). Freud's essay "Dostoevsky and Parricide" can be found in James Strachey and Anna Freud, eds., *The Standard Edition of the Complete Psychological Works of Sigmund Freud*, vol. 21 (London: Hogarth Press, 1966), 175–196.
4 See James L. Rice, "Dostoevsky in Freud's World" (123–158) and "'Dostoevsky and Parricide'" (177–200) in his *Freud's Russia: National Identity in the Evolution of Psychoanalysis* (New Brunswick, NJ: Transaction Publishers, 1993). See also Harvey Mindess, "Freud on Dostoevsky," *American Scholar* 36 (1967): 446–52; and Vladimir K. Kantor, "Freud contra Dostoevskii," in *Tolstoi ili Dostoevskii? Filosofsko-esteticheskie iskaniia v kul'turakh Vostoka i Zapada*, ed. V.E. Bagno (St. Petersburg: Nauka, 2003), 197–207. The version of Dostoevsky's father's murder by his serfs is unsubstantiated. See Frank, "Freud's Case-History of Dostoevsky" in *The Seeds of Revolt*, 379–391. On the medical aspect of Dostoevsky's epilepsy and its relevance to his writing, see James Rice, *Dostoevsky and the Healing Art: An Essay in Literary and Medical History* (Ann Arbor, MI: Ardis, 1985).
5 Earlier examples include Lawrence Kohlberg, "Psychological Analysis and Literary Form: A Study of the Doubles in Dostoevsky," *Daedalus* (Spring 1963): 345–362; Elizabeth Dalton, *Unconscious Structure in* The Idiot (Princeton, NJ: Princeton University Press), 1979; Louis Breger, "Dostoevsky and Medicine," *Slavic Review* 45 (1986): 735–737; and *Dostoevsky: The Author as Psychoanalyst* (New York: New York University Press), 1989.
6 Bernard J. Paris, *Dostoevsky's Greatest Characters: A New Approach to "Notes from Underground,"* Crime and Punishment, *and* The Brothers Karamazov (New York: Palgrave Macmillan, 2008), 15.
7 Ibid., 22.
8 Ibid., 8.
9 "Меня зовут психологом: неправда, я лишь реалист в высшем смысле, то есть изображаю все глубины души человеческой." Notebooks 1880–1881, *PSS* 27: 65. See the discussion in Malcolm Jones, *Dostoevsky after Bakhtin: Readings in Dostoyevsky's Fantastic Realism* (Cambridge: Cambridge University Press, 1990), 49–51; and Scanlan, *Dostoevsky the Thinker*, 137–147.
10 Gary Saul Morson, "Prosaic Bakhtin: *Landmarks*, Anti-Intelligentsialism, and the Russian Countertradition," in *Bakhtin in Contexts: Across the Disciplines*, ed. Amy Mandelker (Evanston, IL: Northwestern University Press, 1995), 57. Morson quotes from Mikhail Bakhtin, *Problems of Dostoevsky's Poetics*, 62. The emphasis is Morson's.
11 "Совершенно другие я понятие имею о действительности и реализме, чем наши реалисты и критики. Мой идеализм—реальнее ихнего." *PSS* 28 Bk 2: 329. See the discussion in Joseph Frank, *Dostoevsky: The Miraculous Years, 1865–1871* (Princeton, NJ: Princeton University Press, 1995), 308.
12 Steven Cassedy, *Dostoevsky's Religion* (Stanford, CA: Stanford University Press, 2005), 134–135.

13 It should also be noted in this context that Russian semiotician Yuri Lotman defines Russian culture as a binary system. Unlike the West, says Lotman, Russian society proceeds according to a strict binary logic of opposition—the chosen option admits no compromise; alternatives are rejected outright and must be annihilated. This situation instigates a repetitive cycle of breakdown and negation. See Yuri Lotman, *Culture and Explosion*, ed. Marina Grishakova, trans. Wilma Clark (Berlin and New York: Mouton de Gruyter, 2009), 166–171.
14 See Alex de Jonge, *Dostoevsky and the Age of Intensity* (New York: St. Martin's Press, 1975).
15 See Cassedy, *Dostoevsky's Religion*, 129–136.
16 De Jonge, *Dostoevsky and the Age of Intensity*, 15–16 and 22–27.
17 Donna Orwin, *Consequences of Consciousness: Turgenev, Dostoevsky, and Tolstoy* (Stanford, CA: Stanford University Press, 2007), 52.
18 See *PSS* 5: 104 and note 63 in Chapter 3, below. The Underground Man disputes Rousseau and other "*hommes de la nature et de la vérité*" who contend that since order and harmony prevail in nature, disorder and disharmony are man-made, and that we need only go back to nature to discover our own true nature (*PSS* 5: 104). For Dostoevsky, this is false, since, as he wrote in his notebook at the time of the death of his first wife, Maria Dmitrievna, man "strives on earth for an ideal, *opposite* to his nature" (*PSS* 20: 175). Here Dostoevsky's thought echoes St. Paul in Galatians: "For the flesh lusteth against the Spirit, and the Spirit against the flesh: and these are contrary the one to the other: so that ye cannot do the things that ye would" (Galatians 5:17).
19 Richard Tarnas, *The Passion of the Western Mind: Understanding the Ideas That Have Shaped Our World View* (New York: Ballantine Books, 1991), 271.
20 Ibid., 351.
21 Charles Taylor, *Sources of the Self: The Making of the Modern Identity* (Cambridge: Harvard University Press, 1989), 181–184.
22 Ibid., 178.
23 Tarnas, *The Passion of the Western Mind*, 76.
24 Ibid., 85–86.
25 Ibid., 99.
26 Ibid., 101–103.
27 Ibid., 103–109.
28 Richard Tarnas, *Cosmos and Psyche: Intimations of a New World View* (New York: Plume Books, 2007), 367–368.
29 Erich Fromm, *Escape from Freedom* (New York: Henry Holt & Co., 1994), 36.
30 Taylor, *Sources of the Self*, 182.
31 Ibid., 186.
32 Ibid., 191.
33 Ibid., 174–175.
34 Ibid., 177.
35 Ibid., 181.

36 Ibid., 135.
37 Ibid., 174.
38 Tarnas, *Cosmos and Psyche*, 484.
39 (Разгадка психологическая; глубокое чувство, человек и русский человек).... Ах, друг мой! Совершенно другие я понятия имею о действительности и реализме, чем наши реалисты и критики. Мой идеализм – реальнее ихнего. Господи! Порассказать толково то, что мы все, русские, пережили в последние 10 лет в нашем духовном развитии, — да разве не закричат реалисты, что это фантазия? А между тем это исконный, настоящий реализм! Это-то и есть реализм, только глубже, а у них мелко плавает.... Глубок реализм – нечего сказать! Ихним реализмом сотой доли реальных, действительно случившихся фактов не объяснишь. А мы нашим идеализмом пророчили даже факты. Случалось. *PSS* 28 Bk 2: 329.
40 See George Pattison and Diane Oenning Thompson, "Introduction: Reading Dostoevsky Religiously," in *Dostoevsky and the Christian Tradition*, ed. Pattison and Thompson (Cambridge: Cambridge University Press, 2001), 1–28. Also see the discussion in "Essay II: Introduction to Current Debate," in Malcolm Jones, *Dostoevsky and the Dynamics of Religious Experience* (London: Anthem Press, 2005), 25–33.
41 Jones, *Dostoevsky and the Dynamics of Religious Experience*, 30.
42 Kireevsky and fellow Slavophiles Aleksei Khomyakov and Konstantin Aksakov linked the holistic principles of integral knowledge and wholeness of spirit (*tsel'nost' dukha*) to the social ideal of organic unity (*sobornost'*). According to Slavophile principles, man is free but cannot develop except in and through membership in society—a greater whole that promotes self-realization and integrated harmony of the interests of its members. See Sarah Hudspith, *Dostoevsky and the Idea of Russianness: A New Perspective on Unity and Brotherhood* (New York: RoutledgeCurzon, 2004), 7–10.
43 For example, Dostoevsky parodied Slavophilism in his ironically titled editorial "Confessions of a Slavophile," in *Diary of a Writer* (PSS 25: 195–196) and mocked its ideology in the contradictory views of Shatov in *The Devils*. See Hudspith, *Dostoevsky and the Idea of Russianness*, 86–87 and 109–115.
44 Never one to align with pre-existing ideological camps, Dostoevsky proposed a middle way to the debate between Westernizers and Slavophiles along with his brother Mikhail and co-contributors to their journal *Vremia* (*Time*) Nikolai Strakhov and Apollon Grigor'ev, adopting a view called *pochvennichestvo* (commonly translated as "native soil conservatism"). See Scanlan, *Dostoevsky the Thinker*, passim; Joseph Frank, *Dostoevsky: The Stir of Liberation, 1860–1865* (Princeton, NJ: Princeton University Press, 1986), passim; and Frank, *Dostoevsky: The Years of Ordeal, 1850–1859* (Princeton: Princeton University Press, 1990), 173.
45 Jones, *Dostoevsky and the Dynamics of Religious Experience*, 40.
46 Ibid., 152–153.
47 Ibid., xi.

48 Cassedy, *Dostoevsky's Religion*, 160. Cassedy suggests that Zosima's views resemble a type of nationalism condemned at an Orthodox Church Council in Constantinople in 1872 that prohibited the establishment of any church along purely ethnic lines.
49 Ibid., 145–146.
50 See the conclusion of Wil van den Bercken, *Christian Fiction and Religious Realism in the Novels of Dostoevsky* (London: Anthem Press, 2011), 123–126.
51 Irina Kirk, "Buddhistic Elements in The Idiot," *Studia Slavica Academiae Scientiarum Hungaricae* 18, nos. 1–2 (1972): 77–84.
52 Michael Futrell, "Buddhism and *The Brothers Karamazov*," *Dostoevsky Studies* 2 (1981): 155–162; "Dostoyevsky and Islam (And Chokan Valikhanov)," *Slavonic and East European Review* 57, no. 1 (January 1979): 16–31. For another description of Buddhistic elements in Dostoevsky, see Aleksandr Fursov, "Vremia, kogda ulybaetsia lotos: Dostoevskii i kitaisskie mudretsy," *Dukhovno-nravstvennoe vospitanie* 6 (2009): 18–20.
53 Sarah J. Young, "Buddhism in Dostoevsky: Prince Myshkin and the True Light of Being," in Sarah Young and Lesley Milne, eds., *Dostoevsky: On the Threshold of Other Worlds*, 220–229 (Ilkeston, England: Bramcot, 2006).
54 Tatiana Kasatkina, *O tvoriashchei prirode slova: ontologichnost' slova v tvorchestve F.M. Dostoevskogo kak osnova 'realizma v vysshem mysle'* (Moscow: IMLI RAN, 2004), 457–458.
55 Rowan Williams, *Dostoevsky: Language, Faith, and Fiction* (Waco, TX: Baylor University Press, 2008), 10.

Notes to Chapter 2

1 Raffaella Vassena, *Reawakening National Identity: Dostoevskii's Diary of a Writer and Its Impact on Russian Society* (New York: Peter Lang, 2007), 47–50.
2 Ibid., 49–50.
3 Letter to Georges Izambard, 13 May 1871. Arthur Rimbaud, *Oeuvres Complètes*, ed. Rolland de Renéville and Jules Mouquet (Paris: Editions Gallimard, 1963), 268.
4 Friedrich Nietzsche, *Die fröhliche Wissenschaft*, §307.
5 Taylor, *Sources of the Self*, 10–11.
6 "У меня есть прожект: сделаться сумасшедшим. Пусть люди бесятся, пусть лечат, пусть делают умным." *PSS* 28.1: 51.
7 "Ужасно видеть человека у которого во власти непостижимое, человека, который не знает, что делать ему, играет игрушкой, которая есть—бог!" Ibid.
8 "Чтоб больше *знать*, надо меньше *чувствовать*, и обратно, правило опрометчивое, бред сердца. Что ты хочешь сказать словом *знать*? Познать природу, душу, бога, любовь…Это познается сердцем, а не умом." Letter of 31 October 1838. *PSS* 28 Bk 1: 53. Emphasis in original.
9 "Проводник мысли сквозь бренную оболочку в состав души есть ум.

Ум—способность материальная…душа же, или дух, живет мыслию, которую нашептывает ей сердце… Мысль зарождается в душе. Ум—орудие, машина, движимая огнем душевным… Притом (2-я статья) ум человека, увлекшись в область знаний, действует независимо от *чувства*, след<овательно>, от *сердца*. Ежели же цель познания будет любовь и природа, тут открывается чистое поле *сердцу*…" *PSS* 28 Bk 1: 54. Translation by Andrew MacAndrew in Joseph Frank and David I. Goldstein, *Selected Letters of Fyodor Dostoyevsky* (Brunswick, NJ: Rutgers University Press, 1987), 10. Emphasis in original.

10 "Ведь дважды два четыре есть уже не жизнь, господа, а начало смерти." *PSS* 5: 118–119.

11 Frank 1976, 103–104. For a detailed examination of Dostoevsky as a Romantic writer, see also Donald Fanger, *Dostoevsky and Romantic Realism: A Study of Dostoevsky in Relation to Balzac, Dickens, and Gogol* (Cambridge, MA: Harvard University Press, 1965).

12 "Я ношусь в какой-то холодной, полярной атмосфере, куда не заползал луч солнечный…Я давно не испытывал взрывов вдохновенья…зато часто бываю и в таком состоянье, как, помнишь, Шильонский узник после смерти братьев в темнице…Не залетит ко мне райская птичка поэзии, не согреет охладелой души." *PSS* 28 Bk 1: 54.

13 "Ежели бы мы были духи, мы бы жили, носились в сфере той мысли, над которою носится душа наша, когда хочет разгадать ее. Мы же прах, люди должны разгадывать, но не могут обнять вдруг мысль." Ibid., 53–54.

14 De Jonge, *Dostoevsky and the Age of Intensity* (New York: St. Martin's Press, 1975), 23–25.

15 "И так везде у Достоевского. Живою тяжестью давят читателя его туманы, сумраки и моросящие дожди. Мрачная, отъединенная тоска заполняет душу. И вместе с Достоевским начинаешь любить эту тоску какою-то особенною, болезненною любовью." V.V. Veresaev, *Zhivaia zhizn': O Dostoevskom, O L've Tolstom, O Nitsshe* (Moscow: Izdatel'stvo "Respublika," 1999), 37.

16 Quoted in Joseph Frank, *Dostoevsky: The Seeds of Revolt, 1821–1849* (Princeton, NJ: Princeton University Press, 1976), 55.

17 Leonid Grossman, *Poetika Dostoevskogo*, vyp. 4 (Moscow: Gosudarstvennaia akademiia khudozhestvennykh nauk, 1925), 35.

18 Mark S. Simpson, *The Russian Gothic Novel and Its British Antecedents* (Columbus, OH: Slavica Publishers, 1986), 90.

19 Ibid.

20 Ibid., 95.

21 Andrei Dostoevskii, *Vospominaniia* (Moscow: Agraf, 1999), 65.

22 Originally a supplement attached to the political portion of French newspapers, the *feuilleton* consisted chiefly of non-political news and gossip, literature and art criticism, a chronicle of fashions, epigrams, charades, and other literary trifles. The *roman feuilleton* carried these conventions over into novel

format, incorporating ethnographic sketches of contemporary urban life. Influenced by the French, the *feuilleton* became a popular genre in Russia's nineteenth-century literary journals.

23 Andrei Dostoevskii, *Vospominaniia*, 69–70.
24 See Frank, *Dostoevsky: The Seeds of Revolt*, 105–112.
25 Ibid., 63–64 and 102–105.
26 Leonid Grossman, *Poetika Dostoevskogo*, 10–12.
27 De Jonge, *Dostoevsky and the Age of Intensity*, 15–16, 25.
28 Ibid., 22–23.
29 Ibid., 29.
30 Ibid., 25.
31 René Girard, *Deceit, Desire, and the Novel; Self and Other in Literary Structure*, trans. Yvonne Freccero (Baltimore, MD: Johns Hopkins Press, 1965), 62–63.
32 *PSS* 1: 120.
33 Laurence M. Porter, "The Devil as Double in Nineteenth-Century Literature: Goethe, Dostoevsky, and Flaubert," *Comparative Literary Studies* 15, no. 3 (1978): 316–317.
34 Andrei Dostoevskii, *Vospominaniia*, 69–70.
35 See Charles E. Passage, *Dostoevski the Adapter: A Study in Dostoevski's Use of The Tales of Hoffmann* (Chapel Hill, NC: University of North Carolina Press, 1954).
36 Ibid., note 7, p. 178.
37 Passage 6.
38 Antony Pogorelsky, *The Double, or My Evenings in Little Russia*, trans. and with an Introduction by Ruth Sobel (Ann Arbor, MI: Ardis, 1988). "Lafertovskaia makovnitsa" appeared in *Novosti literatury* (*The Literary News*) in 1825.
39 Ruth Sobel, "Introduction," in Pogorelsky, *The Double*, 13–14.
40 The story is near in theme to Hoffmann's "Sandman," which also deals with the tragic love of a sensitive young man, endowed with a powerful imagination, toward a doll constructed by a skilful mechanic. Pogorelsky's story lacks Hoffmann's depth and originality, and the author was accused of misunderstanding Hoffmann. See Sobel, 14.
41 "Взгляните на свет: сколько встретите вы кукол обоего пола, которые совершенно ничего иного не делают и делать не умеют, как только гуляют по улицам, пляшут на балах, приседают и улыбаются. Несмотря на то, частехонько в них влюбляются и даже иногда предпочитают их людям, несравненно достойнейшим!" Antonii Pogorel'skii, *Izbrannoe* (Moscow: Sovetskaia Rossiia, 1985), 85. Translation by Sobel, 65.
42 Pogorelsky, *The Double*, 87–101.
43 "А ты не смущайся и не ропщи на то, что вот между нами такое странное теперь обстоятельство: роптать, брат, грешно; это природа! А мать-природа щедра, вот что, брат Яша! Любя тебя, братски любя тебя, говорю." *PSS* 1: 158. Translation by George Bird in Fyodor Dostoevsky, *A Poem of St. Petersburg* (Bloomington: Indiana University Press, 1958), 112.

44 "Если ты меня забудешь, / Не забуду я тебя; / В жизни может всё случиться, / Не забудь и ты меня!" *PSS* 1: 157; Bird (trans.), *The Double*, 111.
45 "…чтоб и ты был спокоен и счастлив. Вот мы теперь все счастливы, так чтоб и ты был спокоен и счастлив. А теперь спокойной ночи желаю тебе. Усни, Петруша, усни." *PSS* 1: 159; Bird (trans.), *The Double*, 114.
46 "Читал ли ты «Емелю» Вельтмана, в послед<ней> «Б<иблиотеке> д<ля> ч<тения>»"—что за прелесть." Letter of 4 May 1845, *PSS* 28 Bk 1: 110.
47 V.A. Koshelev and A.V. Chernov, "Mudraia fantaziia skazochnika," in A.F. Vel'tman, *Serdtse i dumka* (Moscow: Sovetskaia Rossiia, 1986), 11.
48 Andrei Dostoevskii, *Vospominaniia*, 69–70.
49 "Явится ли в ком-нибудь слепая вера, он поселял сомнение; сойдется ли кто с кем-нибудь по чувствам, он внушал подозрение; настанет ли тишина в душе и сердце, он тотчас нагонит облачко, которое разрастется в невзгодье; и везде, где только таится искорка под пеплом, он ее раздует,—везде нашушукает, везде наплетет, все смутит, расстроит." Vel'tman, *Serdtse i dumka*, 35.
50 "Поэта, живущего всегда в воздушном пространстве, он не считал под своим ведением." Ibid., 83.
51 Frank, *Dostoevsky: The Seeds of Revolt*, 179.
52 For analysis of the culturally specific word *sud'ba*, see Anna Wierzbicka, *Semantics, Culture, and Cognition* (New York: Oxford University Press, 1992), 66–67. The concept stems from Russian folk philosophy and is fundamental to the national character and psychology. It often implies an attitude of acceptance or resignation toward one's destiny, even a love for one's fate or suffering.
53 There are brief mentions of Odoevsky in Dostoevsky's letters of 16 November 1845, in which he claims that Vladimir Fyodorovich was begging him (amid the hype surrounding the success of *Poor Folk*) for a visit (*PSS* 28 Bk 1: 115), and February 1, 1846, when he refers to alleged plans of Odoevsky and V.A. Sollogub to write separate articles on *Poor Folk* (neither of which appeared). Ibid., 117.
54 Frank, *Dostoevsky: The Seeds of Revolt*, 179.
55 "Не верь ему,—говорил сей последний,—или, лучше сказать, не верь мне в твоём мире. Там я сам не знаю, что делаю, но здесь я понимаю мои поступки, которые в вашем мире представляются в виде *невольных побуждений*. Там я подарил тебе игрушку, сам не зная для чего, но здесь я имел в виду предостеречь твоего дядю и моего благодетеля от несчастия, которое грозило всему вашему семейству." V.F. Odoevskii, *Kosmorama*, edited with introduction, notes, bibliography, and vocabulary by Roger Cockrell (London: Bristol Classical Press, 1998), 9. Translation by Neil Cornwell in *The Salamander and Other Gothic Tales: Eight Stories by Vladimir Odoevsky* (Evanston, IL: Northwestern University Press, 1992), 96. Emphasis in original.
56 "Злополучный счастливец! Ты—ты можешь всё видеть—всё, без покрышки, без звёздной пелены, которая для меня самого *там* непроницаема. Мои мысли я должен передавать себе посредством сцепления

мелочных обстоятельств жизни, посредством символов, тайных побуждений, тёмных намёков, которые я часто понимаю криво или которых вовсе не понимаю." Ibid. Emphasis in original.

57 "Я видел графа Б. в различных возрастах его жизни... я видел, как над изголовьем его матери, в минуту его рождения, вились безобразные чудовища и с дикою радостью встречал новорождённого. Вот его воспитание: гнусное чудовище между им и его наставником—одному нашёптывает, другому толкует мысли себялюбия, безверия, жестокосердия, гордости; вот появление в свете молодого человека: то же гнусное чудовище руководит его поступками, внушает ему тонкую сметливость, осторожность, коварство, наверное, устраивает для него успехи..." Odoevskii, *Kosmorama*, 30; Cornwell (trans.), *Salamander*, 114.

58 I compare "The Sylph" to Dostoevsky's 1877 story "The Dream of a Ridiculous Man" in "Reasonable to Ridiculous: The Inward Gaze of the Modern Self in Dostoevskii and Vladimir Odoevskii," *Canadian Slavonic Papers* 55, nos. 3–4 (September–December 2013): 343–363.

59 Neil Cornwell, ed., *The Gothic-fantastic in Nineteenth-century Russian Literature* (Amsterdam and Atlanta: Rodopi, 1999), 7–8.

60 Neil Cornwell, *The Life, Times, and Milieu of V.F. Odoyevsky, 1804–1869* (London: Athlone Press, 1986), 110.

61 See Pamela Davidson, ed., *Russian Literature and Its Demons* (New York and Oxford: Berghahn Books, 2000).

62 Porter, "The Devil as Double," 318.

63 Ibid., 319.

64 "Господин Голядкин уже давным-давно знал, что у них там что-то приготовляется, что у них там есть кто-то другой." *PSS* 1: 144.

65 "Увы! он это давно уже предчувствовал!" *PSS* 1: 229. NB: This episode is taken from the alternate ending Dostoevsky gave to the story in the published revision of 1866 (see Chapter 3, this volume).

66 Roger B. Anderson, *Dostoevsky: Myths of Duality* (Gainesville: University of Florida Press, 1986), 2.

67 Ibid., 67.

68 See my discussion in Chapter 3 of Dostoevsky's efforts to revise *The Double* in the mid-1860s.

69 Belinsky wrote, "Every deficiency in *Poor Folk* that was pardonable for a first work appeared to be a monstrous error in *The Double*, and this all stems from one cause: the inability of too rich a talent to define a reasonable measure for the artistic development of his idea and to know its boundaries," and "In *The Double* there is yet another substantial shortcoming: its fantastic coloration. The fantastic in our time has a place only in the madhouse, and not in literature, and it requires the expertise of doctors, not of writers." Vissarion Belinskii, "Vzgliad na russkuiu literaturu 1846-go goda," in V.G. Belinskii, *Sobranie sochinenii v deviati tomakh*, vol. 8 (Moscow: Khudozhestvennaia literatura, 1976–82), 213.

70 Malcolm Jones, *Dostoevsky after Bakhtin: Readings in Dostoyevsky's Fantastic Realism* (Cambridge: Cambridge University Press, 1990), 30.
71 Joseph Frank, *Dostoevsky: The Years of Ordeal 1850–1859* (Princeton, NJ: Princeton University Press, 1990), 173. See also Chapter 1, note 44, and Chapter 4, p. 120.
72 For further discussion on two of these uses of "The Vision of the Neva," see Frank, *Dostoevsky: The Seeds of Revolt*, 133–134.
73 "Какая-то странная мысль вдруг зашевелилась во мне. Я вздрогнул, и сердце мое как будто облилось в это мгновение горячим ключом крови, вдруг вскипевшей от прилива могущественного, но доселе незнакомого мне ощущения. Я как будто что-то понял в эту минуту, до сих пор только шевелившееся во мне, но еще не осмысленное; как будто прозрел во что-то новое, совершенно в новый мир, мне незнакомый и известный только по каким-то темным слухам, по каким-то таинственным знакам." *PSS* 19: 69.
74 "Всё это были странные, чудные фигуры, вполне прозаические, вовсе не Дон Карлосы и Позы, а вполне титулярные советники и в то же время как будто какие-то фантастические титулярные советники …. какое-то титулярное сердце, честное и чистое, нравственное и преданное начальству, а вместе с ним какая-то девочка, оскорбленная и грустная, и глубоко разорвала мне сердце вся их история." *PSS* 19: 71.
75 See Robert Louis Jackson's discussion of the tragedy of naive idealism in the face of evil in *The Insulted and Injured* in *Dostoevsky's Quest for Form: A Study of His Philosophy of Art* (New Haven, CT, and London: Yale University Press, 1966), 10–11.
76 *PSS* 23 Bk 1: 175.
77 Frederick C. Copleston, *Philosophy in Russia from Herzen to Lenin and Berdyaev* (Notre Dame, IN: University of Notre Dame Press, 1986), 145.
78 Ibid., 145–148.
79 Ibid., 143–150.
80 Steven Cassedy, *Dostoevsky's Religion* (Stanford, CA: Stanford University Press, 2005), 134–135.
81 Ibid., 147.
82 Ibid., 146–147.
83 Ibid., 147–148.
84 See Nick F. Gier, "Dialectic: East and West," *Indian Philosophical Quarterly* 10 (January 1983): 207–218.
85 Ibid.
86 David L. Hall and Roger T. Ames, *Thinking from the Han: Self, Truth, and Transcendence in Chinese and Western Culture* (Albany: State University of New York Press, 1998), 8.
87 Ibid., 4.
88 Ibid., 18.
89 Ibid. Emphasis in original.

90 Ibid., 17; the quote is from Richard Rorty.
91 Copleston, *Philosophy in Russia*, 150.
92 Cassedy, *Dostoevsky's Religion*, 122–125.
93 Ibid., 120–121.
94 Ibid., 121.
95 Ibid., 126.
96 Ibid., 136.
97 Ibid., 139–140.
98 *PSS* 20: 191–203. For a discussion of the projected article, see Joseph Frank, *Dostoevsky: The Stir of Liberation, 1860–1865* (Princeton, NJ: Princeton University Press, 1986), 371–374.
99 See Frank, *Dostoevsky: The Seeds of Revolt*, 105–112.
100 "Социалисты хотят переродить человека, *освободить* его, представить его без бога и без семейства. Они заключают, что, изменив насильно экономический быт его, цели достигнут. Но человек изменится не от *внешних* причин, а не иначе как от перемены *нравственной*. Раньше не оставит бога, как уверившись математически, а семейства прежде, чем мать не захочет быть матерью, а человек не захочет обратить любовь в клубничку. Можно ли достигнуть этого оружием? И как сметь сказать заране, прежде опыта, что в этом спасение? И это рискуя всем человечеством. Западная дребедень." *PSS* 20: 171–172. Translation by Frank, in *Dostoevsky: The Stir of Liberation*, 374–375. Emphasis in original.
101 Liza Knapp, *The Annihilation of Inertia: Dostoevsky and Metaphysics* (Evanston, IL: Northwestern University Press, 1996), 22–23.
102 Ibid., 14–16.
103 *PSS* 20: 194; Dostoevsky's emphasis; quoted in James P. Scanlan, *Dostoevsky the Thinker* (Ithaca, NY, and London: Cornell University Press, 2002), 189. Translations here and below by Scanlan.
104 *PSS* 24: 276; Dostoevsky's emphasis; quoted in Scanlan, *Dostoevsky the Thinker*, 189.
105 *PSS* 30 Bk 1: 14–15; quoted in Scanlan, *Dostoevsky the Thinker*, 190.
106 Frederick C. Copleston, *Philosophy in Russia from Herzen to Lenin and Berdyaev* (Notre Dame, IN: University of Notre Dame Press, 1986), 35.
107 Scanlan, *Dostoevsky the Thinker*, 192.
108 "Человек возвращается в массу, в непосредственную жизнь, след<овательно>, в естественное состояние, но как? Не авторитетно, а, напротив, в высшей степени самовольно и сознательно. Ясно, что это высшее самоволие есть в то же время высшее отречение от своей воли. В том моя воля, чтоб не иметь воли, ибо идеал прекрасен." *PSS* 20: 192. Translation by Scanlan, *Dostoevsky the Thinker*, 192.
109 Scanlan, *Dostoevsky the Thinker*, 192.
110 Richard Tarnas, *Cosmos and Psyche: Intimations of a New World View* (New York: Plume Books, 2007), 485.

111 Richard Peace, "Dostoevsky and the 'Golden Age,'" *Dostoevsky Studies* 3 (1982): 74. On the Golden Age in Dostoevsky, also see A. Boyce Gibson, *The Religion of Dostoevsky* (Philadelphia: Westminster Press, 1973), 154–168.
112 So named after the publication of *Vekhi* (*Landmarks* or *Signposts*, 1909), a collection of essays published in reaction to the positivism and materialism that had dominated the century. The Vekhi group critiqued Marxism and favoured the inner spiritual life of the individual over social revolution. See Frederick C. Copleston, *Russian Religious Philosophy: Selected Aspects* (Notre Dame, IN: University of Notre Dame Press, 1988), 17–36.
113 Ibid., 19–20.
114 Ibid., 20.
115 Ksana Blank, *Dostoevsky's Dialectics and the Problem of Sin* (Evanston, IL: Northwestern University Press, 2010), 13. Also see Copleston, *Russian Religious Philosophy*, Chapter 4, "The Human Being: The Concept of Godmanhood," and Chapter 5, "The Concept of Sophia."
116 Ksana Blank, "The Rabbit and the Duck: Antinomic Unity in Dostoevskij, the Russian Religious Tradition, and Mikhail Bakhtin," *Studies in East European Thought* 59, nos. 1–2 (2007): 33.
117 Ibid., 21.
118 Ksana Blank, *Dostoevsky's Dialectics and the Problem of Sin* (Evanston, IL: Northwestern University Press, 2010), 13.
119 Ibid., 22.
120 Ibid., 22–23.
121 Ibid., 10.

Notes to Chapter 3

1 *PSS* 16: 330. See the discussion in Bruce K. Ward, *Dostoevsky's Critique of the West: The Quest for the Earthly Paradise* (Waterloo, ON: Wilfrid Laurier University Press, 1986), 39. Translation by Ward; Dostoevsky's emphasis.
2 Ibid. Dostoevsky's emphasis.
3 See Ward, *Dostoevsky's Critique*, 39–61. On loss of whole meaning, disorder, and "rootlessness," also see Alex de Jonge, *Dostoevsky and the Age of Intensity* (New York: St. Martin's Press, 1975), 90–109.
4 V.V. Veresaev, *Zhivaia zhizn': O Dostoevskom, O L've Tolstom, O Nitsshe* (Moscow: Izdatel' stvo "Respublika," 1999), 41.
5 *PSS* 14: 99–100; quoted in Belknap, *The Structure of* The Brothers Karamazov (The Hague and Paris: Mouton, 1967), 19.
6 "Тут берега сходятся, тут все противоречия вместе живут." *PSS* 14: 100. See Chapter 4 in this volume for my discussion on the principle of complementarity of opposites.
7 Veresaev, *Zhivaia zhizn'*, 67.
8 *PSS* 14: 105. Translation by Belknap, *The Structure of* The Brothers Karamazov, 20.

9 "А что, если [в будущей жизни] одни пауки или что-нибудь в этом роде,—сказал он вдруг.... Нам вот всё представляется вечность как идея, которую понять нельзя, что-то огромное, огромное! Да почему же непременно огромное? И вдруг, вместо всего этого, представьте себе, будет там одна комнатка, эдак вроде деревенской бани, закоптелая, а по всем углам пауки, и вот вся вечность. Мне, знаете, в этом роде иногда мерещится." *PSS* 6: 221.

10 "Мне как будто казалось временами, что я вижу, в какой-то странной и невозможной форме, эту бесконечную силу, это глухое, темное и немое существо. Я помню, что кто-то будто бы повел меня за руку, со свечкой в руках, показал мне какого-то огромного и отвратительного тарантула и стал уверять меня, что это то самое темное, глухое и всесильное существо, и смеялся над моим негодованием." *PSS* 8: 340.

11 "Я не в силах подчиняться темной силе, принимающей вид тарантула." *PSS* 8: 341. See the discussion in Veresaev, *Zhivaia zhizn'*, 85.

12 Beverly Hansen Weisblatt, "The Numinous on Russian Soil: A Depth Psychological Interpretation of Religious Experience in *The Brothers Karamazov*," Master's thesis, Pacifica Graduate Institute (2010): 94–95.

13 Joseph Frank, *Dostoevsky: The Years of Ordeal 1850–1859* (Princeton, NJ: Princeton University Press, 1990); James Rice, *Dostoevsky and the Healing Art: An Essay in Literary and Medical History* (Ann Arbor, MI: Ardis, 1985; George Gibian, "C.G. Carus' *Psyche* and Dostoevsky," *American Slavic and East European Review* 14, no. 3 (1955): 371–382.

14 Frank, *Dostoevsky: The Years of Ordeal*, 173.

15 Ibid., 172–173.

16 Rice, *Dostoevsky and the Healing Art*, 134, 136.

17 Ibid., 134–138.

18 *PSS* 28 Bk 1: 173. For discussion, see Malcolm Jones, *Dostoevsky and the Dynamics of Religious Experience* (London: Anthem Press, 2005), 8.

19 Jones, *Dostoevsky and the Dynamics of Religious Experience*, 8.

20 George Gibian, "C.G. Carus' *Psyche* and Dostoevsky," *American Slavic and East European Review* 14, no. 3 (1955): 376.

21 Ibid.

22 Jung, *Mysterium Coniunctionis*, CW, Vol. 14; quoted in Richard Noll, *The Jung Cult: Origins of a Charismatic Movement* (Princeton, NJ: Princeton University Press, 1994), 42.

23 C.G. Jung, *Four Archetypes: Mother, Rebirth, Spirit, Trickster*, trans. R.F.C. Hull (Princeton, NJ: Princeton University Press, 1970), 3.

24 *PSS* 1: 489.

25 P.I. Avanesov, "Dostoevskii v rabote nad 'Dvoinikom.'" In *Tvorcheskaia istorriia: Issledovaniia po russkoi literature*, edited by N.K. Piksanov, 124–191 (Moscow: Nikitinskie subbotniki, 1927), 161–162.

26 *PSS* 1: 435. Dostoevsky's emphasis. Compare revisions of the two versions and see the discussion in *The Double: Two Versions*, ed. and trans. Evelyn J. Harden (Ann Arbor, MI: Ardis), 1985. Translation here by Harden.

27 Joseph Frank, *Dostoevsky: The Stir of Liberation, 1860–1865* (Princeton, NJ: Princeton University Press, 1986), 371.
28 Ibid., 311–312.
29 *PSS* 16: 329.
30 "Итак, человек стремится на земле к идеалу, *противуположному* его натуре." *PSS* 20: 175. Emphasis in original.
31 "…[закон] развития личности и достижения окончательной цели, которым связан человек." Ibid., 174.
32 "Когда человек не исполнил закона стремления к идеалу, то есть не приносил *любовью* в жертву своего *я* людям или другому существу…он чувствует страдание и назвал это состояние грехом." Ibid., 175. Emphasis in original.
33 See my discussion in Chapter 2, this volume.
34 *PSS* 5: 102–104.
35 "Где у меня первоначальные причины, на которые я упрусь, где основания? Откуда я их возьму? Я упражняюсь в мышлении, а следственно, у меня всякая первоначальная причина тотчас же тащит за собою другую, еще первоначальнее, и так далее в бесконечность. Такова именно сущность всякого сознания и мышления." *PSS* 5: 108.
36 See Carl G. Jung et al., *Man and His Symbols* (London: Aldus Books, 1964), 186.
37 Ibid., 195.
38 Ibid., 192–193.
39 Jung, *Symbols of Transformation*, CW Vol. 5, 1970, 16.
40 Joanna Hubbs, *Mother Russia: The Feminine Myth in Russian Culture* (Bloomington and Indianapolis: Indiana University Press, 1988), xiv–xv.
41 Hubbs, *Mother Russia*, xv.
42 Ibid.
43 Ibid., 213–214.
44 Ibid., 228–229.
45 Richard Avramenko and Jingcai Ying, "Dostoevsky's Heroines: Or, on the Compassion of the Russian Woman" in Richard Avramenko and Lee Trepanier, eds., *Dostoevsky's Political Thought* (Lanham, MD: Lexington Books, 2013), 73–74.
46 Ibid., 75–76.
47 Hubbs, *Mother Russia*, 229–230.
48 Respectively, Robert Louis Jackson, *Dostoevsky's Quest for Form: A Study of His Philosophy of Art* (New Haven, CT, and London: Yale University Press, 1966), 214; and Richard Peace, *Dostoevsky: An Examination of the Major Novels* (Cambridge: Cambridge University Press, 1971), 83.
49 Patricia Flanagan Behrendt, "The Russian Iconic Representation of the Christian Madonna: A Feminine Archetype in *Notes from Underground*," in Alexej Ugrinsky, Frank S. Lambasa, and Valija K. Ozolins, eds., *Dostoevski and the Human Condition after a Century* (New York: Greenwood Press, 1986), 136–137.

50 Ibid., 137–138.
51 Ibid., 139.
52 Ibid., 140.
53 *PSS* 5: 174–175. Quoted in Behrendt, "The Russian Iconic Representation of the Christian Madonna," 141.
54 "…для женщины в любви-то и заключается всё восресенье, всё спасение от какой бы то ни было гибели и всё возрождение, да иначе и проявиться не может, как в этом." *PSS* 5: 176.
55 *PSS* 6: 422.
56 Diana Cusmerenco, "Representations of the Archetype of the Fatal Woman in *The Idiot* by Dostoevsky and *The Most Beloved of Earthlings* by Marin Preda: Natasya Filippovna and Matilda," *Wiener Slavistisches Jahrbuch* 1.1 (2013): 43–61. Another reading interprets Nastasya Filippovna as a Mary Magdalene type or representative figure of the fallen woman. See Richard Peace, "Dostoevsky and the 'Golden Age,'" *Dostoevsky Studies* 3 (1982): 83.
57 Cusmerenco, "Representations of the Archetype of the Fatal Woman," 49–53. Emphasis in original.
58 Ibid., 52.
59 Ibid., 50.
60 Ibid., 51. Emphasis in original.
61 Avramenko and Ying, "Dostoevsky's Heroines," 59.
62 George P. Fedotov, *The Russian Religious Mind*, vol. 3 (Belmont, MA: Nordland Publishing, 1975), 376. Cited in Behrendt, "The Russian Iconic Representation of the Christian Madonna," 140.
63 Avramenko and Ying, "Dostoevsky's Heroines," 81.
64 A similar distinction is made by the Russian Orthodox theologian and philosopher Pavel Florensky in *Iconostasis* (1922). Florensky differentiates between "countenance" [*lik*], the face which reveals the image or likeness of God, and "mask" [*lichina*], an empty form with no metaphysical substance. Florensky comments on Dostoevsky's interpretation of the dichotomy: "As sin possesses a personality, and as the face ceases to be a window through which God's radiance shines, becoming streaked with the always more visible darkness, the face separates from the personality—from, that is, its creative origin—and loses its vitality in becoming a chilling mask of possession by the passions. Dostoevsky well understood this process in his character Stavrogin, whose face had become a stony mask and no longer a real face: such is one of the steps in the disintegration of personality." Pavel Florensky, *Iconostasis*, trans. Donald Sheehan and Olga Andrejev (Crestwood, NY: St. Vladimir's Seminary Press, 1996), 55–56.
65 Bernard J. Paris, *Dostoevsky's Greatest Characters: A New Approach to "Notes from Underground,"* Crime and Punishment, *and* The Brothers Karamazov (New York: Palgrave Macmillan, 2008), 89; also see Paris's discussion of the Underground Man's personality, 3–47.
66 Donna Orwin, *Consequences of Consciousness: Turgenev, Dostoevsky, and Tolstoy* (Stanford, CA: Stanford University Press, 2007), 23.

67 Ibid., 23–24.
68 "Что же собственно до меня касается, то ведь я только доводил в моей жизни до крайности то, что вы не осмеливались доводить и до половины, да еще трусость свою принимали за благоразумие, и тем утешались, обманывая сами себя. Так что я, пожалуй, еще «живее» вас выхожу." *PSS* 5: 178.
69 Orwin, *Consequences of Consciousness*, 7.
70 "Конечно, страшен диссонанс, страшно неравновесие, которое представляет нам общество. *Вне* должно быть уравновешено с *внутренним*. Иначе, с отсутствием внешних явлений, внутреннее возьмет слишком опасный верх. Нервы и фантазия займут очень много места в существе. Всякое внешнее явление с непривычки кажется колоссальным и пугает как-то. Начинаешь бояться жизни." *PSS* 23: 137–138. Italics in original.
71 "Начало личное, начало особняка, усиленного самосохранения, самопромышления, самоопределения в своем собственном Я, сопоставления этого Я всей природе и всем остальным людям, как самоправного отдельного начала, совершенно равного и равноценного всему тому, что есть кроме него." *PSS* 5: 79.
72 James Scanlan, *Dostoevsky the Thinker* (Ithaca, NY, and London: Cornell University Press, 2002), 69.
73 Ibid., 75.
74 *PSS* 20: 172–175. See the chapter "Belief Is Ideal" (115–148) in Steven Cassedy, *Dostoevsky's Religion* (Stanford, CA: Stanford University Press, 2005); and Scanlan, *Dostoevsky the Thinker* (21–24, 49–50, 82–84, and 191–196 passim) for comprehensive analyses of the passage in question.
75 "Закон личности на земле связывает. Я препятствует." *PSS* 20: 172–173.
76 Scanlan, *Dostoevsky the Thinker*, 177.
77 *PSS* 5: 79–80. See Scanlan, *Dostoevsky the Thinker*, 61.
78 *PSS* 20: 172–174. See Cassedy, *Dostoevsky's Religion*, 136; and Scanlan, *Dostoevsky the Thinker*, 82–83.
79 Scanlan, *Dostoevsky the Thinker*, 83.
80 "Сам знаю, как дважды два, что вовсе не подполье лучше, а что-то другое, совсем другое, которого я жажду, но которого никак не найду! К черту подполье!" *PSS* 5: 121.
81 See René Girard, *Resurrection from the Underground: Feodor Dostoevsky* (New York: Crossroad Publishing, 1997), 52–53.
82 Jung 1970, *Four Archetypes*, 76.
83 See Ward, *Dostoevsky's Critique*, 37–38.
84 "Это должно быть нечто ужасно простое, самое обыденное и глаза бросающееся, ежедневное и ежеминутное, и до того простое, что мы никак не можем поверить, чтоб оно было так просто, и, естественно, проходим мимо вот уже многие тысячи лет, не замечая и не узнавая." *PSS* 13: 178.
85 Scanlan, *Dostoevsky the Thinker*, 189.
86 *PSS* 19: 126. See the discussion in Scanlan, *Dostoevsky the Thinker*, 191.
87 Scanlan, *Dostoevsky the Thinker*, 83. See *PSS* 25: 62 and 24: 213.

Notes to Chapter 4

1. C.G. Jung, *The Portable Jung*, ed. Joseph Campbell, trans. R.F.C. Hull (New York: Penguin Books, 1976), 87.
2. Carl Jung 1969, *Psychology and Religion*, CW 11, pars. 130–134; cited in *The Essential Jung*, selected and introduced by Anthony Storr (Princeton, NJ: Princeton University Press, 1983), 90.
3. See chapter 2, "The Structure of Inherent Relationships" (22–53), in Robert Belknap, *The Structure of* The Brothers Karamazov (The Hague and Paris: Mouton, 1967).
4. Ibid., 26–32.
5. Ibid., 39.
6. Ibid., 45; emphasis my own.
7. Ibid., 45.
8. Ibid., 46–47.
9. Ibid., 48.
10. Ibid., 48. Also see my discussion of this epigraph in the Chapter 5 section, "Myths of Death and Renewal."
11. Ibid., 49–50.
12. "Мы уже видели, что юмористические описания его находились во вражде и в противоречии с сентиментально и религиозно построенной фантастикой и романтизмом, к которому он был склонен. Приходится удивляться, – говорит Котляревский, – что при такой душевной организации Гоголь мог так часто забывать о себе, иронизировать тогда, когда хотелось рассуждать и говорить о всякой житейской мелочи и пошлости, когда душа так и рвалась к возвышенном и вечному." I.D. Ermakov, *Psikhoanaliz literatury. Pushkin. Gogol'. Dostoevskii* (Moscow: Novoe literaturnoe obozrenie, 1999), 187. Ermakov is citing Nestor Kotliarevskii, *Nikolai Vasil'evich Gogol', 1829-1842: ocherk iz istorii russkoi povesti i dramy* (St. Petersburg: Tip. M.M. Stasiulevicha, 1911), 518.
13. "Раздражающая отъединенность духа от тела, хилость связи между ними делает героев Достоевского совершенно неспособными к яркой цельной страсти." V.V. Veresaev, *Zhivaia zhizn': O Dostoevskom, O L've Tolstom, O Nitsshe* (Moscow: Izdatel'stvo "Respublika," 1999), 70.
14. "Если не откроется выхода в бездушие в самоубийство или убийство, то останется только один выход—пошлость." Ibid., 71.
15. Nicholas Berdyaev, *Dostoevsky*, trans. Donald Attwater (New York: Meridian Books, 1968), 13; quoted in Ksana Blank, *Dostoevsky's Dialectics and the Problem of Sin* (Evanston, IL: Northwestern University Press, 2010), 8.
16. Blank, *Dostoevsky's Dialectics*, 8.
17. Jung 1969, CW 14, xiii.
18. Ibid., 3.
19. Ibid., 17.
20. "Тут берега сходятся, тут все противоречия вместе живут." *PSS* 14: 100.
21. Belknap, *The Structure of* The Brothers Karamazov, 30–33.

22 *PSS* 15: 129; quoted in Belknap, *The Structure of* The Brothers Karamazov, 33.
23 Ibid.
24 Beverly Hansen Weisblatt, "The Numinous on Russian Soil: A Depth Psychological Interpretation of Religious Experience in *The Brothers Karamazov*," Master's thesis, Pacifica Graduate Institute (2010). For discussion see Weisblatt's chapter, "*Coniunctio* Symbolism in *The Brothers Karamazov*," 65–85.
25 Ibid., 68–69.
26 Ibid., 70.
27 Ibid., 70–71.
28 Ibid., 70–72.
29 Ibid., 73.
30 Ibid., 78.
31 Ibid., 78–79.
32 Ibid., 79.
33 Ibid., 79–80.
34 Ibid., 81–83.
35 Joseph Frank, *Dostoevsky: The Years of Ordeal, 1850–1859* (Princeton, NJ: Princeton University Press, 1990), 206.
36 Ibid.
37 See Bruce K. Ward, *Dostoevsky's Critique of the West: The Quest for the Earthly Paradise* (Waterloo, ON: Wilfrid Laurier University Press, 1986); and Alex de Jonge, *Dostoevsky and the Age of Intensity* (New York: St. Martin's Press, 1975).
38 Gary Saul Morson, "Prosaic Bakhtin: *Landmarks*, Anti-Intelligentsialism, and the Russian Countertradition," in *Bakhtin in Contexts: Across the Disciplines*, ed. Amy Mandelker (Evanston, IL: Northwestern University Press, 1995), 33.
39 *PSS* 25: 115.
40 *PSS* 25: 116–117.
41 William J. Leatherbarrow, "Apocalyptic Imagery in *The Idiot* and *The Devils*," *Dostoevsky Studies* 3 (1982): 44.
42 Ibid.
43 *PSS* 14: 222.
44 Liza Knapp, *The Annihilation of Inertia: Dostoevsky and Metaphysics* (Evanston, IL: Northwestern University Press, 1996), 14. See *PSS* 20: 175.
45 "Словом, идея о бессмертии—это сама жизнь, живая жизнь, ее окончательная формула и главный источник истины и правильного сознания для человечества." *PSS* 24: 46–50.
46 "Косность! О, природа! Люди на земле одни—вот беда!…Всё мертво, и всюду мертвецы. Одни только люди, а кругом них молчание—вот земля!" *PSS* 24: 35. See Ludmila Koehler, "Five Minutes Too Late…," *Dostoevsky Studies* 6 (1985): 113–124. Translation by Koehler, 120–121.
47 Cited in Koehler, "Five Minutes," 121.
48 Koehler, "Five Minutes," 121; *PSS* 13: 49.
49 Koehler, "Five Minutes," 121; *PSS* 8: 326, 339–340.
50 "Учение материалистов—всеобщая косность и механизм вещества, значит смерть.… Учение истинной философии—уничтожение косности, то

есть мысль, то есть центр и Синтез вселенной и наружной формы ее—вещества, то есть бог, то есть жизнь бесконечная." *PSS* 20: 175. Translation by Koehler, "Five Minutes," 121–122.

51 "Bobok" appeared in 1873 in *Grazhdanin* (The Citizen), which would form the basis of Dostoevsky's *Diary of a Writer*.
52 *PSS* 21: 42.
53 See the connection of ideas presented in this tale to the mystical doctrines of Emanuel Swedenborg in Ilya Vinitsky, "Where Bobok Is Buried: The Theosophical Roots of Dostoevskii's 'Fantastic Realism,'" *Slavic Review* 65, no. 3 (Autumn 2006): 523–543. Also see the chapter "Dostoevsky and Swedenborg," in Czeslaw Milosz, *Emperor of the Earth: Modes of Eccentric Vision* (Berkeley: University of California Press, 1977).
54 "'Пред судом божиим во гресех равны.' 'Во гресех!... —И не смейте совсем со мной говорить!'" *PSS* 21: 45.
55 "Религия Достоевского во всяком случае.... лазарет для усталых, богодельня для немощных. Бог этой религии—только костыль, за который хватается безнадежно увечный человек. Хватается, пытается подняться и опереться, но костыль то и дело ломается. А кругом—мрачная, унылая пустыня, и царит над нею холодное 'безгласие косности.'" V.V. Veresaev, Zhivaia zhizn': O Dostoevskom, O L've Tolstom, O Nitsshe (Moscow: Izdatel'stvo "Respublika," 1999), 92.
56 *PSS* 24: 127; Scanlan, *Dostoevsky the Thinker* (Ithaca, NY, and London: Cornell University Press, 2002), 194.
57 *PSS* 18: 55. See Raffaella Vassena, *Reawakening National Identity: Dostoevskii's Diary of a Writer and Its Impact on Russian Society* (New York: Peter Lang, 2007), 23.
58 "Русская идея...будет синтезом всех тех идей, которые...развивает Европа." Quoted in Yuri Seleznev, *Dostoevskii* (Moscow: Molodaiia gvardiia, 1981), 222. For interpretations of the "Russian idea" vis-à-vis Dostoevsky, see Vassena, Hudspith, and Ward, cited above, as well as Linda Ivanits, *Dostoevsky and the Russian People* (Cambridge, UK: Cambridge University Press, 2008).
59 *PSS* 25: 20; see Scanlan, *Dostoevsky the Thinker*, 198.
60 Ward, *Dostoevsky's Critique of the West*, 28.
61 Tim McDaniel, *The Agony of the Russian Idea* (Princeton, NJ: Princeton University Press, 1996), 25.
62 McDaniel, *The Agony of the Russian Idea*, 34. The quote is from *Diary of a Writer* in its first month of publication, January 1873 (*PSS* 21: 36). McDaniel also cites Aleksandr Solzhenitsyn and other advocates of the same principle.
63 Ibid., 22–55. McDaniel is careful to point out, on the other hand, that the Russian idea is not entirely, nor is it exclusively Russian, that in fact many of its elements were borrowed from European social thought.
64 "Это должна быть и проповедь ..." Iurii Seleznev, *Dostoevskii* (Moscow: Molodaiia gvardiia, 1981), 210–211.
65 Martin Malia, *Russia under Western Eyes: From the Bronze Horseman to the Lenin Mausoleum* (Cambridge: Harvard University Press, 1999), 209.

66 *PSS* 14: 267, 286–287. See James Scanlan, *Dostoevsky the Thinker* (Ithaca, NY, and London: Cornell University Press, 2002), 159.
67 Steven Cassedy, *Dostoevsky's Religion* (Stanford, CA: Stanford University Press, 2005), 160–162.
68 Ibid., 167–168.
69 Ibid., 160.
70 See Chapter 1, note 44.
71 Ward, *Dostoevsky's Critique of the West*, 12.
72 Raffaella Vassena, *Reawakening National Identity: Dostoevskii's* Diary of a Writer *and Its Impact on Russian Society* (New York: Peter Lang, 2007), 27–28.
73 Deborah Martinsen, *Surprised by Shame: Dostoevsky's Liars and Narrative Exposure* (Columbus: Ohio State University Press, 2003).
74 Ward, *Dostoevsky's Critique of the West*, 12–13.
75 Ibid., 14–15.
76 Ibid.; emphasis my own.
77 Ibid., 15–16.
78 Joseph Frank, *Dostoevsky: The Mantle of the Prophet, 1871–1881* (Princeton, NJ: Princeton University Press, 2002), 384–387.
79 See Czeslaw Milosz's introduction to Vladimir Solovyov, *War, Progress and the End of History: Three Conversations, Including a Short Story of the Anti-Christ*, trans. Alexander Baksky (Hudson, NY: Lindisfarne Press, 1990). Also see my discussion on Solovyov and the Vekhi group in Chapter 2.
80 Letter of 18 August 1880; cited in Ward, *Dostoevsky's Critique of the West*, 17.
81 See Vassena, *Reawakening National Identity*, 28.
82 Ibid.
83 Ibid., 24–25.
84 Frank, *Dostoevsky: The Mantle of the Prophet*, 385.
85 "Не как мальчик же я верую во Христа и его исповедую, а через большое горнило сомнений моя осанна прошла…" *PSS* 27: 86; Dostoevsky's emphasis.
86 See *PSS* 29 Bk 1: 117.
87 Linda Ivanits, *Dostoevsky and the Russian People* (Cambridge, UK: Cambridge University Press, 2008), 6.
88 See Robert Louis Jackson, *Dostoevsky's Quest for Form: A Study of His Philosophy of Art* (New Haven, CT, and London: Yale University Press, 1966).
89 *PSS* 18: 80, 93. See the discussion in Vassena, *Reawakening National Identity*, 26. Translation by Vassena.
90 Достоевский видел в литературе не просто средство для проведения в жизнь определенных идей, нет—он верил в художественное слово как в силу самостоятельную, духовно преобразующую природу человеческую, созидающую в сознании народа идеал красоты…."; "Если в народе сохраняется идеал красоты и потребность ее, значит есть и потребность здоровья, нормы, а следственно, тем самым гарантировано и высшее развитие этого народа." Iurii Seleznev, *Dostoevskii* (Moscow: Molodaia gvardiia, 1981), 225.

91 *PSS* 19: 51; See Vassena, *Reawakening National Identity*, 26; translation by Vassena.
92 *PSS* 22: 12–13. The Golden Age in Stavrogin's dream in *The Devils* (1871) is also pertinent here. Peace argues that the dreams of the "Golden Age" in versions of Stavrogin, Versilov, and the Ridiculous Man have a polemical aspect, as they offer a refutation of nihilism. 61–78.
93 *PSS* 22: 32–37.
94 *PSS* 22: 39–42.
95 "Еще удивительно, как он дожил, сохранив человеческий образ, а не то что сохранив красоту его. Но он сохранил и красоту своего образа…. Судите русский народ не по тем мерзостям, которые он так часто делает, а по тем великим и святым вещам, по которым он и в самой мерзости своей постоянно воздыхает." *PSS* 22: 43.
96 "Это мы должны преклониться перед народом и ждать от него всего, и мысли и образа." *PSS* 22: 44–45.

Notes to Chapter 5
1 Sibelan Forrester, "Vladimir Propp and the Russian Folktale," preface to Vladimir Propp, *The Russian Folktale*, ed. and trans. Sibelan Forrester (Detroit, MI: Wayne State University Press, 2012), xiii–xxvi.
2 Vladimir Propp, *The Russian Folktale*, ed. and trans. Sibelan Forrester (Detroit, MI: Wayne State University Press, 2012), 55.
3 Ibid., 3–5.
4 Jack Zipes, "Toward Understanding the Complete Vladimir Propp," foreword to Propp, *The Russian Folktale*.
5 Propp, *The Russian Folktale*, 20.
6 Ibid., 24. Propp cites Iosif Tronskii, "Antichnyi mir i sovremennaia skazka" (Leningrad, 1934).
7 Linda Ivanits argues, on the other hand, that this distinction is artificial, in *Russian Folk Belief* (Armonk, NY: M.E. Sharpe, 1988).
8 Propp, *The Russian Folktale*, 23. On the question of genre and Propp's discussion of the relationship of the folktale to myth, see his Chapter 2, "The History of Study of the Folktale," 68–146.
9 Ibid., 20.
10 Forrester, "Vladimir Propp and the Russian Folktale," xiv–xv.
11 Propp, *The Russian Folktale*, 215–216.
12 Forrester, "Vladimir Propp and the Russian Folktale," xiv–xv.
13 Ibid.
14 Ibid., xv.
15 Propp, *The Russian Folktale*, 93.
16 Ibid., 93–94.
17 Ibid.
18 Ivanits, *Russian Folk Belief*, 6.

19 Propp, *The Russian Folktale*, 147. For a description and examination of the characteristics of the wonder tale and their functions, see Propp's Chapter 3, "The Wonder Tale" (147–224).
20 Ibid., 151–172.
21 Ibid., 27–29.
22 Ibid., 5–6.
23 Ibid., 8–11.
24 Maria Carlson, "Fashionable Occultism: Spiritualism, Theosophy, Freemasonry, and Hermeticism in Fin-de-Siècle Russia," in Bernice Glatzer Rosenthal, ed., *The Occult in Russian and Soviet Culture*, 135–152 (Ithaca, NY: Cornell University Press, 1997), 152.
25 "Если бога с земли изгонят, мы под землей его сретим! Каторжному без бога быть невозможно, невозможнее даже, чем некаторжному! И тогда мы, подземные человеки, запоем из недр земли трагический гимн богу, у которого радость! Да здравствует бог и его радость! Люблю его!" *PSS* 15: 31.
26 Interestingly, Freud used the phrase in his epigraph to *The Interpretation of Dreams*. See Richard Tarnas, *The Passion of the Western Mind: Understanding the Ideas That Have Shaped Our World View* (New York: Ballantine Books, 1991), 432. An alternative translation reads: "If I cannot deflect the will of Heaven, I shall move Hell."
27 Ksana Blank, *Dostoevsky's Dialectics and the Problem of Sin* (Evanston, IL: Northwestern University Press, 2010), 48. Curiously, Blank does not note the connection to the descent to the underworld in the *Aeneid*, nor do the editors of the Academy Edition of Dostoevsky's Collected Works (*PSS*).
28 Ibid. It must be noted, moreover, that the name "Karamazov" loosely translates as "black smear," or "smeared with black" (from *kara*- the Turkic root for "black," and the Russian verb *mazat'* – to spread, to smear), which associates the brothers with the earthy force of the underground, as well as conjures the stain of original sin. This is compounded by the fact that the word *kara* in Russian means "punishment," a synonym to *nakazanie*, which appears in the title of *Crime and Punishment*.
29 *PSS* 28 Bk 1: 164; Malcolm Jones, *Dostoevsky after Bakhtin: Readings in Dostoyevsky's Fantastic Realism* (Cambridge: Cambridge University Press, 1990), 46.
30 *PSS* 4: 232.
31 "Когда чувствуешь, что немощна плоть перед таким гнетом впечатлений, что разрывается вся нить бытия, и когда вместе с тем поздравляешь всю жизнь свою с обновлением и воскресением" *PSS* 1: 278.
32 *PSS* 9: 252.
33 As I mentioned in Chapter 3. See Jones, *Dostoevsky after Bakhtin*, 46–47.
34 Ibid., 53.
35 Ibid., 62.
36 Ibid., 45–46, 58, 62.
37 James Scanlan, *Dostoevsky the Thinker* (Ithaca, NY, and London: Cornell University Press, 2002), 50.

38 *PSS* 5: 121, 178. See Jones, *Dostoevsky after Bakhtin*, 12; V.V. Veresaev, *Zhivaia zhizn': O Dostoevskom, O L've Tolstom, O Nitsshe* (Moscow: Izdatel'stvo "Respublika," 1999); and my discussion in Chapter 3.
39 See Jones, *Dostoevsky after Bakhtin*, 192.
40 Joseph Campbell, *The Hero with a Thousand Faces*, 3rd ed. (Novato, CA: New World Library, 2008), 42–43.
41 Ibid., 46.
42 Ibid.
43 Ibid., 49–50.
44 Ibid., 59.
45 "Он не раскрыл ее и теперь, но одна мысль промелькнула в нем: «разве могут ее убеждения не быть теперь и моими убеждениями? Ее чувства, ее стремления, по крайне мере…»" *PSS* 6: 422.
46 "Но тут уж начинается новая история, история постепенного обновления человека, история постепенного перерождения его, постепенного перехода из одного мира в другой, знакомства с новою, доселе совершенно неведомою действительностью. Это могло бы составить тему нового рассказа, — но теперешний рассказ наш окончен." Ibid.
47 Joseph Campbell, *The Hero with a Thousand Faces*, 3rd ed. (Novato, CA: New World Library, 2008), 59–61.
48 Ibid., 61.
49 Ibid., 43.
50 Ibid., 74.
51 Ibid., 77.
52 Ibid., 67–68.
53 Ibid., 81.
54 Ibid., 84.
55 Quoted in John Holman, *The Return of the Perennial Philosophy: The Supreme Vision of Western Esotericism* (London: Watkins Publishing, 2008), 4.
56 Campbell, *The Hero,* 89.
57 Ibid., 35–36.
58 *PSS* 14: 272.
59 *PSS* 14: 262.
60 *PSS* 14: 275–276; Steven Cassedy, *Dostoevsky's Religion* (Stanford, CA: Stanford University Press, 2005), 139.
61 *PSS* 14: 290.
62 *PSS* 14: 328.
63 Bernice Glatzer Rosenthal, ed., *The Occult in Russian and Soviet Culture*, 135–152 (Ithaca, NY: Cornell University Press, 1997), 5.
64 On the meaning and significance of "living nature" in occult doctrine and practice, see Rosenthal, *The Occult in Russian and Soviet Culture*, 3–4.
65 Blank, *Dostoevsky's Dialectics and the Problem of Sin*, 4.
66 Jung 1964, 73.
67 Ibid., 79.

68 Campbell, *The Hero*, 31.
69 Robert Louis Jackson, *The Art of Dostoevsky: Deliriums and Nocturnes* (Princeton: Princeton University Press, 1981), 278.
70 "Есть секунды, их всего зараз приходит пять или шесть, и вы вдруг чувствуете присутствие вечной гармонии, совершенно достигнутой. Это не земное; я не про то, что оно небесное, а про то, что человек в земном виде не может перенести. Надо перемениться физический или умереть. Это чувство ясное и неоспоримое." *PSS* 10: 450.
71 Myshkin's egolessness [*samootverzhennost'*], childlike simplicity, and moral purity [*nravstvennaia chistota*] are qualities prefigured in such precursors of Dostoevsky's invention as the Dreamer from *White Nights* (1848), Colonel Rostanev of *The Village of Stepanchikovo and Its Inhabitants* (1859), Ivan Petrovich of *The Insulted and Injured* (1861), and the Dagestanian tatar Alei of *Notes from the House of the Dead* (1860–1862). See *PSS* 9: 337–338.
72 Jones, *Dostoevsky after Bakhtin*, 14–16.
73 "Ощущение жизни, самосознания почти удесятерялось в эти мгновения, продолжавшиеся как молния. Ум, сердце озарялись необыкновенным светом; все волнения, все сомнения его, все беспокойства как бы умиротворялись разом, разрешались в какое-то высшее спокойствие, полное ясной, гармоничной радости и надежды, полное разума и окончательной причины." *PSS* 8: 188.
74 Dostoevsky told Strakhov about similar personal experiences he had had: "I experience a happiness that is impossible under ordinary circumstances, and of which most people have no comprehension. I feel a complete harmony within myself and in the whole world, and this feeling is so strong, and affords so much pleasure, that one could give up ten years of one's life for several seconds of that ecstasy, perhaps one's whole life." Cited in Malcolm Jones, *Dostoevsky and the Dynamics of Religious Experience* (London: Anthem Press, 2005), 8. Translation by Jones.
75 Blank, *Dostoevsky's Dialectics and the Problem of Sin*, 11.
76 See Vladimir Lossky, "Apophasis and Trinitarian Theology," in Daniel B. Clendenin, ed., *Eastern Orthodox Theology: A Contemporary Reader*, 2nd ed. (Grand Rapids, MI: Baker Academic, 2003), 153–157.
77 Tarnas, *The Passion of the Western Mind*, 98–105.
78 Sarah J. Young, "Dostoevskii's *Idiot* and the Epistle of James," *Slavonic and East European Review* 81, no. 3 (July 2003): 403.
79 "Они дразнят меня теперь тем, что ведь это был только сон. Но неужели не всё равно, сон или нет, если сон этот возвестил мне Истину? Ведь если раз узнал истину и увидел ее, то ведь знаешь, что она истина и другой нет и не может быть, спите вы или живете." *PSS* 25: 109.
80 "Лица их сияли разумом и каким-то восполнившимся уже до спокойствия сознанием, но лица эти были веселы; в словах и голосах этих людей звучала детская радость." *PSS* 25: 112.
81 *PSS* 25: 114; see Scanlan, *Dostoevsky the Thinker*, 166.

82 "В один бы день, в один бы час—всё бы сразу устроилось! Главное—люби других как себя, вот что главное, и это всё, больше ровно ничего не надо: тотчас найдешь как устроиться." *PSS* 25: 119 (Dostoevsky's emphasis).
83 "Я смешной человек. Они меня называют теперь сумасшедшим.... Но теперь уж я не сержусь, теперь они все мне милы, и даже когда они смеются надо мной—и тогда чем-то даже особенно милы. Я бы сам смеялся с ними,—не то что над собой, а их любя, если б мне не было так грустно, на них глядя. Грустно потому, что они не знают истины, а я знаю истину. Ох как тяжело одному знать истину!" *PSS* 25: 104. See Pike: "This narrator…seeks urgently to persuade the reader of a truth which he has witnessed. The nature of that truth, however, is that direct, intuitional 'understanding' or 'perception' of life is pregnant with harmony, whereas rational analysis and categorisation ('the knowledge of laws') is barren." Christopher Pike, "Dostoevsky's 'The Dream of a Ridiculous Man': Seeing Is Believing," in *The Structural Analysis of Russian Narrative Fiction*, ed. Joe Andrew and Christopher Pike (Keele: Department of Russian Studies, Keele University, 1984), 46.
84 "Я видел истину,—не то что изобрел умом, а видел, видел, и живой образ ее наполнил душу мою навеки. Я видел ее в такой восполненной целости, что не могу поверить, чтоб ее не могло быть у людей." *PSS* 25: 118 (Dostoevsky's emphasis). On the Ridiculous Man's experience of truth, see Michael Holquist, *Dostoevsky and the Novel* (Evanston, IL: Northwestern University Press, 1986), 737; and Robin Feuer Miller, "Dostoevsky's 'The Dream of a Ridiculous Man': Unsealing the Generic Envelope," in *Freedom and Responsibility in Russian Literature: Essays in Honor of Robert Louis Jackson,* ed. Elizabeth Cheresh Allen and Gary Saul Morson (Evanston, IL: Northwestern University Press, 1995), 86–104.
85 See Holman, *The Return of the Perennial Philosophy*, 62.
86 "Многое на земле от нас скрыто, но взамен того даровано нам тайное сокровенное ощущение живой связи нашей с миром иным, с миром горним и высшим, да и корни наших мыслей и чувств не здесь, а в мирах иных." *PSS* 14: 290.
87 Refer also to my article, "The Numinous Experience of Ego Transcendence in Dostoevsky," *Slavic and East European Journal* 57, no. 3 (Fall 2013): 388–402.
88 Gary Saul Morson, "Prosaic Bakhtin: *Landmarks*, Anti-Intelligentsialism, and the Russian Countertradition," in *Bakhtin in Contexts: Across the Disciplines,* ed. Amy Mandelker (Evanston, IL: Northwestern University Press, 1995), 85–88.
89 Morson, "Prosaic Bakhtin," 89.

Notes to Conclusion
1 V.V. Veresaev, *Zhivaia zhizn': O Dostoevskom, O L've Tolstom, O Nitsshe* (Moscow: Izdatel'stvo "Respublika," 1999), 85–87.
2 Ibid., 86.
3 Frank, *The Mantle of the Prophet*, 370.

4 Ibid., 292.
5 On Western esoteric sources of perennialism, see John Holman, *The Return of the Perennial Philosophy: The Supreme Vision of Western Esotericism* (London: Watkins Publishing, 2008).
6 Tolstoy studied Plato during the formative years of his writing, and particularly valued the Socratic dialogue as a literary form and method. See Donna Orwin, *Consequences of Consciousness: Turgenev, Dostoevsky, and Tolstoy* (Stanford, CA: Stanford University Press, 2007), 57–70.
7 The principles of Platonism are paraphrased here from Richard Tarnas, *The Passion of the Western Mind: Understanding the Ideas That Have Shaped Our World View* (New York: Ballantine Books, 1991), 41.
8 Ibid., 405.

Bibliography

Anderson, Roger B. *Dostoevsky: Myths of Duality*. Gainesville: University of Florida Press, 1986.

Avanesov, P.I. "Dostoevskii v rabote nad 'Dvoinikom.'" In *Tvorcheskaia istoriia: Issledovaniia po russkoi literature*, edited by N.K. Piksanov, 124–191. Moscow: Nikitinskie subbotniki, 1927.

Avramenko, Richard, and Jingcai Ying. "Dostoevsky's Heroines: Or, on the Compassion of the Russian Woman." In *Dostoevsky's Political Thought*, edited by Richard Avramenko and Lee Trepanier, 73–90. Lanham, MD: Lexington Books, 2013.

Bakhtin, Mikhail. *Problems of Dostoevsky's Poetics*. Edited and translated by Caryl Emerson. Minneapolis: University of Minnesota Press, 1984.

Behrendt, Patricia Flanagan. "The Russian Iconic Representation of the Christian Madonna: A Feminine Archetype in *Notes from Underground*." In *Dostoevski and the Human Condition after a Century*, edited by Alexej Ugrinsky, Frank S. Lambasa, and Valija K. Ozolins, 133–143. New York: Greenwood Press, 1986.

Belinskii, V.G. *Sobranie sochinenii v deviati tomakh*. Moscow: Khudozhestvennaia literatura, 1976–1982.

Belkin, A.A., ed. *F.M. Dostoevskii v russkoi kritike: Sbornik statei*. Moscow: Khudozhestvennaia literatura, 1956.

Belknap, Robert. *The Structure of* The Brothers Karamazov. The Hague and Paris: Mouton, 1967.

Bem, A.L. *O Dostoevskom*. Vol. 2. Prague, 1933.

Berdyaev, Nicholas. *Dostoevsky*. Translated by Donald Attwater. New York: Meridian Books, 1968.

Berman, Art. *Preface to Modernism*. Urbana and Chicago: University of Illinois Press, 1994.

Bernstein, Laurie. *Sonia's Daughter's: Prostitutes and Their Regulation in Imperial Russia*. Berkeley: University of California Press, 1995.

Berry, Thomas. "Dostoevsky and Spiritualism." *Dostoevsky Studies* 2 (1981): 43–49.

Bird, Robert. "Refiguring the Russian Type: Dostoevsky and the Limits of Realism." In *A New Word on* The Brothers Karamazov, edited by Robert Louis Jackson, 17–30. Evanston, IL: Northwestern University Press, 2004.

Blank, Ksana. *Dostoevsky's Dialectics and the Problem of Sin*. Evanston, IL: Northwestern University Press, 2010.

———. "The Rabbit and the Duck: Antinomic Unity in Dostoevskij, the Russian Religious Tradition, and Mikhail Bakhtin." *Studies in East European Thought* 59, nos. 1–2 (2007): 21–37.

Breger, Louis. *Dostoevsky: The Author as Psychoanalyst*. New York: New York University Press, 1989.

———. "Dostoevsky and Medicine." *Slavic Review* 45 (1986): 735–737.

Budanova, N.F., and G.M. Fridlender. *Letopis' zhizni i tvorchestva F.M. Dostoevskogo v trekh tomakh, 1821-1881*. T.1: 1821–1864. Saint Petersburg: Akademicheskii proekt, 1993.

Campbell, Joseph. *The Hero with a Thousand Faces*. 3rd ed. Novato, CA: New World Library, 2008.

Carlson, Maria. "Fashionable Occultism: Spiritualism, Theosophy, Freemasonry, and Hermeticism in Fin-de-Siècle Russia." In *The Occult in Russian and Soviet Culture*, edited by Bernice Glatzer Rosenthal, 135–152. Ithaca, NY: Cornell University Press, 1997.

Carus, Carl Gustav. *Psyche: Zur Entwicklungsgeschichte der* Seele. Pforzheim: Flammer und Hoffmann, 1846.

Cassedy, Steven. *Dostoevsky's Religion*. Stanford, CA: Stanford University Press, 2005.

Copleston, Frederick C. *Philosophy in Russia from Herzen to Lenin and Berdyaev*. Notre Dame, IN: University of Notre Dame Press, 1986.

———. *Russian Religious Philosophy: Selected Aspects*. Notre Dame, IN: University of Notre Dame Press, 1988.

Cornwell, Neil. *The Life, Times, and Milieu of V.F. Odoyevsky, 1804–1869*. London: Athlone Press, 1986.

———, ed. *The Gothic-fantastic in Nineteenth-century Russian Literature*. Amsterdam and Atlanta, GA: Rodopi, 1999.

Cusmerenco, Diana. "Representations of the Archetype of the Fatal Woman in *The Idiot* by Dostoevsky and *The Most Beloved of Earthlings* by Marin Preda: Natasya Filippovna and Matilda." *Wiener Slavistisches Jahrbuch* 1, no. 1 (2013): 43–61.

Davidson, Pamela, ed. *Russian Literature and Its Demons*. New York and Oxford: Berghahn Books, 2000.

De Jonge, Alex. *Dostoevsky and the Age of Intensity*. New York: St. Martin's Press, 1975.

Dalton, Elizabeth. *Unconscious Structure in* The Idiot. Princeton, NJ: Princeton University Press, 1979.

Dostoevskii, Andrei. *Vospominaniia*. Moscow: Agraf, 1999.

Dostoevskii, Fedor. *Polnoe sobranie sochinenii v tridtsati tomakh*. Edited by G.M. Fridlender et al. Leningrad: Nauka, 1972–1990.

Dostoevsky, Fyodor. *The Double, A Poem of St. Petersburg*. Translated by George Bird. Bloomington: Indiana University Press, 1958.

———. *The Double: Two Versions*. Edited and translated by Evelyn J. Harden. Ann Arbor, MI: Ardis, 1985.

———. *Selected Letters of Fyodor Dostoyevsky*. Edited by Joseph Frank and David I. Goldstein. Translated by Andrew MacAndrew. New Brunswick, NJ: Rutgers University Press, 1987.

Ermakov, I.D. *Psikhoanaliz literatury: Pushkin, Gogol', Dostoevskii*. Moscow: Novoe literaturnoe obozrenie, 1999.

Fanger, Donald. *Dostoevsky and Romantic Realism: A Study of Dostoevsky in Relation to Balzac, Dickens, and Gogol*. Cambridge, MA: Harvard University Press, 1965.

Fedotov, George. *The Russian Religious Mind*. Vol. 3. Belmont, MA: Nordland Publishing, 1975.

Florensky, Pavel. *Iconostasis*. Translated by Donald Sheehan and Olga Andrejev. Crestwood, NY: St. Vladimir's Seminary Press, 1996.

Forrester, Sibelan. "Vladimir Propp and the Russian Folktale." Preface to Vladimir Propp, *The Russian Folktale*. Edited and translated by Sibelan Forrester. Detroit, MI: Wayne State University Press, 2012.

Frank, Joseph. *Dostoevsky: The Seeds of Revolt, 1821–1849*. Princeton, NJ: Princeton University Press, 1976.

———. *Dostoevsky: The Stir of Liberation, 1860–1865*. Princeton, NJ: Princeton University Press, 1986.

———. *Dostoevsky: The Years of Ordeal, 1850–1859*. Princeton, NJ: Princeton University Press, 1990.

———. *Dostoevsky: The Miraculous Years, 1865–1871*. Princeton, NJ: Princeton University Press, 1995.

———. *Dostoevsky: The Mantle of the Prophet, 1871–1881*. Princeton, NJ: Princeton University Press, 2002.

Freud, Sigmund. "Dostoevsky and Parricide." In *The Standard Edition of the Complete Psychological Works of Sigmund Freud*, edited by James Strachey and Anna Freud. Vol. 21, 175–196. London: Hogarth Press, 1953–1974.

Fromm, Erich. *Escape from Freedom*. New York: Henry Holt & Co., 1994.

Frye, Northrop. *Anatomy of Criticism: Four Essays*. Princeton, NJ: Princeton University Press, 1957.

Fursov, Aleksandr. "Vremia, kogda ulybaetsia lotos: Dostoevskii i kitaisskie mudretsy." *Dukhovno-nravstvennoe vospitanie* 6 (2009): 18–20.

Futrell, Michael. "Buddhism and *The Brothers Karamazov*." *Dostoevsky Studies* 2 (1981): 155–162.

———. "Dostoyevsky and Islam (and Chokan Valikhanov)." *Slavonic and East European Review* 57, no. 1 (January 1979): 16–31.

Gibian, George. "C.G. Carus' Psyche and Dostoevsky." *American Slavic and East European Review* 14, no. 3 (1955): 371–382.

Gibson, A. Boyce. *The Religion of Dostoevsky*. Philadelphia, PA: Westminster Press, 1973.

Gier, Nick F. "Dialectic: East and West." *Indian Philosophical Quarterly* 10 (1983): 207–218.

Gillespie, Alyssa Dinega, ed. *Dictionary of Literary Biography, Vol. 277: Russian Literature in the Age of Realism*. Detroit, MI: Gale, 2003.

Girard, René. *Deceit, Desire, and the Novel: Self and Other in Literary Structure.* Translated by Yvonne Freccero. Baltimore, MD: Johns Hopkins Press, 1965.

———. *Resurrection from the Underground: Feodor Dostoevsky.* New York: Crossroad Publishing, 1997.

Gor'kii, Maksim. "O karamazovshchine" and "Eshche o karamazovshchine." *Sobranie sochinenii v tridtsati tomakh.* Vol. 24, 146–156. Moscow: Khudozhestvennaia literatura, 1949-55.

Grillaert, Nel. *What the God-seekers Found in Nietzsche: The Reception of Nietzsche's Übermensch by the Philosophers of the Russian Religious Renaissance.* Amsterdam and New York: Rodopi, 2008.

Grossman, Leonid. *Poetika Dostoevskogo.* Vyp. 4. Moscow: Gosudarstvennaia akademiia khudozhestvennykh nauk, 1925.

Hall, David L., and Roger T. Ames. *Thinking from the Han: Self, Truth, and Transcendence in Chinese and Western Culture.* Albany: State University of New York Press, 1998.

Hubbs, Joanna. *Mother Russia: The Feminine Myth in Russian Culture.* Bloomington and Indianapolis: Indiana University Press, 1988.

Harrison, Lonny. "The Numinous Experience of Ego Transcendence in Dostoevsky." *Slavic and East European Journal* 57, no. 3 (Fall 2013): 388–402.

———. "Reasonable to Ridiculous: The Inward Gaze of the Modern Self in Dostoevskii and Vladimir Odoevskii." *Canadian Slavonic Papers* 55, nos. 3–4 (September–December 2013): 343–363.

Holman, John. *The Return of the Perennial Philosophy: The Supreme Vision of Western Esotericism.* London: Watkins Publishing, 2008.

Holquist, Michael. *Dostoevsky and the Novel.* Evanston, IL: Northwestern University Press, 1986.

Hubbs, Joanna. *Mother Russia: The Feminine Myth in Russian Culture.* Bloomington and Indianapolis: Indiana University Press, 1988.

Hudspith, Sarah. *Dostoevsky and the Idea of Russianness: A New Perspective on Unity and Brotherhood.* New York: RoutledgeCurzon, 2004.

Ivanits, Linda. *Dostoevsky and the Russian People.* Cambridge, UK: Cambridge University Press, 2008.

———. *Russian Folk Belief.* Armonk, NY: M.E. Sharpe, 1988.

Ivanov, Vyacheslav. *Freedom and the Tragic Life.* Wolfeboro, NH: Longwood Academic, 1989.

Jackson, Robert Louis. *The Art of Dostoevsky: Deliriums and Nocturnes.* Princeton, NJ: Princeton University Press, 1981.

———. *Dostoevsky's Quest for Form: A Study of His Philosophy of Art.* New Haven, CT, and London: Yale University Press, 1966.

———, ed. *A New Word on* The Brothers Karamazov. Evanston, IL: Northwestern University Press, 2004.

Jones, Malcolm. *Dostoevsky and the Dynamics of Religious Experience.* London: Anthem Press, 2005.

———. *Dostoevsky after Bakhtin: Readings in Dostoyevsky's Fantastic Realism.* Cambridge, MA: Cambridge University Press, 1990.

Jung, C.G. *Analytical Psychology: Its Theory and* Practice. London: Routledge and Kegan Paul, 1982.
———. *The Collected Works of C.G. Jung*, 2nd ed. Translated by R.F.C. Hull, Bollingen Series XX. Princeton, NJ: Princeton University Press, 1966–1970. (Hereinafter CW, followed by name, volume, year.)
———. CW *Symbols of Transformation*. Vol. 5. 1970.
———. CW *Psychological Types*. Vol. 6. 1971.
———. CW *The Archetypes and the Collective Unconscious*. Vol. 9, part 1. 1969.
———. CW *Psychology and Religion: East and West*. Vol. 11. 1969.
———. CW *Mysterium Coniunctionis*. Vol. 14. 1970.
———. *The Essential Jung*. Selected and introduced by Anthony Storr. Princeton, NJ: Princeton University Press, 1983.
———. *Four Archetypes: Mother, Rebirth, Spirit, Trickster*. Translated by R.F.C. Hull. Princeton, NJ: Princeton University Press, 1970.
———. *The Portable Jung*. Edited by Joseph Campbell. Translated by R.F.C. Hull. New York: Penguin Books, 1976.
———. *The Undiscovered Self* with *Symbols and the Interpretation of Dreams*. Translated and revised by R.F.C. Hull. Princeton, NJ, and Oxford: Princeton University Press, 2010.
Jung, C.G., M.-L. von Franz, et al. *Man and His Symbols*. Garden City, NY: Doubleday & Company, 1964.
Kantor, Vladimir K. "Freud contra Dostoevskii." In *Tolstoi ili Dostoevskii? Filosofsko-esteticheskie iskaniia v kul'turakh Vostoka i Zapada*, edited by V.E. Bagno, 197–207. St. Petersburg: Nauka, 2003.
Kasatkina, Tatiana. *O tvoriashchei prirode slova: ontologichnost' slova v tvorchestve F.M. Dostoevskogo kak osnova 'realizma v vysshem smysle'*. Moscow: IMLI RAN, 2004.
Kirk, Irina. "Buddhistic Elements in The Idiot." *Studia Slavica Academiae Scientiarum Hungaricae* 18, nos. 1–2 (1972): 77–84.
Knapp, Liza. *The Annihilation of Inertia: Dostoevsky and Metaphysics*. Evanston, IL: Northwestern University Press, 1996.
Koehler, Ludmila. "Five Minutes Too Late ..." *Dostoevsky Studies* 6 (1985): 113–124.
Kohlberg, Lawrence. "Psychological Analysis and Literary Form: A Study of the Doubles in Dostoevsky." *Daedalus* (Spring 1963): 345–362.
Koshelev, V.A., and A.V. Chernov. "Mudraia fantaziia skazochnika." In A.F. Vel'tman, *Serdtse i dumka*. Moscow: Sovetskaia Rossiia, 1986.
Kostalevsky, Marina. *Dostoevsky and Soloviev: The Art of Integral Vision*. New Haven, CT: Yale University Press, 1997.
Kotliarevskii, Nestor. *Nikolai Vasil'evich Gogol', 1829–1842: ocherk iz istorii russkoi povesti i dramy*. St Petersburg: Tip. M.M. Stasiulevicha, 1911.
Kuleshov, V.I. *"Otechestvennye zapiski" i literatura 40 godov XIX v.* Moscow: Izdatel'stvo Moskovskogo universiteta, 1959.
Lachman, Gary. *Jung the Mystic: The Esoteric Dimensions of Carl Jung's Life and Teachings*. New York: Jeremy P. Tarcher/Penguin, 2013.

Lantz, Kenneth. *The Dostoevsky Encyclopedia*. Westport, CT: Greenwood Publishing Group, 2004.
Leatherbarrow, William J. "Apocalyptic Imagery in *The Idiot* and *The Devils*." *Dostoevsky Studies* 3 (1982): 43–51.
Lermontov, Mikhail. *A Hero of Our Time*. Translated by Vladimir Nabokov with Dmitri Nabokov. Garden City, NY: Doubleday Anchor, 1958.
Lossky, Vladimir. "Apophasis and Trinitarian Theology." In Daniel B. Clendenin, ed., *Eastern Orthodox Theology: A Contemporary Reader*, 2nd ed., 149–162. Grand Rapids, MI: Baker Academic, 2003.
Lotman, Yuri. "The Tradition Generated by *Onegin*." In *Russian Views of Pushkin's "Eugene Onegin."* Translated by Sona Stephan Hoisington, 169–177. Bloomington and Indianapolis: Indiana University Press, 1988.
———. *Culture and Explosion*. Edited by Marina Grishakova. Translated by Wilma Clark. Berlin and New York: Mouton de Gruyter, 2009.
Malia, Martin. *Russia under Western Eyes: From the Bronze Horseman to the Lenin Mausoleum*. Cambridge, MA: Harvard University Press, 1999.
Martinsen, Deborah. *Surprised by Shame: Dostoevsky's Liars and Narrative Exposure*. Columbus: Ohio State University Press, 2003.
McDaniel, Tim. *The Agony of the Russian Idea*. Princeton, NJ: Princeton University Press, 1996.
McReynolds, Susan. "You Can Buy the Whole World: The Problem of Redemption in *The Brothers Karamazov*." *Slavic and East European Journal* 52, no. 1 (2008): 87–111.
Miller, Robin Feuer. "Dostoevsky's 'The Dream of a Ridiculous Man': Unsealing the Generic Envelope." In *Freedom and Responsibility in Russian Literature: Essays in Honor of Robert Louis Jackson,* edited by Elizabeth Cheresh Allen and Gary Saul Morson, 86–104. Evanston, IL: Northwestern University Press, 1995.
Milosz, Czeslaw. *Emperor of the Earth: Modes of Eccentric Vision*. Berkeley: University of California Press, 1977.
Mindess, Harvey. "Freud on Dostoevsky." *American Scholar* 36 (1967): 446–452.
Morson, Gary Saul. *The Boundaries of Genre: Dostoevsky's* Diary of a Writer *and the Traditions of Literary Utopia*. Evanston, IL: Northwestern University Press, 1988.
———. "Prosaic Bakhtin: *Landmarks*, Anti-Intelligentsialism, and the Russian Countertradition." In *Bakhtin in Contexts: Across the Disciplines*, edited by Amy Mandelker, 33–78. Evanston, IL: Northwestern University Press, 1995.
Noll, Richard. *The Jung Cult: Origins of a Charismatic Movement*. Princeton, NJ: Princeton University Press, 1994.
Odoevskii, V.F. *Povesti i rasskazy*. Moscow: Gosudarstvennoe izdatel'stvo khudozhestvennoi literatury, 1959.
———. *Kosmorama*. Edited with introduction, notes, bibliography and vocabulary by Roger Cockrell. London: Bristol Classical Press, 1998.
Odoevsky, Vladimir. *The Salamander and Other Gothic Tales: Eight Stories by Vladimir Odoevsky*. Translated with an introduction by Neil Cornwell. Evanston, IL: Northwestern University Press, 1992.

Orwin, Donna. *Consequences of Consciousness: Turgenev, Dostoevsky, and Tolstoy.* Stanford, CA: Stanford University Press, 2007.
Paris, Bernard J. *Dostoevsky's Greatest Characters: A New Approach to "Notes from Underground,"* Crime and Punishment, *and* The Brothers Karamazov. New York: Palgrave Macmillan, 2008.
Passage, Charles E. *Dostoevski the Adapter: A Study in Dostoevski's Use of The Tales of Hoffmann.* Chapel Hill: University of North Carolina Press, 1954.
Pattison, George, and Diane Oenning Thompson, eds. *Dostoevsky and the Christian Tradition.* Cambridge: Cambridge University Press, 2001.
Peace, Richard. *Dostoevsky: An Examination of the Major Novels.* Cambridge: Cambridge University Press, 1971.
———. "Dostoevsky and the 'Golden Age.'" *Dostoevsky Studies* 3 (1982): 61–78.
Pike, Christopher. "Dostoevsky's 'The Dream of a Ridiculous Man': Seeing Is Believing." In *The Structural Analysis of Russian Narrative Fiction*, edited by Joe Andrew and Christopher Pike, 26–63. Keele: Department of Russian Studies, Keele University, 1984.
Pogorelsky, Antony. *The Double, or My Evenings in Little Russia.* Translated and with an introduction by Ruth Sobel. Ann Arbor, MI: Ardis, 1988.
Pogorel'skii, Antonii. *Izbrannoe.* Moscow: Sovetskaia Rossiia, 1985.
Porter, Laurence M. "The Devil as Double in Nineteenth-Century Literature: Goethe, Dostoevsky, and Flaubert." *Comparative Literary Studies* 15, no. 3 (1978): 316–317.
Propp, Vladimir. *The Russian Folktale.* Edited and translated by Sibelan Forrester. Detroit, MI: Wayne State University Press, 2012.
Rank, Otto. *The Double: A Psychoanalytic Study.* Chapel Hill: University of North Carolina Press, 1971.
Rice, James L. *Dostoevsky and the Healing Art: An Essay in Literary and Medical History.* Ann Arbor, MI: Ardis, 1985.
———. *Freud's Russia: National Identity in the Evolution of Psychoanalysis.* New Brunswick, NJ: Transaction Publishers, 1993.
Rimbaud, Arthur. *Oeuvres Complètes.* Edited by Rolland de Renéville and Jules Mouquet. Paris: Editions Gallimard, 1963.
Rosenthal, Bernice Glatzer, ed. *The Occult in Russian and Soviet Culture.* Ithaca, NY: Cornell University Press, 1997.
Rudicina, Alexandra F. "Crime and Myth: The Archetypal Pattern of Rebirth in Three Novels of Dostoevsky." *PMLA* 87, no. 5 (October 1972): 1065–1074.
Scanlan, James P. *Dostoevsky the Thinker.* Ithaca, NY, and London: Cornell University Press, 2002.
Seleznev, Iurii. *Dostoevskii.* Moscow: Molodaia gvardiia, 1981.
Shamdasani, Sonu. *Cult Fictions: C.G. Jung and the Founding of Analytical Psychology.* New York and London: Routledge, 1998.
Simpson, Mark S. *The Russian Gothic Novel and Its British Antecedents.* Columbus, OH: Slavica Publishers, 1986.
Solovyov, Vladimir. *War, Progress and the End of History: Three Conversations, Including a Short Story of the Anti-Christ.* Translated by Alexander Baksky. Hudson, NY: Lindisfarne Press, 1990.

Stacy, Robert H. *Russian Literary Criticism: A Short History*. Syracuse, NY: Syracuse University Press, 1974.

Tarnas, Richard. *Cosmos and Psyche: Intimations of a New World View*. New York: Plume Books, 2007.

———. *The Passion of the Western Mind: Understanding the Ideas That Have Shaped Our World View*. New York: Ballantine Books, 1991.

Taylor, Charles. *A Secular Age*. Cambridge, MA: Belknap Press, 2007.

———. *Sources of the Self: The Making of the Modern Identity*. Cambridge, MA: Harvard University Press, 1989.

Terras, Victor. *Handbook of Russian Literature*. New Haven, CT: Yale University Press, 1985.

Todorov, Tzvetan. *The Fantastic: A Structural Approach to a Literary Genre*. Translated by Richard Howard. Cleveland, OH: Case Western Reserve University Press, 1973.

Van den Bercken, Wil. *Christian Fiction and Religious Realism in the Novels of Dostoevsky*. London: Anthem Press, 2011.

Vassena, Raffaella. *Reawakening National Identity: Dostoevskii's* Diary of a Writer *and Its Impact on Russian Society*. New York: Peter Lang, 2007.

Vel'tman, A.F. *Serdtse i dumka*. Moscow: Sovetskaia Rossiia, 1986.

Veresaev, V.V. *Zhivaia zhizn': O Dostoevskom, O L've Tolstom, O Nitsshe*. Moscow: Izdatel'stvo "Respublika," 1999.

Vinitsky, Ilya. *Ghostly Paradoxes: Modern Spiritualism and Russian Culture in the Age of Realism*. Toronto: University of Toronto Press, 2009.

———. "Where Bobok Is Buried: The Theosophical Roots of Dostoevskii's 'Fantastic Realism.'" *Slavic Review* 65, no. 3 (Autumn 2006): 523–543.

Walicki, Andrzej. *A History of Russian Thought from the Enlightenment to Marxism*. Translated by Hilda Andrews-Rusiecka. Stanford, CA: Stanford University Press, 1979.

Ward, Bruce K. *Dostoevsky's Critique of the West: The Quest for the Earthly Paradise*. Waterloo, ON: Wilfrid Laurier University Press, 1986.

Weisblatt, Beverly Hansen. "The Numinous on Russian Soil: A Depth Psychological Interpretation of Religious Experience in *The Brothers Karamazov*." Master's thesis, Pacifica Graduate Institute, 2010.

Wierzbicka, Anna. *Semantics, Culture, and Cognition*. New York: Oxford University Press, 1992.

Williams, Rowan. *Dostoevsky: Language, Faith, and Fiction*. Waco, TX: Baylor University Press, 2008.

Wood, James. *The Irresponsible Self: On Laughter and the Novel*. New York: Farrar, Straus and Giroux, 2004.

Young, Donald. "Ermakov and Psychoanalytic Criticism in Russia." *Slavic and East European Journal* 23, no. 1 (Spring 1979): 72–86.

Young, Sarah J. "Buddhism in Dostoevsky: Prince Myshkin and the True Light of Being." In *Dostoevsky: On the Threshold of Other Worlds*, edited by Sarah Young and Lesley Milne, 220–229. Ilkeston, UK: Bramcot, 2006.

———. "Dostoevskii's *Idiot* and the Epistle of James." *Slavonic and East European Review* 81, no. 3 (July 2003): 401–420.

Index

"About the Fact That We Are All Good People" (Dostoevsky), 123–24
Absolute Idea, 45
"accursed questions," 20, 80
Afanasyev, Aleksandr, 126, 129
"A Gentle Creature" (Dostoevsky), 115
The Agony of the Russian Idea (McDaniel), 118, 176n63
A Hero of Our Time (Lermontov), 2
Aksakov, Konstantin, 161n42
alchemy, 16; and Christian symbolism, 107–10; and complementarity of opposites, 105–6; in *Faust*, 79; in psychological structure of Jung, 12
alienation: and Romantic Age despair, 47; spiritual alienation, 18; of Underground Man, 7; of uprootedness, 74
allegory, 7
alterity, 40
Ambrose, Father, 121, 122
Ames, Roger T., 64–65
Anderson, Roger, function of duality myths, 59–60
anima/animus: as archetype, 89–90; stages of development, 84–85
antinomies, duality of, 63–64
apocalyptic imagery, 112–14
apophatic theology, 36, 105, 144
apparent self: and authentic self, 91–92, 132, 172n64; and autonomous personhood, 29–30, 91–92; identification with ego, 93–95; recognition of, 152

Aquinas, Thomas, principle of participation, 32
A Raw Youth (Dostoevsky), 61, 96; *kosnost'* in, 115–16
archetypes: anima/animus, 84–85, 89–90; as aspects of personality, 11; Devil as, 7, 58, 101–2; direct experience, 15; Dostoevskian self, 4, 24–25; double motif, 19, 50–58; dreamer as, 7, 92–93; of the fatal woman, 90, 172n56; feminine archetypes, 84–91; femme fatale, 19, 88, 89–90, 172n56; hero archetype, 142, 151; and higher realism, 15; history of, 8–10; *Imago Dei* (God-image in man), 9; individuation and, 13; Karamazovan nature, 3, 19; mother archetype, 84–85, 86; Mother Russia, 20, 85–86, 88; *Mysterium Coniunctionis*, 20; positive/negative sides of, 13–14; Russian Madonna, 19, 88–89; saintly prostitute, 7, 79, 88, 89, 136; spontaneity, 15; the unconscious, 77–79; underground type, 7, 13–14, 19, 82–83
Aristotle, 64
artistry (*khudozhestvennost'*), 122–23
Atheism (Dostoevsky), 34
Augustine, St., innate self, 32, 33
authentic self: awareness of, 91–92; in myths of initiation, 138–39; of personal transformation, 12, 14, 132, 133–34; recovery of through transcendent arts, 91–92, 152, 172n64

193

Avramenko, Richard, "Dostoevsky's Heroines," 87, 90, 91

Bakhtin, Mikhail, 28, 71
Balzac, Honoré de, 121
behavioural psychology, 27
Behrendt, Patricia F., 89
Belinsky, Vissarion, 6, 16, 61; atheistic socialism, 66; censure of *The Double*, 50, 60, 166n69; criticism of Veltman, 55; *narodnost'* (folk identity), 112
Belknap, Robert: complementarity of opposites, 106–7; Karamazovan nature, 3, 19; on Karamazovism (*Karamazovshchina*), 101–4; spider and insect imagery, 75–76
Berdiaev [Berdyaev], Nicholas, 20; complementarity of opposites, 105; Dostoevsky as mystical realist, 14–15; ideas as expression of human nature, 63; on role of the Russian woman, 87; and the Russian idea, 118; Vekhi group, 69, 169n112
Bernstein, Laurie, 7
Berry, Thomas, 16
Bestuzhev-Marlinsky, Alexander, 54
Bird, Robert, 6
Blank, Ksana, 70; descent to the underworld, 132, 171n27; yin-yang of Dostoevsky's dialectics, 71
"Bobok" (Dostoevsky), 116–17
Bogoroditsa (Mother of God), 90–91
"Book-learning and Literacy" (Dostoevsky), 123
The Brothers Karamazov (Dostoevsky): alchemical imagery in, 107–9; Buddhistic elements in, 36; buffoonery, 102, 103; character types in, 6; contradictory truth of church doctrine, 70–71; descent to the underworld, 131–32, 171nn27–28; devil archetype in, 58, 101; Mysterious Visitor, 20, 66, 140; parricide in, 26, 112; Russian idea, 121–22; spider and insect imagery, 75–76; transformation and resurrection in, 133; underground symbolism of, 3, 99–100. *See also* Karamazovism (*Karamazovshchina*)

Buddhism, 36, 64
buffoonery, 102, 103
Bulgakov, Sergei, 69, 70
Buslaev, Fedor, 129
bylina (epic song), 131
Byron, Lord, 121

Campbell, Joseph, 99; monomyth of the hero's journey, 8, 130, 134–43; personal transformation, 133–34
Carpi, Guido, 121
Carus, Carl Gustav, 12; *Psyche*, 77–79
Cassedy, Steven, 29, 65, 66; antinomies, duality of, 63–64; faith of Elder Zosima, 35–36, 162n48; universalism of the Russian character, 119–20
cataphatic theology, 105
Cervantes, Miguel de, 143
Chamisso, Adelbert von, 50
character types, 6, 23–24; as archetypes, 3–4, 19; attributes, clusters of, 101–4; the buffoon, 102, 103; catalysis and transformation in, 6; Coincidence of Opposites, 20, 104–11; the double, 19, 99; dreamer type, 7, 92–93; emotions, and ideas, 5–6; femme fatale, 19; Golyadkin, as character prototype, 81–82; ideas, as lived experience, 100; Karamazovism (*Karamazovshchina*), 3, 101–4, 156n13; personality, and identity, 25, 26, 93–95; psychological perspective on, 25–29; Russian Madonna, 19, 88–89; self-sacrificial love, 87–88; underground type, 1–2, 3, 7, 19, 79, 82–83

Chernyshevsky, Nikolai, 94
Christianity: and alchemical imagery, 107–10; and dual nature of Christ, 70, 82; founding myth of, 7; Ideal Beauty, and Christ, 122–23; *metanoia*, 144; mysticism, and Russian Christianity, 17, 158n61; mythopoeic narrative, 143; and Neoplatonism, 32; and socialism, 65–69
Coincidence of Opposites, 20, 104–11. *See also* opposites
collective unconscious: psychic reality of, 14, 79; transcendent function of, 17
complementarity of opposites, 19, 105–6, 106–9, 152. *See also* opposites
conscious mind/consciousness: of apparent self, 91–92; confrontation with unconscious, 19, 106; decomposition of, 116–17; as disease, 83–84; and identity, 25; influence of social-political structures on, 69; and moral awareness, 53; rational self-consciousness of modern self, 64–65; reflective consciousness, 40
Copleston, Frederick C., 62, 65
Corneille, Pierre, 121
Crime and Punishment (Dostoevsky): faith, and religion, 151; ghosts, 15; Herald figure, 135; Madonna figure, 89; moral degeneration in, 80; moral rehabilitation in, 150; social revolt of intelligentsia, 112; spider imagery, 76; threshold guardians, 137–38; transformation, 133; water symbolism, 129
cults, and myths, 127, 128
Cusmerenco, Diana, 90, 172n56

Dante, 123, 136, 137
Daoism, 64
death: odour of, 109; and renewal, myths of, 131–34; and resurrection, 20, 90, 132–34

Deceit, Desire, and the Novel (Girard), 26
Decembrists, 120–21
de Jonge, Alex: *Dostoevsky and the Age of Intensity*, 47
de Kock, Paul, 44
depth psychology, 40; archetypal patterning of, 8–9, 10, 153; and the modern self, 7, 156n24; and nonrational modes of perception, 50; shadow archetype, 100
Derzhavin, Gavril, 43
de Saint-Simon, Henri, 66
destiny, Russian concept of, 55, 165n52
Devil, 7, 58; as archetype, 101–2
The Devils (Dostoevsky), 15–16, 29, 36, 87–88; apocalyptic imagery, 113–14; devil archetype in, 101–2; egoism in, 94–95; social revolt of intelligentsia, 112
dialectics: *both–and* dialectic of Dostoevsky, 64, 152; duality-in-unity, 69–71; ideas as expression of human nature, 62–63; socialism and Christianity, 65–69; Western duality, 63–65
Diary of a Writer (Dostoevsky), 34, 118, 119; apocalyptic imagery, 112; on ideas, 5; on portrayal of reality, 4–5; Russian idea, 124; on spiritualism, 16
Dionysius the Areopagite, 105, 144
direct experience, 15
divine grace, interaction with Karamazovism, 103
doppelgänger motif: in *The Double*, 48–49, 58–59; duality of, 19; psychoanalytic studies of, 26; in Russian Romanticism, 50–51; as shadow, 48. *See also* double motif
Dostoevsky, Andrei (brother), 44, 50
Dostoevsky, Fyodor Mikhailovich: *both–and* dialectic of, 64, 152; Carus, influence of, 77–79; criticism of Gogolian social types, 2–3, 155n11; duality, pathological root

of, 39; epilepsy, 26, 39, 65, 66, 112, 144, 181n74; fantastic realism, 60–62; folk sources, use of, 12, 129–30, 131; Gothic horror, 43–44; Hoffmann, influence of, 50; on ideas, 5; influences on, 7, 12, 43–45, 121; *legenda* (legend), use of, 130; moral sickness of, 111; Odoevsky, influence of, 56, 58, 165n53; philosophical influences, 15–16; on portrayal of reality, 4–5; psychological realism of, 27–29; "Pushkin Speech," 86, 119–20; on reality and realism, 28–29, 34; Schellingian idealism, 30, 70; on the Second Coming, 68; on self, 24–25; Siberian exile, 78, 132–33; and Slavophilism, 35, 161n43, 161n44; social-humanitarian Christianity of, 45; on spiritualism, 16; transformation and resurrection cycle, 132–34; "two worlds" metaphysics of, 65–66; Veltman, influence of, 54–55; Western duality of, 63–65

Dostoevsky, Fyodor Mikhailovich: works: "About the Fact That We Are All Good People," 123–24; "A Gentle Creature," 115; "A Petersburg Chronicle," 83; *A Raw Youth*, 61, 96, 115–16; *Atheism*, 34; "A Weak Heart," 61; "Book-learning and Literacy," 123; *Diary of a Writer*, 4–5, 16, 34, 113, 118, 119; *The Eternal Husband*, 95; *The Insulted and Injured*, 62; "Masha entry," 65–66, 94, 95, 116; *Notes from the House of the Dead*, 36; *Notes from Underground*, 1–2, 20, 68, 79–84; "One of Today's Falsehoods," 119; "On Love for the Russian People," 124; "Polzunkov," 102; *Poor Folk*, 61; "Socialism and Christianity," 65–69, 96; "Something about Devils," 123; "The Golden Age in [Your] Pocket," 123, 178n92; "The Landlady," 132–33; "The Peasant Marei," 124; "Unsubstantiated Claims," 115; *Vremia* (journal), 119, 161n44; "White Nights," 7, 92; "Winter Notes on Summer Impressions," 93–94, 95. See also *Crime and Punishment*; *The Brothers Karamazov*; *The Devils*; *The Double*; "The Dream of a Ridiculous Man"; *The Idiot*

Dostoevsky, Mikhail (brother), 41, 93, 161n44

Dostoevsky and the Age of Intensity (de Jonge), 47

Dostoevsky Encyclopedia, The (Lantz), 7

Dostoevsky's Greatest Characters (Paris), 26–27

The Double (Dostoevsky): antecedents to, 50–53; criticism of, 60, 166n69; doppelgänger motif, 26, 48–49, 50–51, 58–59; double as emanation of self, 53–54; Golyadkin, as character prototype, 81–82; Golyadkin, as underground type, 1, 21, 60, 79; Herald figure, 135; madness motif, 58; moral idealism in, 48–49; and *Notes from Underground*, 79–84; parallels with Odoevsky, 58; political dimension of, 80–81; spiritual health, diagnosis of, 78–79; underground idea, creation of, 1

double motif: as archetype, 19, 50–58; and the doppelgänger, 19; in *The Double*, 1, 21; Romantic expressions of duality, 48; as suppressed aspect of personality, 58; in "The Cosmorama," 56–57

doubling: as generative principle of narrative, 49–50; as literary device, 58

dreamer type, 7, 92–93

"The Dream of a Ridiculous Man" (Dostoevsky): apocalyptic imagery, 113; authentic self, shared sense of, 145–47; collective Self of, 69;

expression of authentic self, 143; Herald figure, 135; supernatural aid, 136; transformation and resurrection in, 133; transition of hero in, 138
duality: of antinomies, 63–64; binary logic of opposition, 29, 43, 160n13; and contradiction, 104; of the divided self, 42–43, 46–48; doppelgänger motif, 19, 26; duality-in-unity, 69–71; duality myths, function of, 59–60; *dvoemirie*, "two-worldedness" of, 57, 58; in hero myth, 139; of madness and doubles, 40–42; of opposites, 12, 19, 104–11; reconciliation of opposites, 82; substance dualism, 40; unity-in-duality, 19; in Western discourse traditions, 40
Dumas, Alexandre, 57
dvoemirie, "two-worldedness" of, 57, 58
dvoinik (double), 50
dvuedinstvo (duality-in-unity), 19, 70

Easter motifs, 133
ego: and the apparent self, 93–95; in cultural ethos of Romanticism, 47–48; ego self, 35; ego transcendence, 20–21, 150
egoism, and morality of self-interest, 93–95
eidos, 13
Eleusinian Mysteries, 132
Enlightenment: modern reason, and the archetypal vision, 9–10; and the modern self, 33–34; rationalist thought of, 41
Ermakov, Ivan, 25, 104
essentialism: and individuation, 18; and the unconscious mind, 14
The Eternal Husband (Dostoevsky), 95
Eugene Onegin (Pushkin), 2, 86
Eve, in anima development, 84
evil, in Gothic horror genre, 44

faith, 25; and conception of belief, 29; credibility of, 36, 151
fantastic realism, 60–62; "Bobok," 116–17
fatal woman archetype, 90, 172n56
Faust (Goethe), 58, 136, 137
Fedorov, Nikolai, 16
Fedotov, George, 91
feeling, and reason, 41–42, 51–53, 114
feminine archetypes, 19, 20, 84–91; role of women in regeneration of society, 86–88
femme fatale archetype, 19, 88, 89–90
Fichte, Johann Gottlieb, 17
Flaubert, Gustave, *La Tentation de saint Antoine*, 58
Florensky, Pavel, 70; countenance vs. mask, 91, 172n64
folk creativity, folkloric character of, 129
folklore: devil archetype in, 58; the Devil in, 101–2; Mother Russia, 85–86; of the Rusalka, 90; *sud'ba* (destiny), 55, 165n52
folk mysticism. *See* mysticism
folk religion, and occultism, 131
folk tales: archetypal patterning of, 153; genre and classifications of, 129–30; influence on literary development, 130–31; interconnectedness of, 126–27; *legenda* (legend) genre, 130; relationship to myth, 127–28; and unconscious processes of the psyche, 10–11; wonder tale, origins of, 126
Forrester, Sibelan, 128
Fourier, Charles, 66
Frank, Joseph: links between *The Double* and *Notes from Underground*, 81–82; mutual moral responsibility, 151–52; philosophical influences on Dostoevsky, 17, 45, 56, 77, 158n61; Romantic metaphysics, 42

Frank, Semyon, 69
freedom, 25
free will: and external subjection, 115; and human nature, 67–68; and identity, 25; and moral law, 94
French Utopian Socialism, 45
Freud, Sigmund, 8, 10, 26
Fridlender, G.M., 121
Fromm, Erich, 32
From New York to San Francisco and Back to Russia (Ogorodnikov), 15–16
Frye, Northrop, 11
Futrell, Michael, 36

German Idealism, 17, 20
German Romantic Idealism, 8, 16, 45
German Romanticism: doubling technique of, 50; influence on Dostoevsky, 77, 149; influence on Jung, 12, 77
Gibian, George, 77, 78, 112
Gier, Nick F., 64
Girard, René: *Deceit, Desire, and the Novel*, 26
Gnosticism, 11, 15, 138
god-man, ideal of, 9, 20, 62, 108, 142
Godmanhood, concept of, 70
Goethe, Johann Wolfgang von, 7; *Faust*, 58, 136, 137; Urbild/Urtype, 12
Gogol, Nikolai, 50; duality, and contradiction, 104; *legenda* (legend), use of, 130; social types of, 2–3, 155n11; "The Nose," 50
"The Golden Age in [Your] Pocket" (Dostoevsky), 123, 178n92
Golyadkin: as character prototype, 81–82; as Herald, 135; inertia of, 83, 84; parallels to Underground Man, 79–84; as underground type, 1, 21, 60, 79. *See also The Double*
Gorky, Maxim, on Karamazovism (*Karamazovshchina*), 3, 156n13
gothic horror genre, 43–44; "Bobok," 116–17

Grigor'ev, Apollon, 161n44
Grimm, Brothers, 129
Grimm, Jacob, *German Mythology*, 129
Grishin, D.V., 115
Grossman, Leonid, 43, 45

Hall, David L., 64–65
Handbook of Russian Literature (Terras), 2
Hegel, Georg Wilhelm Friedrich, 17, 40, 63–64, 65; *Philosophy of History*, 78
Helen, in anima development, 84
Heraclitus, 40, 105
Hermeticism, 16
heroes: divided self, of Romantic protagonists, 42–43, 46–48; personal authenticity of sacred quest, 59–60. *See also* monomyth
hero myth. *See* monomyth
Herzen, Alexandr, 16
Hinduism, 64
Hoeller, Stephan, 138
Hoffmann, E.T.A., 50, 121; *Der Magnetiseur*, 41; "Sandman," 164n40
Hoffmannism, and Russian Romanticism, 50–51
Holy Fool, 7
Homer, 121, 123
Horney, Karen, 26
Hubbs, Joanna, *Mother Russia*, 85, 86, 87–88
Hudspith, Sarah, 121
Hugo, Victor, 45, 66, 121
humanity, and man as mystery, 4
human nature: as composite of animal/spiritual nature, 96–97; dialectic of, 62–63; and free will, 67–68; in Gothic horror genre, 44; and the unconscious, 77
human society, stages of, 66–68

"I": of Christ as humanity's ideal, 65–66; Law of Personality, 66; spontaneity of the self-conscious "I," 92–93

idealism: Christian idealism, 37; consciousness, and intuition, 29–30; deconstruction of, 82; as mystical doctrine, 14
The Idiot (Dostoevsky), 29, 36, 102, 112; apocalyptic imagery, 113–14; *kosnost'* in, 116; spider imagery, 76
Imago Dei (God-image in man), 9, 20, 62, 70, 108, 142
individuation: archetypes, role of in, 13; categories of, 19; and essentialism, 18; intuition and, 14; and the shadow self, 8–9
industrialization, responses to, 46
industrial transformation, 16
inertia, 73; contradiction between inner freedom and external subjection, 115; and decomposition of consciousness, 114–18; as *kosnost'*, 115–17; as law of nature, 67; life as annihilation of, 115; of Underground Man and Golyadkin, 83, 84
initiatory experience, and ego transcendence, 138–39
insect imagery: as *kosnost'*, 116; of the underground, 74–76
insensibility (*kosnost'*), 115–17
The Insulted and Injured (Dostoevsky), 62
intelligentsia: apocalyptic imagery of, 112–14; estrangement from the people, 120–21; illness among, 111–12; positivist attitude of, 146; uprootedness of, 112
intuition: consciousness and, 29–30; and individuation, 14; in opposition to reasoning, 91
irrationality, otherworld of, 43
Isaeva, Maria Dimitrievna (first wife of Dostoevsky), 65, 94
Islam, 36
Ivanits, Linda, 122, 129
Ivanov, Vyacheslav, 5

Jackson, Robert Louis, 6, 122, 142
Jones, Malcolm, 35, 78; fantastic realism, 60; resurrection, and spiritual rebirth, 133
Jung, Carl, 40, 73; alchemy, and transformation, 12, 105–6, 107–8; *Allegoria Merlini*, 108; *anima/animus*, 84–85; archetypal patterning, 8–9; archetypes, theory of, 11–14; collective unconscious, 14, 17, 79; complementarity of opposites, 19, 105–6, 106–9, 152; hero archetype, 142; influence of Carus on, 77, 79; *Memories, Dreams, Reflections*, 17–18; *Mysterium Coniunctionis*, 20, 105–6; mysticism and, 17; shadow self, 8–9, 95, 100; transcendence, and transformation, 132; the unconscious, 77–79, 95–96
Jungism, 17–18

Kant, Immanuel, 9, 10, 40, 41; *Critique of Pure Reason*, 78
Karamazov, Alyosha: spiritual epiphany of, as rebirth, 140–41; supernatural aid to, 137; transformation through visionary narrative, 107, 109–11; as underground type, 3
Karamazov, Dmitri, 106–7
Karamazov, Ivan, 80, 114
Karamazovan nature, 3, 19, 107
Karamazovism (*Karamazovshchina*), 3, 101–4, 156n13; clusters of attributes, 101–3, 107; complementarity of opposites, 106–9; underground symbolism of, 99–100
Khomyakov, Aleksei, 161n42
khudozhestvennost' (artistry), 122–23
Kireevsky, Ivan, 35, 161n42
Kirk, Irina, 36
Knapp, Liza, 67
Koehler, Ludmila, 115–16
kosnost' (insensibility/inertia), 115–17

Kraevsky, Andrei, *Notes of the Fatherland* (journal), 55–56

Lacan, Jacques, 40
Lachman, Gary, 17, 18
"The Landlady" (Dostoevsky), 132–33
Lantz, Kenneth, *The Dostoevsky Encyclopedia*, 7
Law of Love, 20, 91–97
Law of Personality, 20, 82, 91–97, 115, 118, 144; "I" of Christ as humanity's ideal, 66
Lazhechnikov, Ivan, 45, 50
Leatherbarrow, William J., 113–14
Lebensphilosophie, 157n41
legenda (legend), moralizing nature of, 130
Lermontov, Mikhail, 6; *A Hero of Our Time*, 2
literary tropes: complementarity of opposites, 100; doubling, 48, 49–50; duality, 100; feminine archetypes, 86
Lotman, Yuri, 6
Luther, Martin, 64

madness motif: in *The Double*, 58; in "The Cosmorama," 56
Madonna archetype, 88–89
magic, disengagement with, 32–33
Maikov, Apollon, 28
Malia, Martin, 119
Marxism, and traditional Russian culture, 128
Mary Magdalene as archetype, 7, 79, 88, 89, 136
Masalsky, K.P., 45
"Masha entry," 65–66, 94, 95, 116
materialism, as *kosnost'*, 116
Matushka Rus' (Mother Russia), 85–86
McDaniel, Tim, *The Agony of the Russian Idea*, 118, 176n63
mechanistic determinism, 67
Memories, Dreams, Reflections (Jung), 17–18

mental health, role of in psychological portraiture, 27
mental illness: among intelligentsia, 111–12; madness motif, 56, 58
modern identity, and human agency, 31–34
modernity: binary logic of opposition, 29, 160n13; conflicts of, 18, 19; disenchantment of, 146–47; and interiority of the self, 48; and Law of Personality, 91–97; nihilistic materialism of, 91–92, 149–50; problem of the modern self, 29–34; and spirituality, 108–9; and traditional Russian culture, 128; and the true self, 149–50; and Western thought, 150
monomyth, 8, 130, 134–43; archetypal patterning of, 138; call to adventure, 134–36; crossing the threshold, 90, 137–38; duality in, 59, 139; the Herald, 135; initiation, 138–39; rebirth, 137, 139–43; refusal of the call, 135; Siberian Shamanic tradition, 138; supernatural aid, 135, 136–37
moral idealism: and concepts of self, 62; in *The Double*, 48–49, 58–59; as transcendental end of reason, 77–78
moral illness, 111–12
moral regeneration, and the Vekhi group, 69–70, 169n112
Morson, Gary Saul, 28, 112, 147
mother archetype, 84–85, 86
Mother Russia, 85–86; duality of, 88; as Earth Mother, 20, 90–91; eternal womanhood of, 91
murder, organizing pattern of, 7
Mysterium Coniunctionis (Jung), 20, 105–6
mysticism: complementarity of opposites, 105; Dostoevsky as mystical realist, 14–15; folk mysticism, influence on Jung, 12; ghosts, 15, 116–17
myth(s): archetypal patterning of, 8, 153; contrast between traditional

and modern mythmaking, 59–60; cross-cultural cycles of, 125; death and renewal, 125; duality myths, function of, 59–60; founding myth of Christianity, 7; as higher-order reality, 127; initiation and funeral rites, 126, 128; personal authenticity of sacred quest, 59–60; as reference point for reality, 12, 157n41; relationship to folk tales, 127–28; structural patterns of, 7–8; and unconscious processes of the psyche, 10–11; vision narrative as transformation myth, 143–47; wonder tale, 127, 128, 130. *See also* monomyth; wonder tale

nadryv, emotional outbursts of, 102–3
narodnost' (folk identity), 112
national identity/nationalism: and the intelligentsia, 112; of Mother Russia, 20, 85–86; religious nationalism, 119–20; of Russia, 2, 8; Russian idea, 118, 119; and the Russian self, 34–37
native soil conservatism (*pochvennichestvo*), 60, 120, 161n44
Natural School: realism, and the Romantic fantastic, 60–62; social realism of, 6, 50–51
nature mysticism, 36, 120, 139–40, 141–42, 162n48
Naturphilosophie, 78; influence on Dostoevsky, 77; influence on Jung, 12, 77; living nature principle, 141–42
Neoplatonism, 16, 20, 152; and Christianity, 32
Nicholas of Cusa, 105
Nietzsche, Friedrich, *The Gay Science*, 40
nihilism, refutation of, 123, 178n92
nihilistic materialism, 91–92, 149–50
Noll, Richard: *The Jung Cult*, 11–12, 157n41; *Jungism*, 17–18

Notes from the House of the Dead (Dostoevsky), 36
Notes from Underground (Dostoevsky): censored passage, 82; Christian idealism in, 37, 68; and *The Double*, 79–84; insect imagery, 75; underground motif, 1–2, 20

occultism, 15–16, 17, 131
Odoevsky, Vladimir, 16, 30; influence of on Dostoevsky, 56, 58, 165n53; *Russian Nights*, 50; "The Cosmorama," 51, 56–57; "The Living Corpse," 55; "The Sylph," 57; "two-worldedness" of *dvoemirie*, 57, 58
Ogorodnikov, P.I., *From New York to San Francisco and Back to Russia*, 15–16
"One of Today's Falsehoods" (Dostoevsky), 119
"On Love for the Russian People" (Dostoevsky), 124
opposites: Coincidence of Opposites, 20, 104–11; complementarity of opposites, 19, 105–6, 106–9, 152; duality of, 19, 40; as literary trope, 100; tension between as generative force of, 12; unification of, 142
Orwin, Donna, 92–93
the Other, 40
Ozmidov, Nikolai, 24

pan-human brotherhood, 35; authentic self, shared sense of, 145–47; of universal Christlike love, 70
Paris, Bernard, *Dostoevsky's Greatest Characters*, 26–27
parricide, 26, 112
Peace, Richard, 69
"The Peasant Marei" (Dostoevsky), 124
Perovsky, Alexei. *See* Pogorelsky, Antony
persona, 19

personality, and identity: *lichnost'*, 93–95; of Underground Man, 26
Peter the Great, 120
Petrashevsky Circle, 81, 111
Plato, 31, 144, 152, 183n6; Allegory of the Cave, 40, 147; "*archetype*," use of as term, 9
pochvennichestvo (native soil conservatism), 60, 120, 161n44
Pogorelsky, Antony: *The Double, or My Evenings in Little Russia*, 50, 51; "The Pernicious Effects of an Unbridled Imagination," 52, 164n40; "The Poppy-Seed-Cake Woman of the Lafertov Quarter," 50, 51–52
polyphony, concept of, 28, 91, 126
"Polzunkov" (Dostoevsky), 102
Poor Folk (Dostoevsky), 61
Porter, Laurence, 49–50, 58
Prince Myshkin, 29, 97; epilepsy, pre-seizure state of mind, 112; expression of authentic self, 143–45, 181n71; numinous experiences, 20
Propp, Vladimir, 126–31; *Historical Roots of the Wonder Tale*, 126, 127, 128; *Morphology of the Folktale*, 126, 127; *The Russian Folktale*, 126
Psyche (Carus), 77–79
psychoanalytic studies: of Dostoevsky works, 25–29; of Underground Man, 26–27
Pushkin, Aleksandr, 6; *Contemporary* (journal), 55; "Egyptian Nights," 75; *Eugene Onegin*, 2, 86; "The Queen of Spades," 50
Pygmalion, 52

Racine, Jean, 121
Radcliffe, Ann, 43, 121
Rank, Otto, 26
Raskolnikov: spider imagery, 76; supernatural aid, 136; transformation of, 133; unconscious roots of disease, 78, 112

rational egoism, and the modern self, 36–37
rational empiricism, and Romantic poetics, 53
realism: fantastic realism, 60–62; as metaphysical concept, 4–5
reason, 25; disengaged reasoning, 33, 91; emergence of modern mind, 32–33; and feeling, 41–42, 51–53, 114; as material faculty, 41; and moral conscious, 146
rebirth: in founding myth of Christianity, 7; in hero myth (monomyth), 137, 139–43
Reformation, Protestant: authoritarian social structures, 32
religion, and religious symbolism: apophatic theology, 36, 105, 144; in beliefs of Dostoevsky, 63–64; and direct experience, 15, 35–37; folk religion, 131; illuminative transformation, 144–45; *Imago Dei* (God-image in man), 9; as participation mystique, 134; psychological need for, 14; saint and sinner, coincidence of, 64; Siberian Shamanic tradition, 138; spirituality, and Russian national identity, 34–35
religious nationalism, 119–20
Renaissance: authoritarian social structures, 32
repentance, and spiritual redemption, 78–79
Rice, James, 77, 78
Rimbaud, Arthur, 40
roman feuilleton, 44–45, 163–64n22
Romantic Idealism. *See* German Romantic Idealism
Romanticism: archetypes in, 9; binary oppositions of, 43; disengaged reason, critique of, 30–31, 91, 160n18; divided self, of Romantic protagonists, 42–43, 46–48; doppel-

gänger motif, 19, 48; ideal self of, 37; Natural School realism, and the fantastic, 60–62; quest for lost unity, 30–31; *roman feuilleton*, 44–45, 163–64n22; self-awareness, and the transcendental, 42–43
Romantic nationalism, 45
Rosenblium, L.M., 115
Rousseau, Jean-Jacques, 123
Rudicina, Alexandra, "Crime and Myth," 7
Russia: *bylina* (epic song), 131; national identity of, 2, 8; Peter the Great, 120; scientific materialism of intellectual society, 62; secular literature, development of, 131; *skazka* (folk tale), 131
Russian character: innate goodness in, 123–24; of the Underground Man, 2
Russian Idea, 118–24, 176n63; and Coincidence of Opposites, 20; and European culture, 120; as pan-human unification, 118; problems with, 119–20; redemptive suffering, spiritual wealth of, 118–19
Russian Madonna archetype, 19, 88–89
Russian Orthodox theology: contradictory truth of, 70; Divine Wisdom, and living nature, 142; legacy of Neoplatonism on, 144; Madonna figure, 88–89; motifs of, 35–36; mysticism and, 17, 158n61; rebirth and resurrection, 133
Russian Realism, 3, 6, 8
Russian Romantic Gothic, 57
Russian Romanticism, and Hoffmannism, 50–51

Saint-Simonian New Christianity, 45
Sand, George, 45, 66, 121
Sapientia, in anima development, 84
Scanlan, James, 15, 68, 94–95, 97
Schelling, Friedrich Wilhelm, 12, 17, 78, 141–42
Schellingian idealism, 30, 70

Schiller, Friedrich, 17, 121, 123
Scholastics, "problem of universals," 9
scientific materialism of Russian intellectual society, 62
Scott, Walter, 45, 121
Seleznev, Yuri, 123
self: apparent self, 29–30, 91–92, 132; as archetype, 4, 24; authentic self, 12, 91–92, 132; buffoons, and the apparent self, 102; culture-bound character of, 64–65; depth psychology, and the modern self, 6–7, 156n24; dialogic "I," 25, 65–66; divided self, of Romantic protagonists, 42–43, 46–48; holistic vision of, 68–69; and human agency, 31–34; individuation, and the shadow self, 8–9, 19; and the "I" of Christ, 65–66; modern self, evolution of, 18, 67–69, 149–50; moral ideals in concepts of self, 62; notions of in Romanticism, 42–43, 46–48; personality, and identity, 93–95; plurality of, 64–65; Romantic individualism of, 46–48; Romantic perceptions of, 48; the Russian self, 34–37; universal self, 12, 153
self-awareness: anima as connection to the unconscious, 84–85; and crisis of modernity, 146–47; and ecstatic fusion, 144–45, 181n74; as heightened consciousness, 83–84; in the hero myth, 134; individuation, and the shadow self, 8–9; salvationist theory of transformation, 143; and the transcendental, 42–43
self-consciousness of Russian literary tradition, 92–93
self-narrative, projection onto history, 114
self-sacrificial love, 87–88, 89
self-will, and the Christ ideal, 97
shadow self: as archetype, 100; awareness of, and individuation, 8–9, 19;

and ego identity, 95; transformation, and the authentic self, 125–26
Shakespeare, William, 121, 123
shamanism, 36
Simpson, Mark S., 44
Skabichevsky, Aleksandr, 39, 62
skazka (folk tale), 131
Slavophilism, 35, 63, 161n42, 161n43, 161n44
socialism: atheistic socialism, 66; and Christianity, 65–69
social realism, 5–6
social revolt of intelligentsia, 111–12
Soloviev [Solovyov], Vladimir, 20, 68, 69, 118, 121
"Something about Devils" (Dostoevsky), 123
Sophia, concept of, 70
Speshnev, Nikolai, 111
spider imagery: as *kosnost'*, 116; of the underground, 74–76
spirit, law of: transcendence over laws of nature, 67–68
spiritualism, 15–16, 131
spiritual rebirth, in *coniunctio* archetype, 109–11
Stoics, 31
Strakhov, Nikolai, 161n44
sud'ba (destiny), 55, 165n52
Sue, Eugène, 44, 57
Sufi mysticism, 36
Sulié, Frederick, 44

Tarnas, Richard, 31; archetypes of ancient myths, 9, 10; depth psychology, and the modern self, 7, 156n24; expression of archetypes, 153
Taylor, Charles, 64; enchantment, and disenchantment, 32–33; identity, and human agency, 31–34; reflective consciousness, 40
Terras, Victor, *Handbook of Russian Literature*, 2

Theseus, and the minotaur, 135, 136
theurgy, 70
Tikhomirov, L.A., 121
Tolstoy, Leo, 152, 183n6; *legenda* (legend), use of, 130
Totleben, E.I., 111
transcendence: higher unity as ideal of, 20; over laws of nature, 67–68; psychological need for, 26
transcendentalism, Russian, 158n61
transcendent self, 93–95
transformation: and alchemical transmutation, 15; of authentic self, 12, 14, 125–26; and complementarity of opposites, 105–6, 152; of consciousness, 107; dynamics of, as underground, 73–77; and ego transcendence, 20–21, 37; illuminative transformation, 144–45; of the individual in Russian society, 6; industrial transformation, 16; as key to character type, 6; and the modern self, 149; opposites, tension between as generative force of, 12, 19; rebirth narratives, 132–33; and resurrection, 20, 90, 132–34; salvationist theory of, 143; of shadow self, 125–26; socialism and Christianity, 65–69; and the underground, 19, 20–21; as upward-pointing archetype, 13–14; visionary experiences of, 97; in vision narratives, 150–51
Truth, ecstatic vision of, 143
Turgenev, Ivan, *Diary of a Superfluous Man*, 92
"two-worldedness" of *dvoemirie*, 57, 58

unconscious mind/unconsciousness: archetypal unconscious, 77–79, 95–96; collective unconscious, 14, 17, 79; confrontation with conscious, 19, 106; imagery associated with, 74–76; role in spiritual

well-being, 77–78; and the underground, 19
Underground Man: as archetypal outsider, 7; creation of, 81; critique of Rousseau, 30, 160n18; mechanistic determinism of, 67; parallels to Golyadkin, 79–84; psychoanalytic view of, 26–27; resistance to rational empiricism, 41; and the Russian personality, 2; self-absorption of, 92, 94; as social-cultural type, 1–2, 82–83
underground motif: as analogy for the unconscious, 74; as archetype, 13–14, 19; in *The Brothers Karamazov*, 3, 99–100; descent to underworld, 90, 131–32, 171nn27–28; in *The Double*, 1–2, 20; in hero myth, 134, 135; imagery associated with, 74–76; as literary innovation, 82–83; in monomyths, 135–36; in *Notes from Underground*, 1–2, 20; and rejection of the sacred, 115; and transformation, 19, 20–21, 73–77; and the unconscious mind, 19, 71; uprootedness, and alienation of, 74
unity: immanence of, 126; and Law of Love, 95; Romantic quest for, 30–31; as transcendental ideal, 151, 153; and universal brotherhood, 152; of utopian socialism, 150
unity-in-duality (*dvuedinstvo*), 19
"Unsubstantiated Claims" (Dostoevsky), 115
Urbild/Urtype, 12
Utopian Socialism, 45, 111

Van den Bercken, Wil, 36
Vassena, Raffaella: Russian idea, 121–23
Vekhi group, 69–70, 169n112
Veltman, Aleksandr (A.F.), 50; *Emelya*, 54; *Heart and Mind*, 51, 54–55; *The Lunatic*, 54

Veresaev, Vikenty: on faith, 151; *kosnost'*, 117; on melancholy, 43; on spiders and insects, 75; unity/disunity of life, 96, 105
Vienna Psychoanalytic Society, 26
violence, organizing pattern of, 7
Virgin Mary, in anima development, 84
vision narrative, 62; of pan-human brotherhood, 70; self-transformation in, 150–51; as transformation myth, 143–47; "two worlds" metaphysics, 65–66
Voltaire, 121, 123
von Wrangel, Baron, 78
Vremia (journal), 119, 161n44

Ward, Bruce K., 74, 118
Weisblatt, Beverly, 77, 142; alchemy, and Christian symbolism, 107–9; "The Numinous on Russian Soil," 107
Western duality, dialectic of, 63–65
Western humanism, and decline of God-consciousness, 32
"White Nights" (Dostoevsky), 7, 92
Williams, Rowan, 36
"Winter Notes on Summer Impressions" (Dostoevsky), 93–94, 95
women: feminine archetypes, 84–91, 172n56; mother archetype, 84–85, 86, 136; role of Russian woman in regeneration of society, 86–88; Russian Madonna figure, 19, 88–89; saintly prostitute, 7, 79, 88, 89, 136
wonder tale: origins of, 127, 128; structural motifs of, 130

Ying, Jingcai: "Dostoevsky's Heroines," 87, 90, 91
Young, Sarah, 36

Zagoskin, M.N., 45
zanimatel'nost (captivating-ness), 45–46

Zipes, Jack, 127
Zosima, Elder: comparison to Ridiculous Man, 147; contradictory truth of church doctrine, 70; death, and putrefaction, 109; and divine grace, of Karamazovism, 103; expression of authentic self, 143; Father Ambrose as basis for, 121; nature mysticism of, 36, 120, 139–40, 141–42, 162n48; religious nationalism, 119; repentance, and spiritual redemption, 78–79; as supernatural aid, 137; transformation, and the underground, 20–21

www.ingramcontent.com/pod-product-compliance
Lightning Source LLC
Chambersburg PA
CBHW052138070526
44585CB00017B/1881